Praise for *Anything*

"Dana Goodyear's new book, about being a wallflower at the American food orgy, won me over on its second page."

—*The New York Times*

"Food editors need people like [Dana Goodyear]. Anyone who can write so wisely and entertainingly about eating rarities is a rarity herself."

—*Slate*

"It is precisely because I am not a foodie that I found such immense pleasure in reading Dana Goodyear's *Anything That Moves: Renegade Chefs, Fearless Eaters, and the Making of a New American Food Culture.* It was like reading Bruce Chatwin on Patagonia or Ryszard Kapuscinski on Ethiopia, maybe even Norman Mailer on war. I don't want to be there, but I want to have already been there."

—*Newsweek*

"When most people picture the job of a food writer—especially one who works at *The New Yorker*—visions of white tablecloths, sumptuous sauces, and delicately perfumed desserts probably come to mind. Dana Goodyear . . . has had her share of those meals . . . in researching *Anything That Moves*, which explores the fringes of America's current foodie movement, Goodyear piled her plate with luxuries of a different kind. Ox penis, fertilized duck eggs, whale meat, cow throats, stinkbugs, marijuana pesto—the author ate it all in the name of food reportage. Goodyear's extreme eating doesn't just come from an appetite for thrills. She wants to understand how and why America is moving out of its peanut-butter-and-jelly dark ages into a veritable renaissance . . . the overall effect is of sharing a story-packed meal with Goodyear, an experience any real gourmand would savor—as long as you can occasionally opt not to have what she's having."

—*Entertainment Weekly*

"Goodyear is an extraordinarily adept reporter and observer. I can't think of another writer who could have done justice to the material. . . . Highly enjoyable and memorable journey through the brave and strange new world of avant-garde cuisine."

—*The Boston Globe*

"I don't think I've ever used the word *disgusting* as a compliment, but here goes. Goodyear's riveting, hilarious, disturbing, and downright disgusting new book is the perfect antidote to a Martha Stewart Thanksgiving. This journalistic thriller, set among the culinary avant-garde, is all about dangerous eating. A rose-haired tarantula spider roll. Frog fallopian tubes. And the most extreme: an unhatched chick, eaten whole. But this story isn't meant to gross you out; it's a window onto a world of chefs, purveyors, farmers, scavengers, and gonzo foodies." —Dani Shapiro, *More*

"Addictive, educational, and gross." —*Elle*

"Goodyear is a witty writer with a sly humor that makes her a genial guide to such a strange and diverse counterculture."

—*Los Angeles Times*

"Like any good exploration of an avant-garde subculture, Goodyear populates her stories with all sorts of fascinations. . . . What *Anything That Moves* does better than talk about weird food is profile the obsessives who eat it. They're an esoteric group whose influence is slowly seeping into the mainstream. You won't want to adjust your dietary habits, but in a lot of ways, [they're] already changing." —*Grantland*

"*Anything That Moves* is frenetic and fascinating and turns the stomach." —*Bloomberg Businessweek*

"Venturing deep into the underground foodie culture, *New Yorker* contributor Goodyear plunges into the world of dedicated individuals who routinely skirt the boundaries imposed by common culinary practices and tastes. . . . Goodyear's exploration of this engrossing and morally complex topic provides a solid footing for hearty conversations." —*Kirkus* (starred review)

"Poet and *New Yorker* staff writer Goodyear is an insightful, vivid, and smart commentator on food. Here she focuses on the reinvention of food in modern America, exploring the highs, lows, and surprises of cutting-edge foodie culture." —*Library Journal*

"Dana Goodyear may be our finest longform food journalist. The *New Yorker* staff writer . . . has written for that magazine on California's unpasteurized milk movement and Los Angeles's underground Wolvesmouth restaurant. She does not disappoint here, in an exploration (partly culled from her *New Yorker* pieces) of what she calls 'the outer bounds of food culture,' which includes everything from the Las Vegas food scene (a frightening notion) to head-to-tail butchering. Anyone who writes about eating 'stinkbugs' is worth reading." —*Atlantic Wire*

"In *Anything That Moves*, Dana Goodyear takes as her subject the outer edges and extremes of American food culture and shows us, with grace, quiet humor, and poetic precision, how closely the weird mirrors the typical. Reporting on the margins of food culture, she reveals much about the broader comedy of manners and morals in American life."

—Adam Gopnik, author of *The Table Comes First: Family, France, and the Meaning of Food* and *Paris to the Moon*

"Dana Goodyear is one of the most complete and authoritative voices in food journalism today. *Anything That Moves* so accurately describes the remaking of our modern food culture in America that I swear I can taste it. Combining serious thought and intelligent perspective with writing that is entertaining and inspiring, this is an important book and a delightfully fun read. I loved it."

—Andrew Zimmern, host of *Bizarre Foods with Andrew Zimmern*

"Dana Goodyear takes us on a wild romp through the fringes of today's extreme dining scene. The journey is exciting, eye-opening, a little scary at times, and always fascinating. I couldn't put *Anything That Moves* down."

—Barry Estabrook, author of *Tomatoland: How Modern Industrial Agriculture Destroyed Our Most Alluring Fruit*

"Finally the 'foodie movement' finds a voice I trust. With a poet's empathy and a reporter's nose for story, Goodyear brings us the high-minded adventurers and flash hucksters who are setting the future course of American food. This book has permanently changed my view of the plate, by revealing the politics, culture, sex, and crime that lie behind."

—Tom Mueller, *New York Times*–bestselling author of *Extra Virginity: The Sublime and Scandalous World of Olive Oil*

ANYTHING THAT MOVES

Renegade Chefs, Fearless Eaters, and the Making of a New American Food Culture

DANA GOODYEAR

RIVERHEAD BOOKS
NEW YORK

RIVERHEAD BOOKS
Published by the Penguin Group
Penguin Group (USA) LLC
375 Hudson Street
New York, New York 10014

USA · Canada · UK · Ireland · Australia
New Zealand · India · South Africa · China

penguin.com
A Penguin Random House Company

Portions of this book have appeared in different form in *The New Yorker.*

The Library of Congress has catalogued the hardcover edition as follows:

Library of Congress Cataloging-in-Publication Data

Goodyear, Dana.
Anything that moves : renegade chefs, fearless eaters, and the making of a new American food culture / Dana Goodyear.
p. cm.
ISBN 978-1-59448-837-5
1. Food—Social aspects—United States. 2. Food habits—United States. 3. Cooking—Social aspects—United States. 4. Extremists—United States. 5. Cooks—United States. 6. Gourmets—United States. 7. United States—Social life and customs—1971– I. Title.
GT2853.U5G66 2013 2013025054
394.1'2—dc23

First Riverhead hardcover edition: November 2013
First Riverhead trade paperback edition: November 2014
Riverhead trade paperback ISBN: 978-1-59463-287-7

Printed in the United States of America
1 3 5 7 9 10 8 6 4 2

BOOK DESIGN BY AMANDA DEWEY

For Rummy and Willa, my darlings

CONTENTS

ANYTHING THAT MOVES

INTRODUCTION

Bugs, horse, brains, whale; leaves, weeds, ice cream flavored with lichen-covered logs. The disturbingly familiar and the alarmingly rare, the unregulated, illegal, and indeterminate. A new American cuisine is forming, one marked by extreme and challenging ingredients. Animals never before considered or long since forgotten are emerging as delicacies. Parts that used to be for scrap are centerpieces. Ash and hay are fashionable ingredients, and you pay handsomely to breathe flavored air. I haven't yet heard of an American chef with the nerve to serve actual dirt—in Tokyo you can get a fancy dirt soup, and compost is an ingredient at one of Spain's most celebrated restaurants—but a high-end meal in this country feels incomplete these days without a little mound of "soil" made from cocoa or coffee. Going out to a nice dinner often precipitates a confrontation with a fundamental evolutionary question: Is that food?

My relationship to food is that of an acrophobe to a bridge: unease masks a desire to jump. A well-fed child with the imagination of a scrounger, I remember holing up in the back of the station wagon eating the dog's Milk-Bones, which were tastier than you might expect. Thinking of the sorrel that grew under our swing set still makes me drool. In winter—we lived outside Cleveland at that point—we drizzled maple syrup on the snow. My mother, who taught herself to cook by reading Elizabeth David, made everything from scratch, down to the English muffins. (She says I once asked her peevishly if it wouldn't be more convenient to buy some frozen food.) My father hunted. We always had a meat freezer full of doves from the eastern shore of Maryland and elk from the Rockies.

As I grew older, I remained curious. When I was in college, I got a summer job in Hong Kong at the *South China Morning Post*. After being teased in the lunchroom by a Singaporean colleague for being squeamish, I tried chicken feet. In Hanoi, I went to a dog restaurant and ate seven courses of "hornless goat." (Back home, I told my disgusted family that dogs may have been domesticated to serve as a source of meat in lean times. They still thought I was gross.) In Africa, I ate African animals; in South America, South American ones. But at home I was a "normal" eater—no chicken feet, no pets.

Until I started hanging out with foodies. Coined by the critic Gael Greene in 1980 to describe the devoted fans of an untrained Paris housewife who cooked in heels, the word *foodie* has taken on a new life in the age of social media. An American foodie documents what she eats with the avidity of a competitive birder, and publishes the images online for the world to see. So-called food porn is the most popular content on Pinterest, one of the fastest-growing websites in history, and it dominates the photo-sharing sites Instagram and Flickr. It's everywhere on TV. And, as with any fetish, the more outlandish and rarefied a find, the more a foodie likes it.

In "The Food Wife," a 2011 episode of *The Simpsons,* Marge and the kids become thrill-seeking food bloggers, sampling pig snouts, walrus moustaches, pine-needle sorbet, and a "regret course" of human tears. Matthew Selman, who wrote the episode and considers it a love letter to his kind, arranges family trips around restaurant reservations and finds himself ordering "the most organy, taily, brainy, nosy thing in the world—*because* it's exciting and dangerous." He has a hard time with the terminology, though. "I wish there was a word other than 'foodie,'" he says. "How about 'super food asshole' or 'pretentious food jerk'?" But somehow this piggy, cute, overweening word is right. *Gourmet* is too grand—too faux—for this movement; *epicure* is too ancient. We needed a word in English—a keen, young, democratic word—to describe the epidemic of food love.

Late-Roman eating habits are, to us, the emblem of the society's decadence, a forerunner of and justification for its fall. According to Patrick Faas, a historian of Roman food, "Rome became the giant stomach of the world, devouring everything," during its five hundred years of imperial rule. The rich considered birds' brains a delicacy and relished moray eels, which they kept in swimming pools at home. (Vedius Pollio, a friend of Augustus, supposedly preferred his eels fattened on human flesh.) In the third century AD, Emperor Elagabalus served coxcombs, peacock heads, and, as an accompaniment to womb-in wild sow, peas with gold, lentils with onyx, beans with amber, and rice with pearls—dishes it is not too hard to imagine in a high-end restaurant today.

Elagabalus was beheaded and, by the standard we apply to Rome, we are due for a comeuppance, too. The big picture about food is frightening: the Western diet overexploits unsustainable resources and, increasingly, our bad habits are being embraced by rapidly industrializing countries with large populations. In the aftermath of Michael Pollan's *The Omnivore's Dilemma,* which demonstrated the problem with a food system devoted to beefsteak and corn, Americans are opening up to previously unthinkable alternatives. In ambitious restaurants, the mainstream twentieth-century Western diet, with its narrow array of acceptable animals and plants, is being questioned. Most of what I consider here is eaten for pleasure—it is expensive, nonessential—but often it refers to necessity, the kind of deep, bone-licking eating that people do when they must milk every last calorie.

Daniel Pauly, a marine ecologist who studies global fisheries, believes that we are not so much changing our preferences as reacting to forces we choose to deny. "This idea of 'liking things' is actually a reflection of the pressure on the environment," he says. "You like what you can get. I grew up in Switzerland eating lots of horse meat because it was cheaper, and so I liked horse meat. China has had an immense population for a long time and cannot afford to be very selective. They eat anything that moves." *Anything that moves*: using that phrase about another culture's eating habits used to be an insult. Now it is a foodie-to-foodie brag, used to celebrate unchecked appetite. Taken another way, it speaks to the hidden side of food culture, where markets are created and desire is conjured; it's a seller's guiding principle. But Pauly is a scientist interested in evolutionary tactics—he admires survival—and, like the foodies who have adopted the expression as their proud credo, he means it as a compliment.

Writing this book, I set out to explore the outer bounds of food culture, where the psychological, rational, legal, ethical, and indeed physical limits of edibility are being tried—and sometimes overturned. What I found was a collection of go-betweens, chefs, and adventurous eaters—scofflaws, innovators, and crusaders—who are breaking with convention to reshape the American palate. Eating alongside them tested my stamina and tolerance for risk. There were things I was surprised to learn I could not bring myself to eat, and others I was disturbed to discover I relish. In our contemporary cuisine, I see anxiety behind the hedonism and resourcefulness tricked out as decadence. After centuries of perfecting the ritual of "civilized" dining, there is a furious backpedaling, a wilding, even among the chefs who employ the most cutting-edge techniques. At the same time, the traditional foods of poverty are being recast as elite. It is the height of sophistication to tear the meat from an animal's bones with your teeth and bare hands. To look at the food for sale in our best restaurants, you'd think that our civilization had peaked and collapsed; what we see on our plates is a post-apocalyptic free-for-all of crudity and refinement, technology and artlessness, an unimaginable future and a forgotten past.

In the past couple of years, extreme foodie-ism has become astonishingly mainstream. In December 2012, when talk of the Mayan apocalypse was in the air, Gevork Kazanchyan, a former L.A. County health inspector, hosted a multicourse dinner, with craft-beer pairings, at a barbecue restaurant in Long Beach—hardly a culinary epicenter. Advertising the event, Kazanchyan had called for only "brave, open-minded diners with no medical nor psychological restrictions on what they can consume." It was an outrageous requirement—whose diet contains *no* restrictions?—but it was only slightly more explicit in its demands than what high-end restaurants today routinely ask of their patrons. Beside each place setting was a stack of sealed envelopes containing descriptions of the courses, which were to be kept secret until after each was served—taste first, judge later.

Kazanchyan is in the unfortunate position of loving food yet knowing too much about microbiology to be at ease when eating it. Sometimes, the food-safety geek in him prevails. "It was a bunch of new-age gastro-enthusiasts versus me," he told me, describing a recent party at his house. "A buddy of mine who's a craft cocktailian and Ph.D. student in organic chem came over and was making egg-based cocktails. I was like, 'Dude, why are you not using pasteurized eggs?' He's like, 'Dude, it's one in twenty thousand.' I'm like, 'It doesn't make it a permissible safe practice.'" In November 2012, Kazanchyan published a cover story in the *Journal of Environmental Health* about the potential hazards of artisanal cocktails: fresh produce, raw eggs, and hand-shaped ice. "Unfortunately, theatrical components may not be quite so compatible with applicable public health regulations," he wrote—even though they taste "all sorts of good."

Sixty people showed up to the dinner in Long Beach. I sat down next to a guy named Thad, who was in his mid-twenties, with dark, slick-backed hair, dark jeans rolled at the cuff, argyle socks, and a leather jacket. He was from West Virginia, and he still had a bit of a twang. Across the table were his friends Erika and Kevin. The three of them had met a few years earlier, working at an Apple store deep in the San Fernando Valley. They were ordinary young aspiring professionals. I asked Thad what brought him. "The food," he said emphatically. "I'm hoping for brains. Hearts. Bone marrow."

Erika was from Bolivia, accustomed to all of those things but afraid of most seafood. She let on that she was a little nervous. "Nervous means excited," Kevin said. He was half Salvadoran and half Vietnamese, an unflappable eater. He's had eel heart, still beating, and he's pretty sure he's eaten dog, marked as "meat," in Vietnamese restaurants in L.A. With Filipino friends he tried *balut,* an unhatched duckling, cooked in its shell and eaten entire: eyes, beak, feathers, and bones. *Balut*, a Manila street food, has a reputation among American foodies for being one of the most psychologically challenging things you can eat. A blogger who writes with equanimity about eating python calls it his "culinary heart of darkness." To me, the idea was horrifying in its simplicity: an unmediated encounter with food, and with lots of parts—feathers, beak—that are decidedly *not* food. And not so much as a sprig of parsley to distract the eye.

Thad grew up eating green beans boiled to gray and burned pork chops and, when he was of age, drinking Miller Lite. After getting hooked on food porn on TV, he decided to read Anthony Bourdain, the former chef whose uninhibited approach to eating has inspired a nation of food adventurers. Thad became obsessed with finding the kinky stuff. "You can eat anything," he said. "There's so many stipulations, like 'Oooooh the texture, oooooh sweetbreads.' But if it's prepared the right way it can be great." He started eating at places where he could get pigs' ears and tails and organ meats, and he has accepted that there are certain kinds of finicky girls he can no longer date. Being in Los Angeles gives him a huge advantage. "You can find just about everything if you look," he said.

The first course came out: a Kumamoto oyster in a petri dish, in a matrix of coriander-flavored agar gel, with habanero cotton candy and several oils that, through the use of tapioca maltodextrin, had been made to resemble "a festering disease." Erika looked dubious. "No preconceptions, no fear," Thad said, digging into the awful, slippery, gummy mess.

We ate *huitlacoche*—corn fungus—alongside snails and black trumpet mushrooms. "We wanted this to be a little uncomfortable," the chef said. "*Huitlacoche* is the most famous of the gross decomposers. Farmers used to get really upset when they'd find it on their corn, until they figured out that they could sell it for three times per pound what corn costs. It's ridiculously expensive—ours cost thirty-one dollars a pound."

Accompanying the course was a Belgian brown beer made with deer sinews and tendons from a Chinese apothecary, and birds' nests that the brewer stole from his mother.

"I'm waiting for the body parts," Thad said. When a course of octopus tentacles came out, still wiggling, Kazanchyan provided instruction. "Pulverize the tissue," he said. "It needs to stop moving before you swallow it." Otherwise, he said, the tentacles might lodge in the throat—a problem that is said to cause several deaths a year in Korea, and makes live octopus among the most dangerous foods in the world. "Right up there with blowfish and rhubarb," he said. "Now we're talking," Thad said. Everybody chewed for a long time. A sucker attached itself to the inside of Thad's lip.

"I'm offended by the word *foodie,*" Thad said at last. By this time he was drinking my beer.

Kevin pointed at him. "*You're* a foodie," he said. "You have a list."

"What is the definition?" Thad said, tucking into a stuffed lamb heart. "Wanting to explore and eat anything out of the norm? We're becoming more open. Young people are more open. I am not a foodie, Goddamn it. I just like good food."

Jonathan, a strawberry-blond roaster at an artisanal coffee shop in Orange County, espoused a more complex view. Late in history, with America's institutions crumbling around them, he and his friends felt mistrustful, even paranoid. They had retreated into Home Ec, believing that if the worst were to happen, at least they'd know how to pickle their own vegetables. "Our generation feels lost," he said. "We're wanting to be self-sufficient." Near the end of the meal, Thad got his marrow. It was made into a ridiculously rich crème brûlée, which was served in a hollowed-out femur bone the chef had sawed himself.

So is foodie-ism greed or resourcefulness? If it were a matter of survival, there would be no difference. But this movement is about pleasure—pleasure heightened at the brink of calamity. Thad flashed a bright white smile and said, "If this is the end of the world, give me a fork and a knife."

PART I

SQUISHY OR SWANK?

One

THE SCAVENGER

Before I ever met Jonathan Gold, I saw him, at the far end of the bar at a pizzeria, packed tight in a black leather jacket; a cascade of graying red hair curling over his shoulders; twitchy, restless blue eyes scanning the room with the herky-jerky motion of an ink-jet printer. His broad, pale, freckled hands were crossed on the counter; the sleeves of his jacket ended a good two inches above his wrists. By then I'd been reading him in the *LA Weekly* and hearing his views on food recited like gospel among my friends for a couple of years. When, in 2007, Gold won the Pulitzer Prize for criticism, a first for a food writer and for the *Weekly,* I asked him to meet me for lunch. I was curious about the man and the food, but more than that, I was curious about the purchase that his fringy approach to eating seemed to be gaining on American cuisine. He wrote, "Let me know whether you'd rather go squishy or swank." Squishy, I replied, and so it began, with a bowl of rubbery abalone porridge and the promise of an adventure.

Gold's dauntless approach to eating has spread to inform a new generation of American eaters. For twenty-five years, he has been chronicling the city's carts and stands and dives and holes-in-mini-malls; its Peruvian, Korean, Uzbek, Isaan Thai, and Islamic Chinese restaurants; the places that serve innards, insects, and extremities. He works the bottom of the food chain, telling his readers where to get crickets, boiled silkworm cocoons, and fried grasshoppers, of which he writes that "the mellow, pecan-like flavor isn't bad." His readers learn to appreciate the sweet rewards of the repulsive, the dangerous, the emotionally complex. "He got me into *sesos* tacos"—brains—"and *uni*, chicken feet, pig's ears, and lots of organ meat," a downtown nightlife entrepreneur told me. The only thing Gold fears is scrambled eggs; his first food memory is of pushing away a plate of them.

Selling food depends on euphemism—if we really knew what we were eating, the thinking goes, we would reject it—and often critics further empurple the industry's own florid prose. Gold is a disabuser, a champion of the real. His descriptions repel as much as they beckon; the pleasure of his prose, in the service of ghastly sounding dishes, is itself an argument that something can be awful and delightful at the same time. Sea cucumbers, he writes, "breathe through their anuses, and when attacked, some of them defend themselves by farting out sections of their poisonous, sticky lungs. The particular, ganky texture expressed by the title ingredient in bird's-nest soup is supposed to come from the fondness of the swallows in question for impaling and sucking the mucus from sea cucumbers." Writing about a Uighur restaurant in Koreatown—"a nondescript corner dining room where northeastern Chinese cooks prepare the Beijing version of Xinxiang barbecue for a Korean-speaking clientele"—he recommended what he called "the winciest dish in town: a sharp, glistening steel skewer stabbed through thin coins of meat sliced from a bull penis, which bubble and hiss when they encounter the heat of the fire, sizzling from proud quarters to wizened, chewy dimes." To him, blowfish-eating is "heightened by danger, flavored with death."

As the patron saint of foodies, Gold rightly suspects that he has encouraged what he calls the "dining as sport" crowd. "These are the guys who say, 'I'll see your live octopus and raise you a chicken foot. Oh, so you're going to eat small intestine full of undigested cow's milk?'" he said. "That's actually a good dish. You can get it at just about any taqueria, but you really have to trust the guy." One avid reader told me, "He has a lot to do with people eating at restaurants with a C from the health department. He trumpeted that really loudly, like 'I do not care! This is going to make me sick and I'm interested in endangering myself.'" Another told me that he was once laid up for two weeks after eating Korean beef-liver sashimi at a restaurant recommended by Gold. "I feel that because he's willing to eat this stuff, it's almost like a dare," he said. "I have to try it, even if it's horrifying."

Alice Waters, the chef at Chez Panisse, in Berkeley, and the mother figure of organic, farm-to-table dining, says that Gold is a harbinger of where American eating needs to go: toward diversity, away from monoculture. Gold reveals, before the U.S. Census Bureau does, which new populations have come to town, where they are, and what they're cooking up. In 2009, he announced a migration from Mexico's Distrito Federal. How did he know? Because you could now get DF-style *carnitas* in Highland Park, "loose and juicy, spilling out of the huge $1.99 tacos like Beyoncé out of a tight jumpsuit." It was the same month that the Centers for Disease Control confirmed the first two U.S. cases of swine flu, both in California, which had most people looking askance at pork. Gold looked at it sidelong, and bit. He recommended the *tacos de nana*—pig uterus—"chewy yet forgiving, pink and yet not, whorled in swoops and paisley shapes that defy Euclidean geometry."

Early in my apprenticeship, Gold took me through Historic Filipinotown. Filipino is one of the few kinds of cooking that Gold can't stand. "It's as if you took the worst of the U.S., Spanish, Asian, and Pacific Island cuisine and mixed them into one thoroughly unwholesome . . . I try, I really try," he told me once. Our destination was the Brooklyn Bagel Bakery, which was started in 1953 by immigrants from New York and is, he says, the single source of every good bagel in Los Angeles.

Looking back, I could have been hurt. Bagels? I got the sense that Gold, who is a gentleman, didn't want to scare me, at least not right away. We got four water bagels and three salt. In the car, tearing hunks from the one he had designated a roadie, he said, "You probably don't eat bagels. Too pure." It was a damning view of my potential and a barely veiled challenge. In any case, Brooklyn Bagel was only a pit stop. We had just had a so-so Guatemalan meal (*chiles relleños,* tamales, pounded-pumpkin-seed stew, and *kakik de gallina,* a chicken dish that he'd never seen on a menu before), and were on the way to

Mama's Hot Tamales Café, off MacArthur Park, near Langer's Deli (the source of the city's best pastrami). "This is one of the gnarlier, gnarlier drug zones in L.A.," he said, circling Mama's block. "I was here with my mother, on our way to Langer's, and people were trying to sell her crack." An apartment where he lived for ten years, until the 1992 riots trashed the neighborhood and he moved to Pasadena, was just a couple of miles away.

At Mama's, we had a chicken tamale with red sauce and a pork tamale with green. Gold took a pound of coffee beans to go, and then we swung back west, to hit a Peruvian restaurant owned by Koreans that sits in a median, next to a car wash, and specializes in spit-roasted chicken and grilled beef heart. "It's not the *best* grilled beef heart you've ever had," he said. He was picking up a chicken for supper and, since he was there, ordered a fermented-corn drink and half a chicken to stay. I smiled weakly and said nothing. At that point, I hadn't had any grilled beef heart, ever, as I'm sure he had deduced.

Gold eats at three hundred to five hundred restaurants every year. "Food rewards obsessiveness," he says. His friend Robert Sietsema told me that, during three years starting in the late nineties, when Gold was working in New York as the restaurant critic at *Gourmet,* Sietsema, who was the restaurant critic for the *Village Voice* and presumably accustomed to eating a lot, gained twenty-five pounds. "We really put on the feed bag," he said. Not long before we talked, Sietsema said, Gold had visited. "He and I went on a typical binge. We started with porchetta sandwiches, then went to David Chang's bakery for focaccia with kimchi, then we had salty-pistachio soft-serve ice cream, cookies, and coffee milk. Then we went to a pizzeria famous for its artichoke slice, where we also had a Sicilian slice, and then we took the train to Flushing and visited a new Chinese food court and had half a dozen Chinese dishes there. Then we went to the old food court down the street, visited three more stalls, and had a bunch of things, including lamb noodles, and then Jonathan had to go to dinner somewhere. After dinner, he stopped by my apartment, and we went out to another three-course dinner." Sietsema told me, "Jonathan once said, 'We don't write about food, we write about eating.'"

When Gold took the job at *Gourmet*, maître d's around the city hastened to get a bead on his appearance. The word went out: "Biker." Wednesday was bear night in the West Village, where he lived, and he became an object of desire. "I felt like I was walking around naked," he says. Gold has been mistaken for the chef Jonathan Waxman—"another hairy Californian"—and for Mario Batali, though, according to him, "I'm much better-looking than Mario." Gold was a music journalist in the eighties and nineties. His hip-hop name, given to him by Snoop Dogg and Dr. Dre, is Nervous Cuz. He is sly and erudite, withdrawn in person and in print exuberant. The avant-garde composer Carl Stone, who has titled many of his pieces after restaurants that Gold has introduced him to, considers him the S. J. Perelman of food.

Gold grew up in South Central, the eldest of three boys. His mother, Judith, was the librarian at a rough public school, a witty, lively woman who had been a magician's assistant and a minor theater actress. His father, Irwin, an aspiring academic, studied under Joyce-scholar Richard Ellmann but got polio before he could finish his dissertation. He became a probation officer; Roman Polanski was one of his cases. The filmmakers behind the documentary *Roman Polanski: Wanted and Desired* used Irwin's copious, finely written probation report in their research. He was passionate about classical music, literature, and comfort food (Chicago-style hot dogs, all-you-can-eat buffets, lunch-counter burgers); aiming to please him, Jonathan took up cello, reading, and eating. In spite of his efforts, he failed to win his father's approval: Irwin claimed never to have read his columns. After his father died, Jonathan cleaned out Irwin's car and found a complete file of his columns in the trunk and Verdi's *Requiem* in the tape deck.

At sixteen, Gold left the house. It was the late seventies; he stayed with friends and, he says, in the months before the Iranian Revolution, squatted in Beverly Hills houses that had been bought but not yet occupied by families from Tehran. On the strength of his cello playing, he went to UCLA, where for a time he lived in his practice room. During his freshman year, Gold took a course in cultural geography and was assigned to make an ethnic map of a block of Beverly Boulevard not far from downtown. The city's variegated, unassimilated complexity began to dawn on him. At a laundromat, he saw Salvadorans saving dryers for Salvadorans, and overheard Mexicans who spoke not Spanish but Nahuatl. The 7-Eleven, he noticed, was owned by Koreans. Just as important, the block included Shibucho—one of the first Japanese restaurants, Gold says, to expel patrons for ordering California rolls—and he tried sushi. Later, for a class that he took with the performance artist Chris

Burden, Gold made a piece that involved going to every Jewish deli in the city and buying two water bagels using only pennies; one he ate and one he saved to hang behind plastic on the studio wall. That was how he discovered the Brooklyn Bagel Bakery.

After graduating UCLA, Gold was living on Pico Boulevard, above a kosher butcher in an Iranian Jewish enclave, and working at a legal newspaper downtown. Taking the bus east on Pico every day, he passed through Korean, Nicaraguan, Salvadoran, Oaxacan, and Jaliscan neighborhoods. As an experiment, he set out to try every restaurant—places that served *pupusas,* chili fries, Korean barbecue—along the boulevard. He gave himself a year, at the end of which he planned to join the Foreign Service, so that he could go off and have adventures around the world. When he was finished eating Pico, he realized that he could have just as exotic a life without ever leaving Los Angeles.

For years, Gold's itinerant eating seemed purposeless; then, suddenly, as with the caterpillar in the Eric Carle book, there was a glorious, fully realized point to it. John Powers, a film critic who met Gold at the *Weekly* in the mid-eighties, when Gold was a proofreader there, says, "He has the flâneur instinct. In all those years, when his peers were very busy professionally writing, Jonathan was professionally wandering around not writing. By background, inclination, and practice, he has always been the one who knows the most stuff close to the ground." Even now, his approach can be exhausting and, to others, anticlimactic. Jervey Tervalon, a novelist who often accompanies Gold on his food tours, remembers weeks spent looking for good blood sausage soup. "The relentlessness of that search!"

he said. "The leads led here and there and finally ended with a big frothy bowl of something that looked like it had a scab on top."

At the *Weekly,* when Gold was in his mid-twenties, he met Laurie Ochoa, a beautiful, dark-haired intern who had just finished college, and wooed her with dollar seats for the Los Angeles Philharmonic at the Hollywood Bowl and a slice of his mother's peach pie. They got married, over a roast pig, in 1990, and she has been his dining companion and first reader ever since. (She was his editor at *Gourmet* and at the *Weekly.*) They have two children, Leon, who is ten, and Isabel, nineteen. Isabel grew up on tentacles but can't abide anything spicy; Leon has spent his childhood ordering chicken and rice in places that specialize in blood and tripe.

The formal rigor that Gold applied to his early eating jags has become a recurring motif. He likes a culinary picaresque, and often takes the kids. They have accompanied him on hot dog, hot chocolate, and gelato sprees. The day he decided to find the city's best espresso, he traveled with David Kendrick, then the drummer for Devo. After twenty-seven shots, Gold—sweating, trembling, and talking too loudly—met up with Ochoa and some friends for dinner. He started to panic and begged the group not to get dessert. When Ochoa ordered tiramisu, he burst into tears, ran out of the restaurant, and took the bus home.

Los Angeles is an immigrant city positioned between two major foci of historical necessity eating, Latin America and Asia. This is where Gold concentrates his efforts. Interesting cuisine, he believes, often comes out of poverty. "I have my thing," he says. "Traditional—I hate the word 'ethnic'—restaurants that serve some actual hunger people have, rather than something they tell themselves they must have." Plus, there is George Orwell's rule of thumb: the fancier the restaurant, the more people who have dripped sweat into your food. For a period in the late eighties, Ochoa told me, Gold had a theory that you could tell a great restaurant based on three factors: the curtains in the window, the look of the sign, and the music that was playing (the worse, the better). One day, in Westminster, a Vietnamese enclave, he found a place with all the indicators, down to the perfectly tattered lace curtains. "We order and the waiter says, 'You don't want this dish,'" Ochoa said. "Now, we've been told that many times. We said, 'No, we really, really want it.' 'No, you don't,' he said. We said, 'We want to eat what Vietnamese people eat.' So they brought the dish out finally. It was boar, and the pieces actually had hair still on them. At this point we *had* to eat it because we'd made this whole big deal. It was pretty foul, and it wasn't just the hair."

Gold drives twenty thousand miles a year in search of food. "I go into a fugue state, like the Aboriginal dreamtime, when you go on long, aimless walks in the outback," he says. "That's how I feel driving on the endless streets of Los Angeles County." Any given afternoon will find him heading east from Pasadena into the far reaches of the San Gabriel Valley, an expansive territory of suburban cities and unincorporated towns northeast of Los Angeles whose culinary significance Gold has long asserted. "When the world's great food cities are being discussed, Paris and Tokyo and Taipei and Rome, it would not be unreasonable to include among them . . . San Gabriel, Calif., population 30,072, which up until a few years ago was noted chiefly for the patty melts at Sandi's Coffee Shop," he wrote in 1992. "Consider this: the city of San Gabriel has at least 50 restaurants worth recommending, far more than Beverly Hills or Cincinnati, and scarcely fewer than Los Angeles' entire Westside."

Over the past thirty years, the San Gabriel Valley has transformed from working-class white suburbs of faded bowling alleys and German restaurants into a place where it is possible to live quite comfortably speaking nothing but Chinese. In the seventies, Frederic Hsieh, a Chinese immigrant, successfully pitched the San Gabriel Valley city of Monterey Park to wealthy Taiwanese as "the Chinese Beverly Hills"; by 1990, according to *The Ethnic Quilt,* a book about the demographics of Southern California, the city was 36 percent Chinese and known as Little Taipei. Eating in the San Gabriel Valley, Gold has observed that, unlike in New York, where immigrants quickly adapt their cooking styles to reflect the city's collective idea of "Chinese food," the insular nature of Los Angeles allows imported regional cuisines to remain intact, traceable almost to the restaurant owners' villages of origin. "The difference is that in New York they're cooking for us," Gold told me. "Here they're cooking for themselves."

Gold's car is a green pickup: toothpicks in the cup holder, mint-flavored Scope in the passenger's footwell. "Alice Waters gave me total shit when I bought it," he told me. "I told her, 'You know how many organic turnips I can fit in the back of this truck?' I just thought it was beautiful. It's big, and I'm big." One day, we alighted at a mini-mall in Rowland Heights, deep in the SGV. "This is the rich Chinese neighborhood," he said. From his pocket he pulled the folded-up flap of an envelope, which was covered with notes scrawled haphazardly in pencil. He wanted to try No. 1 Noodle House, where the specialty is Saliva Chicken. "So hot it makes your mouth water, which is the best of all possible reasons it might be called that," he said. He had learned about the restaurant in the Chinese-language Yellow Pages. Gold doesn't speak or read any language but English; he has strong deductive skills, and Google Translate helps. When in doubt, he points.

The noodle shop was closed. Gold consulted his notes, and we drove a hundred yards to another mini-mall. "We just did something very Californian," he said. "Drove from one shopping center across the street to another." There was a Szechuan restaurant with a string of red chilies draped over the door and a B in the window, a grade given by the county health inspector and posted by law. (Gold subscribes to another rating system, where A stands for "American Chinese," B is "Better Chinese," and C is "Chinese food for Chinese," but he admits that, for years before the grading system was in place, he walked around with constant low-level food poisoning.) He sat down and perused a menu that had been awkwardly translated into English: "Steamed Toad" was the name of one entrée. The waitress came, and he pointed to *dam-dam* noodles, dumplings, wontons, pork, and a fish special. From a cold case, he chose pig's ear. It was my first. It was oddly flavorless, but the texture reminded me of biting on a knuckle, unstable and unforgiving at once. "Some places they just slice the ear," Gold said. "Here they sliced it and pressed it into a kind of terrine, so this is probably a good place." As I chewed, my hand kept wanting to reach up and touch my own ear as a reference point.

"*Cha,* please," he said, ordering tea.

"Huh?" the waitress said.

"*Cha*—tea," he said.

"Oh, *tea*."

The fish arrived, blue-lipped and bathed in chilies and oil. "Spicy," Gold said, tasting it. "The dumplings are good, too. And I suspect they smoke their own pork here. It's good, but I don't think it's enough better than the other good Szechuan place, which is twenty miles closer to L.A." The food was heavy. "They're cooking the peasant version of these dishes," he said. "Oil is a sign of generosity."

Before heading back, Gold wanted to check out a fast-food restaurant called Malan Han Noodle, in yet another mini-mall. "This place in China is the equivalent of McDonald's," he said as he approached the door. "It's the biggest chain, and it's owned by a big petroleum company. The noodles it serves are a specialty of Lanzhou, which is known for being one of the most polluted cities in China—and for its hand-pulled noodles." Inside, Gold sat down and ordered a couple of bowlfuls—large round noodles in beef broth, noodles with brown sauce. The kitchen was visible from the dining area. "Note the Mexican guy rolling out the dough and tossing the noodles," he said, tucking into his soup. "I don't know why, but that always makes me extremely happy."

In foodie mythology, Gold's traverse of Pico has the significance that Siddhartha's search for enlightenment does in Buddhism. Kate Krader, the restaurant editor of *Food & Wine,* says, "The fact that he saw the potential of every restaurant, big and small, fancy and humble, has empowered a lot of people to see the glory in the coffee that's served at their coffee shop, not to mention the person who's making the perfect grilled cheese sandwich just down the block from them." Without him, Krader says, Yelp, a site where amateurs post reviews, would not exist as we know it. For Yelpers, tweeters, bloggers, and other eating documentarians, Gold is also the one to beat.

Javier Cabral, a would-be protégé of Gold, started writing a blog called *The Teenage Glutster: Food, Adolescence, Angst, Hormones and a Really, Really Fast Metabolism* when he was sixteen and a junior in high school. (Now that he's of age, he blogs at *The Glutster.*) When I first met him, at a Vietnamese-Chinese restaurant with Corinthian columns, wedding bunting, a mural of Angkor Wat on the wall, and the whiff of cleaning fluid in the air, he was nineteen, six feet three, and weighed 135 pounds. He was wearing a purple hooded sweatshirt, a T-shirt with a picture of a pineapple on it, and thick-soled purple leopard print T.U.K.s. At the time, he was living with his parents, first-generation immigrants from Mexico, in the back room of their secondhand-furniture store in East Los Angeles.

In addition to being Cabral's "food role model," Gold was his informant on this restaurant's unofficial Cambodian menu. From it, Cabral ordered steamed coconut fish cakes, king crab with scallions and jalapeños, and a salad made of a bitter, green, mulberry-shaped fruit. "*Sdao* is a typical herb in Cambodia," he said. "Like a broccoli texture with a super-medicinal aftertaste. It's a shame they don't have deer today, which is why I came."

In his early teens, Cabral told me, he was "non-food-conscious," eating fast food all the time. When he learned about

PETA, he became a vegan. "I started to get brainwashed," he said. "But that was my gateway, and it led me to get more interested in food." The real transformation came when, in an act of self-preservation—to get away from the temptations of East L.A.: punk rock and beer—he decided to move in with his sister in Alhambra, in the San Gabriel Valley, so he could attend "a high-achieving Asian-driven school." He picked up an *LA Weekly* looking for information about punk shows, and noticed that many of the restaurants being reviewed were within walking distance of his school. While his classmates went in packs to In-N-Out, he'd go alone for Szechuan takeout, which he'd eat in the back alley. "I learned from Jonathan Gold that food writing doesn't need to be so hosh-posh, snobby, and froufrou," the Glutster told me. "It can be ghetto." So he started his own blog. "At first, I was the only food blogger in L.A. with no pictures, because I couldn't afford a camera."

Several years ago, the Glutster's mother took him to a healing mass at La Iglesia Nuestra Señora de la Soledad, his local parish, in the hope that it would cure him of his fascination with food, which she finds worrisome. He left before the service ended, and, taking a walk around the neighborhood, came upon the day's true "revelation," as he put it on his blog: a Oaxacan spot, Moles La Tia, that served twenty varieties of mole. Later, Gold reviewed the restaurant and credited the Glutster with the find, thereby putting him on the food-blogging map.

Over lunch, Cabral told me it had been five years since he ate fast food. With Gold's guidance, he has explored delicacies from the neighborhood where he grew up—goat stew and tongue tacos—which he'd never tried before. He eats his way through any food festival he can score tickets to. At one, he ran into his mentor after trying food from every vendor and sometimes going back for seconds. "So, Mr. Gold, how do you deal with this nasty, disgusting feeling of repulsement?" he asked. "Ach, you'll get used to it," was the answer. Cabral's solution was to walk the five miles home to East L.A.

Not long after his discovery of Moles La Tia, Cabral found out about a place called Pal Cabron, which was serving street food from Puebla, the state just north of Oaxaca. In a post that reflected something of Gold's penchant for the earthily figurative, he rhapsodically chronicled the "Avocado, Chipotle, and the ever acquired taste of Papalo, an herb that smells like if a really thirsty deer just walked on top of it." In other words, it tasted of deer pee, and that was a good thing. This time, when Gold wrote up the restaurant, a week later, he didn't cite the Glutster's review. Cabral tweeted in protest—"J. Gold . . . give me credit!"—to no avail.

Pal Cabron, which has since closed, was in the heavily Mexican neighborhood of Huntington Park. Bricia Lopez, whose parents opened Guelaguetza, the city's first Oaxacan restaurant, is a glamorous young fixture of the L.A. food scene. She started Pal Cabron with her brother. They decorated the inside of the restaurant with bright colors and murals of dishy women, each embodying a different saucily named sandwich from her menu: La Tuya (Yo Momma), La Tetanic (The Double-D), La Muy Muy. The doorway was painted with the screen icons of Facebook, Twitter, and Yelp. The place, according to its décor, was a product of foodie social media; survival, in this off-the-beaten-path location, would depend on Gold's pilgrims.

After we had gorged on Cambodian food, the Glutster suggested we make a trip to Pal Cabron, to get his favorite *cemita,* a sandwich of seasoned lamb and *quesillo*, served on a crunchy, house-made sesame roll. He was emboldened by his recent reviewing triumphs. "Gold used to be my role model. Now he's—dare I say it?—my competition," he mused. "A role model–slash–supercelebrity–slash–archenemy." Cabral has many times offered himself up to Gold as an assistant; he wants to help him put together a long-promised follow-up to *Counter Intelligence*, a compendium of reviews Gold published more than a decade ago. But Gold has been elusive. "Probably he's scared because he knows I'm going to dethrone him one day," Cabral speculated. He walked through the restaurant and chose a table facing the back wall. There, Bricia had commissioned another mural, this one depicting Jonathan Gold, eyes cast down and smiling over a little double chin, next to his *LA Weekly* review. His arm was outstretched, with one hand gently touching the Glutster's computer screen.

To Gold's readers, his reviews have the ontological status that *The New York Times* has for people who follow the news: he doesn't write about it because it is; it is because he's written about it. In the spring of 2009, he published a column titled "The New Cocktailians," about the movement of dandified bartenders who pair suspenders with tattoos and treat drinks as a culinary art, shopping at farmers' markets for fresh produce and educating customers about the origins of the gin fizz. By fall, all food-minded Los Angeles understood, without knowing exactly how or why it knew, that a cocktail moment was in full swing.

Then Gold hosted a benefit event at Union Station, the train depot downtown. There were concoctions from New Cocktailians (Manhattans made with Luxardo cherries, champagne drinks with absinthe-citrus foam), paired with morsels from some of Gold's favorite highbrow places. Gold, wearing a gray suit and a pale pink tie covered in pink velvet polka dots, stood with Ochoa at a cocktail table. "The chefs are going to freak out if you don't eat anything," she said, and went to get him a plate.

Ochoa came back with a pig slider and a pig's ear, a deep-fried, molten triangle, uncomfortably soft. "I definitely encourage a certain kind of cooking," Gold said, popping the ear and then the slider into his mouth. Then he went to search for bacon-wrapped matzoh balls: the ultimate transgression.

The food nerds were out in force: bloggers from the local sites that track Gold's every move. Neil Kohan—thirty-one, receding hair, camera slung over his shoulder—sipped a Manhattan and declared Gold the Thom Yorke of food writing. (His blog, *Food Marathon*, chronicles his eating itineraries, many of them heavily informed by Gold.) Another blogger urged Gold to try her drink—twelve-year-old Scotch, ginger syrup, fresh lime juice, soda water, and crushed ice, also made from Scotch. He sipped. "It's delicious," he said. "But something about it tastes a little like pool water, too."

Following in Gold's footsteps can be hazardous. For many years, at the *Weekly,* Gold produced an annual list called "99 Essential L.A. Restaurants." Ken Baumann, an actor, attempted to eat at every one, but ended up having part of his colon and small intestine removed—Crohn's disease—after ticking off only twenty-eight. Gold's last list for the *Weekly* came out in the fall of 2011. Jenji Kohan, the creator of *Weeds,* and her husband, Christopher Noxon, a writer, decided to tackle it. They are committed eaters and devotees of Gold, and they felt they needed some way to structure their dining. "If you have a curator and you have a project that allows you to focus down, it gives you clarity," Noxon says.

By June, Kohan and Noxon were on their sixtieth of the "99": Lukshon, an upscale restaurant owned by Sang Yoon, the chef Gold credits with starting the national plague of "Changes and Modifications Politely Declined" when he added that language to the menu at his burger place, Father's Office. I met them there for dinner.

"Jonathan Gold says we have to get the squid, and we listen to Jonathan Gold over all things," Kohan said as we sat down. She had on a red cardigan and cat's-eye glasses. Noxon, thin and fair, added tea-leaf salad, Manila clams, Chinese black mushrooms, garlic pork belly. The waiter suggested lamb belly roti; we got two. "He's got a tender tummy, which was a problem initially," Kohan said. "I have an iron stomach. My mother cooked like a cafeteria—mediocre food and a *lot* of it."

"At a certain point, I would have taken a pill for daily caloric intake," Noxon said. "Now I get angry if I have something that isn't delicious. I get depressed."

Once they both cared, choosing where to eat grew complicated. "It was hugely contentious and difficult," Noxon said. "An unbelievable ordeal. Where are we going to eat? What continent?" Sometimes they would spin the globe to settle it. Now they have three children, who bicker in the car on Saturday mornings about whether to go to Golden Deli, a Vietnamese spot in San Gabriel that is perennially on the "99," or to La Cabañita, in the far-flung town of Montrose, for Mexican. Charlie, the eldest, is thirteen. "He is the most adventurous, and the most limited," Kohan said—allergic to dairy, sesame, and cashews. A few years ago, he decided to keep kosher, though his parents aren't observant, and now he avoids pork and shellfish, except on Purim. "He found a loophole in the literature that says on Purim you are 'not yourself,' so for one day a year it's blue crab hand rolls and pork soup dumplings, the things he misses."

At the end of dinner, Noxon said, "Those mushrooms are amazing and I will crave them." They were meaty and deep, with a touch of smoke, like the dregs of a pot of Lapsang souchong. They agreed that the food was tasty, but that it was the kind of place that years of reading Jonathan Gold had taught them to deplore: inauthentic, impersonal, what he calls an "AmEx restaurant." "It's really good, but it's bullshit," Noxon said. "Third generation."

In a fancy restaurant, Gold will wear a rumpled suit and a soft bluish button-down and pay with a credit card issued in the name of his high-school algebra teacher. He has special cell phone numbers that he uses just for reservations. "It's like *The Bourne Identity* in slow motion," he says.

The first piece he wrote for a "slick"—the now defunct *California* magazine, edited by the late Harold Hayes—was a review of Chasen's, which had been an entertainment-industry staple for fifty years. To Gold, it reeked of Reaganomics and other things that he despised. He wrote that it was "a swell place to celebrate a seventy-fifth birthday or a contra incursion," and that the famous chili was "distinguishable from a bowl of Dennison's only by a couple of chunks of sirloin, a 1,600 percent price differential and three guys"—the servers—"who look like they stepped out of a 1935 gangster B-movie." He has his regrets. "Although I didn't do Chasen's in"—it was around for another decade—"I certainly put a lance in its side," he says. "But, looking back, I really miss Chasen's. And kiwi vinaigrette and magical caviar snakes and braised cantaloupe with black corn fungus and all the things I thought were the future back then—a lot of that food was just silly."

Accessible food has always been of greater interest to Gold—but it depends on what you mean by accessible. "The democracy of really fine dining is something I've always liked about L.A.," he says. "In New York, the most expensive restaurant is always the best. That's not necessarily the case here." In 1990, he started writing about Renu Nakorn, an Isaan Thai place twenty miles southeast of downtown, next to a working dairy farm. After his reviews, large numbers of white people started coming in. They ordered what he had ordered: slimy bamboo salads, fermented fish, and intensely spicy dishes—authentic regional Thai food that the owners, Bill and Saipin Chutima, were worried the customers would send back. Jeffrey Steingarten, the food critic for *Vogue,* made a pilgrimage (the Chutimas said that his post-prandial cigar was disrupted by the stench of cows), and so did Mark Bittman, of *The New York Times.* When the Chutimas moved to Las Vegas and opened a new place, Lotus of Siam, Gold called it the best Thai restaurant in North America; in 2011, Saipin, who does the cooking, won a James Beard award.

Gold, who has a competitive streak, put it this way once: "As the Italians say of Christopher Columbus, when he discovered America, it stayed discovered."

As a kid, Gold guzzled hot sauce. Several years ago, on a tip from a diner who had discovered a secret, untranslated menu of southern Thai specialties at an ordinary strip-mall Thai place called Jitlada, Gold paid a visit. After eating there a few times, he brought his friend Carl Stone, the composer, who carries a card in his wallet that says, more or less, in Thai, "Yes, I know I'm not Thai, but please give me the food as spicy as I request." They ordered *kua kling*, a dry-beef curry, and asked for it "Bangkok hot."

The *kua kling* was the spiciest Gold had ever had. "It was glowing, practically incandescent," he told me. "You bite into it and every alarm in your body goes off at once. It's an overload on your pain receptors, and then the flavors just come through. It's not that the hotness overwhelms the dish, which is what people who don't understand Thai cooking always say, but that the dish is revealed for the first time—its flavor—as you taste details of fruit and turmeric and spices that you didn't taste when it was merely extremely hot. It's like a hallucination. You're floating in some high, tasting the most magnificent things you've ever tasted in your life. I've never been able to get them to make it that hot again." Stone said it hurt to pee for three days afterward. He said, "I thought, How in the world could I have gotten the clap?"

That day, the owner, a voluble woman named Jazz, came over to their table and started chatting. She mentioned that she had been praying every day in her Buddha room for Jonathan

Gold to come in and review her restaurant. Did they know him or know what he looked like? she asked. Stone says, "I was going to throw out a red herring—'He's tall and thin with a full head of hair'—but Jonathan started laughing and introduced himself." Gold, in his review, praised the "delicious, foul-smelling yellow curries" and the "strange, mephitic fragrances" of wild tea leaves and stinky beans, and said that Jitlada was "the most exciting new Thai restaurant of the year."

Mark Gold, the youngest of the Gold sons, runs the marine conservation organization Heal the Bay; he finds Jonathan's eating habits atrocious and enumerates his brother's gustatory offenses on his blog, *Spouting Off.* "I have gone to dim sum in San Gabriel when he tried to order shark fin soup," Mark wrote. "I said OMDB! I went to a restaurant with him in Chicago when he was the lead grub guy at *Gourmet* magazine. There, he nearly ordered wild-caught sturgeon until I complained vociferously."

Right before I met him, Jonathan made his first trip to Seoul. When he got back, he wrote about eating live octopus, or *sam nak ji,* which he described as "one of the most alarming dishes in the world." After the piece came out, Mark told me, "Needless to say, I did not participate in that sadistic torture of a wonderful marine animal. I'm not going to eat live shrimp. I'm not going to eat octopus. I haven't had shark or swordfish in twenty-five years. I said to him, 'What do you think an octopus is? You need an ecology class.' He's all, 'It doesn't have a backbone.'"

Of course, Gold didn't need to go to Korea to eat live

octopus. One night he took me to a divey strip-mall restaurant with a picture of a smiling mermaid and a halibut on the sign, and a Korean golf show playing on the television set. He had guessed based on the halibut that they'd have live shrimp and *sam nak ji*. "If you're going to have live halibut you'll have *sam nak ji*," he said. "It's like ham and eggs." It turned out they were out of shrimp—the next shipment was coming at eleven o'clock that night, flown in fresh from Korea—but they had the octopus. "How do I put this delicately?" he said as we sat down. "It's a very male food. We're going to get a lot of winks and nods."

Gold said he thought that the space had once been occupied by Alex Donut, one of three places in town to get Thai food in the late seventies. "I probably wouldn't think it was good now, but that was a thousand Thai meals ago," he said. "I thought it was amusing to eat all the little green nachos in a jar of vinegar, too."

Korean sashimi came to the table—big hunks of white tuna, with the taste and texture of chilled butter; fresh-killed halibut—along with pickled mackerel eggs and sea squirts. The squirts glistened orange and tasted of brine. "These things are essentially taking over the fricking sea," Gold said. "The taste is strong, iodine-y, but not unpleasant—but some people are totally grossed out by them." The bluefin on the table went untouched. "It's the equivalent of going on the Serengeti and eating the lion," Gold said. "My brother hates this argument, but I don't like it because it's boring. Things that are at the top of the food chain are boring. They all taste the same."

Then the proprietor, suppressing a smile, produced the main event, a plate of slippery gray tentacles, squirming anxiously. "It'll try to climb up the chopstick," Gold said, dousing a tentacle in sesame oil to loosen the grip of its suckers. "I don't actually know that much about octopus physiology. Most people say that the octopus is dead, and just twitching, but I don't know. It looks pretty alive to me."

Gold bit into the octopus. "I thought I was completely full from lunch, but this is invigorating food," he said. More courses came—broiled eel and broths and a greasy red kimchi pancake and, finally, crab claws covered in a sticky glaze, lustrous as a ceramic sculpture by Jeff Koons.

He was a tad disappointed about missing the unsettling experience of eating live shrimp. "It freaks me out," he told me. "You're picking up an animal whose carapace has been stripped off by the chef. Its eyeballs are going back and forth on its eyesticks and it's madly trying to swim away. Prawns don't have a great deal of intelligence but they know when they're going to die. You're killing something with your teeth, and whatever the pleasure of that—and the flavor, I've got to admit, is incredibly, hedonistically sweet—it feels wrong. You're not supposed to kill things with your teeth."

Two

GRUB

The roots of extreme foodie-ism extend back to the beginning of the American gourmet industry, when squishy and swank were often one and the same. The business, which, in 2012, represented 10 percent of retail food sales and was worth nearly $86 billion, was built by a handful of largely forgotten European refugees on the backs of a menagerie of creatures most people in this country would gag to see on a plate of food.

At first, the specialty-food trade was based on comforting people with the familiar. During World War II, as thousands of Jews fled Europe for the United States, Jewish importers, most of them working from offices on Hudson and Varick Streets in lower Manhattan, supplied other émigrés with items from home. Only when the salesmen began to penetrate the uptown carriage-trade shops and department stores newly devoting floor space to imported food in spiffy packaging, did the stuff become known as "specialty." Mario Foah, who arrived from Naples in 1939, at the age of eighteen, got his start peddling panettone, a product from the north of Italy that was exotic to the southern Italians he was trying to sell to. Later, he diversified to cookies and candy. "It was strictly a Christmas business," Foah, who is ninety-three, told me. "The rest of the year we managed by starving and eating samples from our suppliers." Business was conducted in cash; according to one old story I heard, dealers kept their money in secret compartments in their shoes.

Storytelling and salesmanship were inseparable, and an aura of personal sophistication proved useful. Ted Koryn was the quintessential New York food pitchman: small and suave, hilariously funny, fluent in four languages and conversant in a handful of others. He was born in Amsterdam to a wealthy family; only French was spoken in his grandmother's dining room, and when his mother went out at night a maid had to stay up till she returned to help her undress. Left alone there during the war—his mother and stepfather had gone "on holiday" to the United States just before the Nazis invaded—he hid out on a boat with two friends, and slept in the boathouse at night. In 1942, his stepfather's uncle was able to trade his art collection for exit visas, and Koryn rejoined his family in New York. There he signed on to a Dutch attachment to the Air Force and was trained in aerial photography at Yale.

After the war, Koryn started a food business, selling mainly French products no one had ever heard of before, like Pommery mustard, Lu Biscuits, and Evian water (which never took off for him). His first wife, Miriam Metzger, was the daughter of Joe

Metzger, who co-founded Dannon yogurt in the Bronx. (The company, which began as Danone in Spain and got its original yogurt cultures from the Pasteur Institute, struggled to connect with U.S. consumers until Miriam's brother, Juan, suggested putting fruit in the bottom of the cup.) Koryn rode around Manhattan in a chauffeured limousine, and socialized constantly with an eclectic group of friends, from the cartoonist Will Eisner to the truffle-selling Urbanis and Xaviera Hollander, a former call girl who wrote *The Happy Hooker.* If he wanted someone to play poker with, he sent the car.

Koryn traveled extensively throughout Europe, always shopping for products to import. It was a good time to get deals: European manufacturers, their domestic economies destroyed, were willing to front product for the chance to enter a potentially vast American market. Purveyors played the edges. "If it was illegal or not one hundred percent, even the better," Tim Metzger, Koryn's nephew, told me. "They loved to press the rules." Bob Lape, a food journalist who started "The Eyewitness Gourmet" segment on WABC-TV in 1970, met Koryn in the middle of a blizzard, when he persuaded him to come visit his factory. Koryn was one of two men Lape called "the hungry ones." The other was Murray Klein, the legendary manager and part owner of the New York specialty store Zabar's, where Koryn sold white truffles and beluga caviar.

In the 1950s, opening a can of mushroom soup and pouring it over a casserole was a culinary event. "They were putting crap in Jell-O and calling it an aspic," John Roberts, a veteran of the food business, says. "Change was not valued. Food was not an adventure." Mario Foah told me, "If you said to the man on the street, 'I'd like to introduce you to gourmet foods,' he'd say, 'Spell it!'" In 1952, Foah, Koryn, and several others decided to form a monthly lunch club that could function as a trade association, lobbying in Washington against tariffs on European products and other issues affecting them. They called themselves the National Association for the Specialty Food Trade, or NASFT.

In 1955, the association put on its first event, the National Fancy Food and Confection Show, at the Sheraton-Astor Hotel in Manhattan. The war had sent a generation of Americans abroad, and the idea was to re-create foreign eating experiences: French mustard, Swiss chocolates, German sausages. The association's president put a note in the brochure, celebrating the inauguration of a marketplace for novel foodstuffs. "This being our first effort, there may be much to criticize and we beg your indulgence for any shortcomings or omissions," he wrote.

One of the omitted would not indulge the oversight. Max Ries, a savvy Chicago-based purveyor, who had been barred from exhibiting—he posed a threat, most likely—ran a limousine from the Sheraton-Astor to another hotel nearby, where he had set up a show of only his products. After a few years, the New Yorkers relented and gave him a booth, which became a major attraction. To his first show, Ries brought an aerosol can filled with liquid cheese spread and a gift basket that cost $300, about $2,500 today. It included a barrel-based table, four chairs, and sixty imported delicacies. Ries came away with sixty-five orders. The next year, he displayed a brightly painted Sicilian cart with an umbrella, loaded with treats. Beautiful models passed out samples. "A lot of people didn't like him," Foah told me. "But I admired him. He made people talk about the industry."

A few months after Ries's show debut, *Fortune* named his company the country's largest importer, estimating its business at $6,500,000 a year, and overall specialty-food sales as high as $200 million, double what they had been in the show's first year. Commercial jetliners were making international travel, and therefore international eating, increasingly accessible. Suburbanites had money, time, and space to entertain; they needed something provocative and delicious to impress their guests at cocktail parties. Curiosity and snobbism, the piece concluded, were leading the way to "a greater sophistication of American taste." The *Los Angeles Times* reported on a "gourmet cult which reaches now from lavish Park Avenue apartments to the grass-roots split-level homes of the Middle West." The country was in the midst of a "great delicacy boom."

Ries, an outsider and a self-reinventor, helped create a taste for the freaky in a society devoted to beefsteak, glamorizing the seemingly repulsive and making it into a symbol of elegance. After a lucrative career as a textile manufacturer in Germany, he arrived in Chicago in 1939 and started selling imported European cheeses out of the back of a station wagon on Route 41, store by store. Soon he employed a brigade of German-Jewish refugees to go on the road for him. They drove all day and for dinner ate canned peaches and ice cream. Within a few years, Ries had diversified: an early price list shows Norwegian goat cheese, Bahamian mustard, chow mein noodles, Cuban rock lobster, and Hawaiian Punch.

Ries was dashing; slim and refined, he wore handmade suits and twirled—never chewed—his cigars. In order to make his company sound more "American," he called it Reese Finer Foods. He developed new foods—baby corn, blue-cheese salad dressing, shelf-stable croutons—and sold them alongside other then-exotic fare like water chestnuts. When a shipment of artichokes arrived in rusty, dented cans, Ries packed them in glass with vinaigrette, and called them marinated artichokes. He couldn't boil water, according to his son, but he had a flair for presentation. Reese Finer Foods helped introduce teriyaki sauce to the United States by attaching a Japanese yen coin to every bottle sold ("Gives you a yen for Oriental food"); their barbecue sauce came with a whisk attached. In 1958, the *Los Angeles Evening Herald Express* announced, "Something wonderful has happened and no longer do you need ever again to get garlic on your finger tips!" Reese had invented roll-on garlic oil.

While other importers looked mainly to Europe, Ries sought unfamiliar snacks in Asia and Latin America. He brought tinned sparrows and French-fried grasshoppers from Japan, and ants from Bogotá. The Illinois candy-maker he hired to cover the ants with chocolate is said to have called Ries in a panic when the 500-pound shipment arrived; workers were threatening to quit the line. Once a year, Ries and his employees went to Asia to look for products and ideas. Reese sold tinned lion, tiger, elephant, and whale; pickled rooster combs, espresso, Lindt chocolate; Canadian muskrat, reindeer steaks from Lapland, and diamondbacks from Ross Allen, a snake-wrestling celebrity herpetologist with a ranch in Florida.

Ancient Romans sold the meat of exotic, imported panthers, hippos, lions, and giraffes killed in death matches at the circus; Reese did the modern equivalent, tinning creatures culled from zoos. "The zoos would furnish lists of animals they had to dispose of," an employee later told a newspaper reporter. "Reese would buy a carcass at a high price and give it, frozen, to a cannery for processing." When Ries went to a stock show in Chicago and noticed that no one was bidding on the bison—not then considered food—he bought the whole lot for forty cents a pound, and canned the meat with wine. "He took great food that nobody knew they wanted and got them to buy it," Stewart Reich, Ries's great-nephew, told me. "Max—I don't want to say he churned it out, but he had a supply line and discovered the soft part of the market and exploited it." At a "Fashion Show of Foods" Ries put on in Milwaukee in the mid-fifties, he said, "Eating habits are in the mind."

As early as 1965, Ries predicted the foodie movement, and its turn toward the more inclusive, inventive cuisines of Latin America and Asia. "More people today can afford more of the so-called 'exotic' foods which previously were available only to persons of great wealth," he said. "With this increased affluence has also come a new spirit of adventure about eating." His evidence that the babyish palate of America was maturing was that people had begun to take their baked potatoes with sour cream instead of sweet butter.

"They were Marco Polo type of guys," Reich says. "They

were definitely in the entertainment business." One year Reese had overstock of its Spooky Foods gift set—chocolate-covered ants, bees, grasshoppers, and caterpillars—so it hired Bela Lugosi to appear in his Dracula costume with the product, which promptly sold out. Alienation was part of the appeal. Reich, who still works in the food business, considered Ries a mentor and an example; the month that *Jaws* opened in theaters Reich hawked shark-meat pâté wearing a scuba suit and took out an advertisement that read, "This is your chance to bite back."

One of Ries's most valued employees was Morris Kushner, a former writer on Groucho Marx's *This Is Your Life*, who started as a West Coast representative and rose to company president. He lived in the guest quarters of a sprawling mansion in Encino and was married to Naudjia de Morozova, a thin, flamboyant woman who dressed in fur, claimed to be a Russian countess, and ate little besides chocolate. Kushner, who wore checked suits, a tweed trilby, and a moustache, was from Nebraska. His pedigree in food was long: his uncle was a grocer in Lincoln, and Kushner apprenticed with him in his youth. After the war, he worked for a wholesaler in Los Angeles that supplied Hollywood with chutney, caviar, and foie gras. In a book on the industry, he boasted of having been one of the first to bring smoked oysters from Japan to the United States, as part of General MacArthur's plan to revive the Japanese economy by appealing to American hostesses.

"I set out to design our private label and felt that I needed something other than merely the words 'Smoked Oysters,'" Kushner wrote. The one other similar product available at the time was a crabapple smoked oyster from the Pacific Northwest. "I searched through Japanese literature and history books. . . . From *Madame Butterfly* and the Cherry Blossom Festival, I assumed that Japan had an abundance of cherry trees, so I labeled our product 'Cherrywood Smoked Oysters.'" When he later met with the president of the Smoked Oyster Association in Hiroshima, he learned that the Japanese had been flummoxed by his first order, and had gone out in search of precious cherrywood to authenticate the label's claim. "Needless to say, that was the only time cherrywood was ever used in that manner, and subsequent orders were smoked with the cheaper kindling scrap wood." But, he concluded proudly, "cherrywood smoked" became the industry standard. "I relate this little tale to illustrate how a product can be upgraded in the eyes of the beholder with a little label imagery."

The successful food seller was part carnival barker, part con man. If an item wasn't moving, Kushner's advice was to mark it up: a $75 jar of truffles is more intriguing than the same jar for $45. Another rule of thumb: "The food broker must never lie to a buyer, or better yet, never get caught lying." In the mid-forties, when most specialty-foods dealers were trying to keep their products *out* of supermarkets for fear that mass marketing and availability would destroy their mystique (and their profit margins), he persuaded a Southern California grocery store to designate a gourmet section. They called the improvised area—a plywood shelf resting on large, foil-wrapped juice cans—"the importation center," because most of the items came from abroad. By 1970, the Safeway in Washington, D.C., stocked nearly five thousand gourmet items, among them staples of the

Reese line like rattlesnake, kangaroo, and Bengal tiger meat. They may not have been a large part of the business, but they served a purpose: "shelf-warmers" tended to start selling faster when placed near such attention-grabbing exotics.

In 1968, Craig Claiborne, the food editor of *The New York Times*, wrote with amusement about Reese's elephant meat, which "the foremost food authority in Florida" was planning to serve in an omelet at her husband's restaurant in Miami. (Her source: Bloomie's.) The following year, the federal Endangered Species Conservation Act was passed, significantly expanding the prohibitions against selling certain animals, and Reese's swashbuckling period came to an abrupt end. In 1973, Congress signed the Endangered Species Act, a broader law that is still in place. That year, after tins of Reese's smoked whale meat were discovered for sale in the Gourmet Foods Shop at Macy's in New York, investigators confiscated a large supply from a Reese warehouse in the Bronx, fined the company, and made it promise not to sell any more endangered species in the state.

As the market changed, Kushner tried to live down his association with the "gimmicky" foods that had set Reese apart from its competitors. Kushner saw food both as a mark of status and as a democratizer, a powerful social vehicle for the eighties striver. "Tonight you can eat as well as Rockefeller," he'd say. In 1982, he told *The New York Times*, "When people can't afford mink coats, Cadillacs, or beautiful homes, they reward themselves with good cheeses they can afford. It's accessible luxury." By then, specialty foods had moved out of the "gourmet ghetto" and onto the supermarket's main shelves—the Grey Poupon alongside the ballpark mustard—and America had changed because of it. There were limits—Kushner didn't think *balut* would ever "go down"—but people had accepted previously spurned exotics like raw oysters, rabbit, and mussels. Kushner took to greeting visitors to the food show by saying, "Welcome to Wonderland, where today's specialties become tomorrow's staples!"

In overcoming the resistance to certain foods, Frederick J. Simoons, the author of the classic text on culinary taboos *Eat Not This Flesh,* says timing is everything, and there is usually more than one factor at play. When Emperor Meiji ate beef—a sacrilege in Buddhist Japan—it was because the country was ready to embrace the West. Noritoshi Kanai, the eighty-eight-year-old president of Mutual Trading Company, which imports gold flakes and matsutake essence to sell to high-end sushi restaurants like Masa and Nobu, introduced sushi to the United States in the 1960s. Because sushi is raw and handled without gloves in front of the customer, everyone told him that the American public would never accept it. The convergence of three factors, he says, changed their minds: the food pyramid, which emphasized fish; the rise of the Japanese car; and *Shōgun*, the best-selling novel by James Clavell.

Insects, the wiggly, bridge-party shockers that helped get America excited about eating, are back, and this time around they may, like Evian, be here to stay. The conditions are promising. America's food intelligentsia bemoans the industrial-scale farming and food processing of the present, and forsees a *Mad Max* future. Insects are danger-tinged but eco-friendly, and little explored as food. Once a staple on *Fear Factor,* they were featured on *Top Chef Masters* a few seasons ago; the winning dish was tempura-fried crickets with sunchoke-carrot purée and blood-orange vinaigrette. During the London Olympics, the celebrated Danish chef René Redzepi, whose restaurant, Noma, has repeatedly been named the best restaurant in the world, served a tasting menu at Claridge's, the five-star Mayfair hotel. The eight-course meal cost more than $300 a head and featured chilled live ants, flown from Copenhagen, on cabbage with crème fraiche. "When you bite into the ants, they release the flavor of lemongrass; what you taste is light and citrusy, in contrast to the edible soil you have just consumed," the *Bloomberg* food critic wrote.

Guelaguetza, the Oaxacan restaurant opened by Bricia Lopez's parents, serves a scrumptious plate of *chapulines a la Mexicana*—grasshoppers sautéed with onions, jalapeños, and tomatoes, and topped with avocado and Oaxacan string cheese. Lopez says that more and more Anglo hipsters—Jonathan Gold readers—are coming in to order them. "Eating grasshoppers is a thing you do here," she said. "Like, 'Oh my God, I ate a grasshopper, *woo.*'" She went on, "There's more of a cool factor involved. It's not just 'Let's go get a burrito.' It's 'Let's get a *mole'* or 'Let's get a grasshopper.'" According to the FDA, insects sold as human food must be raised specifically for the purpose in a facility that follows "good manufacturing processes"; "wildcrafting" is not condoned, for fear of pesticide contamination or disease, nor is diverting bugs from the pet-food stream. The USDA, which typically handles meat, doesn't contemplate insects at all. Until a citation from the health department prompted them to set up a certified facility in Oaxaca, the Lopezes got the *chapulines* they served at Guelaguetza from friends and relatives, who packed them in their carry-ons when they visited from Mexico.

The contemporary vogue for bugs reflects not only a desire for novelty but also a degree of pragmatism, and that may guarantee their staying power. José Andrés, a winner of the James Beard Foundation's Outstanding Chef award, makes a very popular *chapulín* taco—sautéed shallots, deglazed in tequila; chipotle paste; and Oaxacan grasshoppers, in a handmade tortilla—at his Washington, D.C., restaurant Oyamel. He sees bug-eating as both a gastronomic experience (he recommends the mouthfeel of a small, young, crispy *chapulín)* and a matter of survival. "We need to feed humanity in a sustainable way," he says. "Those who know how to produce protein will have an edge over everyone else. World War Three will be over control of water and food, and the insects may be an answer."

According to the ecologist Daniel Pauly, Mexico's tradition of insect-eating arose from a lack of alternatives. Before the arrival of the Europeans, there were neither cows nor horses nor other large mammals that could be easily domesticated. The same went for the rest of Latin America: this is why Peruvians, and tourists to Cuzco, eat guinea pigs. "Even the Aztec killing machine was not able to reduce the population sufficiently," he says. "That Mexico developed a taste for bugs may be related to population pressure." He went on, "Why are we even contemplating eating insects? Because we are gradually running out of things to eat."

* * *

Demographers have projected that by 2050 the world's population will have increased to nine billion, and the demand for meat will grow with it, particularly in dense, industrializing countries like China and India. In 2010—a year in which, according to the United Nations, nearly a billion people suffered from chronic hunger—the journal *Science* published a special issue on food security, and included a piece on entomophagy, the unappealing name by which insect-eating properly goes. Acknowledging that the notion might be "unappetizing to many," the editors wrote, "The quest for food security may require us all to reconsider our eating habits, particularly in view of the energy consumption and environmental costs that sustain those habits."

From an ecological perspective, insects have a lot to recommend them. They are renowned for their small "foodprint"; being cold-blooded, they are about four times as efficient at converting feed to meat as are cattle, which waste energy keeping themselves warm. Ounce for ounce, many have the same amount of protein as beef—fried grasshoppers have three times as much—and are rich in micronutrients like iron and zinc. Genetically, they are so distant from humans that there is little likelihood of diseases jumping species, as swine flu did. They are natural recyclers, capable of eating old cardboard, manure, and by-products from food manufacturing. And insect husbandry offers an alternative to the problem of factory farming: bugs *like* teeming, and thrive in filthy, crowded conditions.

In late 2010, a group of scientists at Wageningen University, in the Netherlands, published a paper concluding that insects reared for human consumption produce significantly lower quantities of greenhouse gases than do cattle and pigs. "This study therefore indicates that insects could serve as a more environmentally friendly alternative for the production of animal protein," the paper said. One of its authors was Arnold van Huis, an entomologist who is working to establish a market for insect-based products in the Netherlands, with funding from the Dutch government; the agriculture ministry recently gave him a million euros to research insect husbandry. "We have a food crisis, especially a meat crisis, and people are starting to realize that we need alternatives, and insects are just an excellent alternative," van Huis said.

On a trip to Africa, in 1995, when van Huis was on sabbatical, he traveled to a dozen countries, interviewing locals about their relationship with insects. Half the people he spoke with talked about eating them, and he finally overcame their reluctance—born of centuries of colonial opprobrium—to share some with him. "I had termites, which were roasted, and they were excellent," he said. When he got home, he offered a bag of termites to Marcel Dicke, the head of his department. Dicke liked them, and the two men started a popular lecture series that addressed insects' potential as a food source. After van Huis and Dicke organized an insect festival that drew twenty thousand people, they were approached by several mealworm and cricket farmers who had been serving the pet-food industry but were interested in diversifying. "We know that Western peoples have some difficulties psychologically with ingesting insects, so we are looking at some ways of introducing them into food so that people will no longer recognize them," van Huis said. Insect flour was one option. "Another possibility is that you can grind insects and make them into a hot dog or a fish stick," he said. Together, van Huis and Dicke helped get mealworms and processed snacks like BugNuggets into the Dutch grocery chain Sligro.

The Dutch are, for reasons of geography, especially concerned about the effects of global warming; they are also progressive when it comes to food development. But entrepreneurs in the United States are starting to explore edible insects, too. Matthew Krisiloff, a student at the University of Chicago, recently started a company called Entom Foods, which is working on deshelling insects using pressurization technology in the hope of selling the meat in cutlet form.

"The problem is the *ick* factor—the eyes, the wings, the legs," he said. "It's not as simple as hiding it in a bug nugget. People won't accept it beyond the novelty. When you think of a chicken you think of a chicken breast, not the eyes, wings, and beak. We're trying to do the same thing with insects, create a stepping-stone, so that when you get a bug nugget you think of the bug steak, not the whole animal." But before he can bring a product to market, he must overcome a daunting technical challenge. Insect protein does not take the form of muscle, but is, as he put it, "goopy."

In Dicke's opinion, simply changing the language surrounding food insects could go a long way toward solving the problem that Westerners have with them. "Maybe we should stop telling people they're eating insects," he said. "If you say it's mealworms, it makes people think of ringworm. So stop saying 'worm.' If we use the Latin names, say it's a *Tenebrio* quiche, it sounds much more fancy, and it's part of the marketing." Another option, Dicke said, is to cover the bugs in chocolate, because people will eat anything covered in chocolate.

The practice of ethical entomophagy started haphazardly. In 1974, Gene DeFoliart, who was the chair of entomology at the University of Wisconsin, was asked by a colleague to recommend someone who could talk about edible insects as part of a symposium on unconventional protein sources. Then, as now, entomology was more concerned with insect eradication than cultivation, and, not finding a willing participant, DeFoliart decided to take on the project himself. He began his talk—and the paper he eventually published—with a startling statement: "C. F. Hodge (1911) calculated that a pair of houseflies beginning operations in April could produce enough flies, if all survived, to cover the earth forty-seven feet deep by August," he said. "If one can reverse for a moment the usual focus on insects as enemies of man, Hodge's layer of flies represents an impressive pile of animal protein."

DeFoliart, who died in early 2013, envisioned a place for edible insects as a luxury item. The larvae of the wax moth (*Galleria mellonella*) seemed to him to be poised to become the next escargot, which in the late eighties represented a three-hundred-million-dollar-a-year business in the United States. "Given a choice, New York diners looking for adventure and willing to pay $22 for half a roasted free-range chicken accompanied by a large pile of shoestring potatoes might well prefer a smaller pile of *Galleria* at the same price," he wrote. He and a handful of colleagues, including Florence Dunkel, now a leading entomophagist and a professor at Montana State University, in Bozeman, began to study and promote the potential of what they called "mini-livestock." In *The Food Insects Newsletter*, their journal, they reported the results of nutritional analyses and assessed the efficiency of insects like crickets—the most delectable of which, entomophagists are fond of pointing out, belong to the genus *Gryllus*.

A couple of years ago, a group of DeFoliart's disciples gathered at a resort in San Diego for a symposium on entomophagy at the annual conference of the Entomological Society of America. Because there is no significant funding available for entomophagy research, it has never been taken seriously by most professional entomologists. Dunkel, who in her half century in academia has many times heard colleagues discourage interested graduate students, often finds herself at odds with others in her field. It was a relief, then, to be among the like-minded. "Your soap-moth-pupae chutney—I'll never forget how that tasted!" she said, introducing a colleague from the Insectarium, in Montreal, which holds a bug banquet every other year. The entomophagists hoped to capitalize on the momentum they perceived. "We don't have to be the kooky, nerdy entomologists who eat bugs because we're crazy," an entomologist from the University of Georgia said. "Twenty years ago, sushi was the *eww* factor; you did not see sushi in grocery stores. Now it's the cultural norm."

At the conference, Dunkel talked about her frustration working in West Africa, where for decades European and American entomologists, through programs like USAID and the British Desert Locust Control Organization, have killed grasshoppers and locusts, which are complete proteins, in order to preserve the incomplete proteins in millet, wheat, barley, sorghum, and maize. Her field work in Mali focuses on the role of grasshoppers in the diets of children, who, for cultural reasons, do not eat chicken or eggs. Grasshoppers contain essential amino acids and serve as a crucial buffer against kwashiorkor, a protein deficiency that impedes physical and neurological development. In the village where Dunkel works, kwashiorkor is on the rise; in recent years, nearby fields have been planted with cotton, and pesticide use has intensified. Mothers now warn their children not to collect the grasshoppers, which they rightly fear may be contaminated.

Mainly, the entomophagists bemoaned the prejudice against insects. "In our minds, they're associated with filth," Heather Looy, a psychologist who has studied food aversions, said over dinner after the symposium. "They go dirty places, but so do fungi, and we eat those all the time. And you don't want to know about crabs and shrimp and lobster." Crabs, shrimp, and lobster are, like insects, arthropods—but instead of eating fresh lettuces and flowers, as many insects do, they scavenge debris from the ocean floor.

This injustice—lobster is a delicacy, while vegetarian crustaceans like wood lice are unfit for civilized man—is a centerpiece of the literature of entomophagy. *Why Not Eat Insects?*, an 1885 manifesto by Vincent M. Holt, which is the founding document of the movement, expounds upon the vile habits of the insects of the sea. "The lobster, a creature consumed in incredible quantities at all the highest tables in the land, is such a foul feeder that, for its sure capture, the experienced fisherman will bait his lobster-pot with putrid flesh or fish which is too far gone even to attract a crab," he writes.

As it is, contemporary Westerners tend to associate insects with filth, death, and decay, and, because some insects feed on human blood, their consumption is often seen as cannibalism by proxy. Holt takes pains to stress that the insects he recommends for eating—caterpillars, grasshoppers, slugs—are pure of this taint. "My insects are all vegetable feeders, clean, palatable, wholesome, and decidedly more particular in their feeding than ourselves," he writes. "While I am confident that they will never condescend to eat *us,* I am equally confident that, on finding out how good they are, we shall some day right gladly cook and eat *them.*"

Holt's compelling, albeit Swiftian, argument addresses the food problems of his day—"What a pleasant change from the labourer's unvarying meal of bread, lard, and bacon, or bread and lard without bacon, would be a good dish of fried cockchafers or grasshoppers"—but he is innocent of the nuances of food marketing. Among the sample menus he supplies are offerings like "Boiled Neck of Mutton with Wire-worm Sauce and Moths on Toast." At dinner in San Diego, it occurred to me that this naïveté had carried down. I was sitting next to Lou Sorkin, a forensic entomologist at the American Museum of Natural History who is also an expert on bedbugs, probably the most loathed insect in the United States today. He had arrived at his latest culinary discovery, he said, while experimenting with mediums for preserving maggots collected from murder victims. Realizing that citrus juice might denature proteins as effectively as a chemical solution, and might be more readily available in the field, he soaked large sarcophagid maggots in baths of grapefruit, lemon, lime, and pomelo juice, and *voilà*! Maggot ceviche. "It's a little chewy," he said. "But tasty."

Food preferences are highly local, often irrational, and defining: a Frenchman is a frog because he considers their legs food and the person who calls him one does not. In Santa María Atzompa, a community in Oaxaca where grasshoppers toasted with garlic, chili, and lime are a favorite treat, locals have traditionally found shrimp repulsive. "They would say 'some people' eat it, meaning 'the coastal people,'" Ramona Pérez, an anthropologist at San Diego State University, says. When she made scampi for a family there, she told me, they were appalled; the mother, who usually cooked with her, refused to help, and the daughters wouldn't eat. The coast is less than a hundred miles away.

Eighty percent of the world eats bugs. Australian Aborigines like witchetty grubs, which, according to the authors of *Man Eating Bugs,* taste like "nut-flavored scrambled eggs and mild mozzarella, wrapped in a phyllo dough pastry." Mealworms are factory-farmed in China; in Venezuela, children roast tarantulas. Besides, as any bug-eater will tell you, we are all already eating bugs, whether we mean to or not. According to the FDA, which publishes a handbook on "defect levels" acceptable in processed food, frozen or canned spinach is not considered contaminated until it has fifty aphids, thrips, or mites per hundred grams. Peanut butter is allowed to have thirty insect fragments per hundred grams, and chocolate is OK up to sixty. In each case, the significance of the contamination is given as "aesthetic."

In fresh vegetables, insects are inevitable. One day, cleaning some lettuce, I was surprised by an emerald-green pentagon with antennae: a stinkbug. I got rid of it immediately—force of habit. But daintiness about insects has true consequences. As Tom Turpin, an entomologist at Purdue University, said, "Attitudes in this country result in more pesticide use, because we're scared about an aphid wing in our spinach."

The antipathy that Europeans and their descendants display toward eating insects is stubborn, and mysterious. Insect consumption is in our cultural heritage. The Romans ate beetle grubs reared on flour and wine; ancient Greeks ate grasshoppers. Leviticus, by some interpretations, permits the eating of locusts, grasshoppers, and crickets. (The rest are unkosher.) The manna eaten by Moses on his way out of Egypt is widely believed to have been honeydew, the sweet excrement of scale insects. Turpin thinks it comes down to expedience. Unlike bugs found in the tropics, those found in Europe do not grow big enough to make good food, so there is no culinary tradition, and therefore no infrastructure, to support the practice. He told me, "If there were insects out there the size of pigs, I guarantee you we'd be eating them."

The next stinkbug I came across I ate. It was lightly fried, and presented on a slice of apple, whose flavor it is said to resemble. (I found it a touch medicinal.) This was in a one-story white clapboard house in the West Adams neighborhood of Los Angeles, with a skateboard half-pipe in the backyard. The house had been rented by Daniella Martin and Dave Gracer, two advocates of entomophagy, under false pretenses. "We told them we were scientists," Martin said, giggling. In fact, Martin, who used to be an Internet game-show host, writes a blog called *Girl Meets Bug*; she and Gracer, an English instructor who travels the country lecturing on entomophagy and has been writing an epic poem about insects for the past fourteen years, were in town to compete in a cooking competition at the Natural History Museum's annual bug fair.

Martin, who is in her mid-thirties, with a heart-shaped face and a telegenic smile, stood at the counter in the small kitchen pulling embryonic drones—bee brood—from honeycomb. They were for bee patties, part of a "Bee L T" sandwich she was going to enter in the competition. But, finding them irresistible, she fried up a few to snack on. "It tastes like bacon," she said rapturously. "I'm going to eat the whole plate unless someone gets in there." I did: the drones, dripping in butter and lightly coated with honey from their cells, were fatty and a little bit sweet, and, like everything chitinous, left me with a disturbing aftertaste of dried shrimp.

Gracer opened the freezer and inspected his bugs: housefly pupae, cicadas, and, his favorite, ninety-dollar-a-pound katydids from Uganda. "They're very rich, almost buttery," he said. "They almost taste as if they've gone around the bend."

"Dave, where's the tailless whip scorpion?" Martin said, and Gracer produced an elegantly armored black creature with a foreleg like a calligraphy flourish. "I'm thinking about doing a tempura type of fry and a spicy mayonnaise," Martin, who also worked for a number of years in a Japanese restaurant, said. First, she flash-fried it to soften the exoskeleton, and then she dipped it in tempura batter. To her knowledge, no one had ever before eaten a tailless whip scorpion. "All right, people, let's make history," she said, using a pair of chopsticks to lower it back into the pan, where it sizzled violently. I decided right there on a new policy, one I thought would pass muster with Gold: I will eat disgusting things, but only those with long established culinary traditions.

When the scorpion was finished, she put it on a plate, and she and Gracer sat down on a couch to feast on what looked like far too much bug for me, and yet not nearly enough to satisfy hunger. Gracer pulled off a pincer. "There's something—that white stuff—that's meat!" he cried, pointing to a speck of flesh. "That's meat!" Martin repeated excitedly, and exhorted him to try it. He tasted; she tasted. "Fish," Gracer said. "It has the consistency of fish." Martin split a leg apart and nibbled. In a few bites, they had eaten all there was. "That was really good," she said.

The following morning, in a tent on the front lawn of the Natural History Museum, Gracer faced Zack (the Cajun Bug Chef) Lemann, an established bug-cooker from New Orleans, who dazzled the judges—most of them children—with his "odonate hors d'oeuvres," fried wild-caught dragonflies served on sautéed mushrooms with Dijon-soy butter. Children are often seen as the great hope of entomophagy, because of their openness to new foods, but even they are not without prejudices. Gracer, who presented stinkbug-and-kale salad, had neglected to account for the fact that kids don't like kale.

A five-year-old approached Lemann afterward. "Excuse me, can I eat a dragonfly?" he said. Lemann cooked one for him. The boy picked the batter off, revealing a wing as elaborately paned as a cathedral window, and then bit into it: his first bug. His little brother, who was three, came over and asked for a bite. "Good," he pronounced.

"Who's going to eat the head?" their mother asked.

"I will," the five-year-old said. "Once somebody licks the mustard off."

The last round of the day matched Martin against Gracer. He was making Ugandan-katydid-and-grilled-cheese sandwiches. Drawing on her Japanese-restaurant experience, Martin decided to make a spider roll, using a rose-haired tarantula bought from a pet store. She held up the spider and burned off its hair with a lighter, and then removed its abdomen. "The problem with eating an actual spider roll, made with crab, is that they're bottom feeders," she said. "This spider probably ate only crickets, which ate only grass." She whipped up a sauce and added a few slices of cucumber, and then presented her dish to the judges, warning them brightly to "be very careful of the fangs!"

A young girl with curly hair lunged eagerly at the plate. "If it's in sushi, I'll eat it," she said. When she had tried a piece, she declared, "It's sushi. With spiders. It's awesome."

Four-fifths of the animal species on earth are insects, and yet food insects are not particularly easy to find. Home cooks can call Fred Rhyme, of Rainbow Mealworms, who provided the Madagascar hissing cockroaches for *Fear Factor*. He sells more than a billion worms a year; the sign at the edge of his farm, a conglomeration of twenty-three trailers, shotgun houses, and former machine shops in South Los Angeles, says, "Welcome to Worm City, Compton, Cal., 90220½. Population: 990,000,000." The farm supplies six hundred thousand worms a week to the San Diego Zoo. "It's mostly animals we feed," Rhyme's wife, Betty, who is the company's president, told me. "The people are something of an oddity."

I wasn't in the market for more mealworms. I had gone to visit Florence Dunkel, the entomologist, in Montana, and eaten plenty of them, fried up in butter, in her kitchen. They smelled of mushrooms and tasted of sunflower seeds. The flavor was unobjectionable, but not reason enough to eat something that reminded me of the time I was halfway through a sleeve of extra-crumbly Ritz crackers before I realized that the crumbs were moving. I wanted to see if bugs could be transcendent, and I knew who would know. "One of the biggest successes of the local New Cocktailian movement is the mezcal-based Donaji at Rivera downtown, which Julian Cox serves in a rocks glass rimmed with toasted-grasshopper salt," Jonathan Gold wrote to me. I duly went to the restaurant and ordered the Donaji, a $14 cocktail named after a Zapotec princess. The salt tasted like Jane's Krazy Mixed-Up Salt, crushed Bac-Os, and fish-food flakes; the bartender recommended it as a rub for grilled meat.

Gold also mentioned that I might try Laurent Quenioux, at Bistro LQ, an old acquaintance of his. Gold's 2006 review of Quenioux's wild hare stew—"a soft, gloriously stinky Scottish hare stewed in something approximating the traditional *foie gras*–inflected blood"—was one of the pieces for which he won the Pulitzer. To me, Gold wrote, "He occasionally has *escamoles*, giant ant eggs, on the menu. They're very seasonal, early spring I think, so you'd have to call." It was winter. I would have to wait.

Escamoles are not actually eggs but immature *Liometopum apiculatum*. A delicacy since Aztec times—they were used as tribute to Moctezuma—they are still a prized ingredient in high-end Mexico City restaurants, where they are known colloquially as Mexican caviar. Exquisitely subtle, palest beigy-pink, knobbly as a seed pearl, they command a market price of around $70 a pound.

Like humans, *Liometopum apiculatum* ants are opportunists; they will eat anything they can overpower, and, because they do not sting, they tear their prey to shreds. (They are also ranchers, tending flocks of aphids and defending them from lady beetles, in exchange for the aphids' surplus honeydew.) They burrow under boulders or at the base of trees, and live in colonies of up to fifty thousand members. Traditionally, they were hunted only by experienced *escamoleros*—the irrepressible image is of an ant with a Tejano hat with a lasso—but, according to Julieta Ramos-Elorduy, a biologist who studies food insects at the National Autonomous University of Mexico, their desirability has invited poachers, who overharvest and destroy the nests. The ants, which are most readily available in the state of Hidalgo, are also found in the southwestern United States. High prices have inspired North American foragers to get in on the business. "Recently at San Juan market in Mexico City, monopolizers informed us that small airplanes loaded with tons of the product arrived from the United States and sold it to the highest bidders," Ramos-Elorduy wrote in a 2006 paper.

You can't really buy *escamoles* in America. The head chef at José Andrés's Oyamel, in D.C., has scoured local markets for them without success, though once, on a tip from a lady who overheard him complaining to his barber about their unavailability, he discovered some frozen Thai ant larvae (labeled as "puffed rice") in an Asian grocery store in Virginia. José Andrés himself told me that he considers *escamoles* a delicacy, and if he could get them he'd put them on the menu at Minibar, his acclaimed six-seat restaurant.

At the first sign of spring, I called Quenioux. He had just closed Bistro LQ because of a problem with the lease, and said he was trying to get some *escamoles* to serve at Starry Kitchen, a downtown lunch counter owned by Nguyen and Thi Tran, who had previously run it as an underground supper club out of their apartment. Quenioux was about to start a pop-up there called LQ@SK. "Basically, you need to smuggle them," he said of the ants. His connection, a Mexican man living near Hidalgo who brought them in foam cups in his carry-on luggage, didn't work anymore; the last two times Quenioux had placed an order, he'd prepaid, only to have his shipment confiscated by Customs at LAX.

A week before the soft launch of Quenioux's residency at Starry Kitchen, he told me that he had a line on some *escamoles.* He knew a guy who knew a guy who would bring them across the border from Tijuana; we simply had to drive down to a meeting place on the U.S. side and escort them back. We set a time, and I went to a street corner in Pasadena, near where Quenioux lives; when I arrived, a red Toyota Corolla was waiting. The window came down partway, and I heard someone call my name.

Originally from Sologne, France, Quenioux—pronounced "kin*you*"—grew up hunting, learned pastry in Paris at Maxim's, and worked in Nice alongside the German-born chef Joachim Splichal, who brought him to Los Angeles in the early eighties. He is a gentle person, with huge, pale green eyes, a bald-shaved head, a set of prayer beads around his wrist, and the endearingly antisocial habit of seeing everything he encounters as potential food: the deer near Mt. Wilson, which he hunts with a bow and arrow; the purple blossoms of the jacaranda trees; a neighbor's chicken, which he killed and cooked when it came into his yard. Usually, he eats chicken only when he's home in France; he thinks American chickens are disgusting.

Certain laws just don't make sense to Quenioux, like the one that prohibits him from serving a dessert made from chocolate hot-boxed with pot smoke. "What's one gram of marijuana, just to have the smoke infuse the chocolate?" he said. When he read in the news that there was to be a mass culling of fifty thousand wild boars that had crossed from Texas into Chihuahua and were destroying everything in their path—not fit for consumption, warned a government official—his first thought was, Shit, can we get a few of those? "Tamales!" Daniel, his sous-chef, said. "With salsa verde!"

As for the *escamoles,* "We do it for the culinary adventure," Quenioux said. He has made blinis with ant eggs and caviar, and a three-egg dish of *escamoles,* quail eggs, and salmon roe.

He has fantasized about making an *escamole* quiche, and, using just the albumen that drains out when the eggs are frozen, meringue. His signature dish is a corn tortilla resting on a nasturtium leaf and topped with *escamoles* sautéed in butter with epazote, shallots, and serrano chilies, served with a shot of Mexican beer and a lime gel. Insects are, to him, like any other ingredient: a challenge and an invitation. "Let's do gastronomy with bugs," he said. "Let's make something delicious."

Quenioux talked about *escamoles* all the way down south—their delicate eggy qualities, their wildness, their unexpected appearance ("condensed milk with little pebbles in it"), the responsibility he feels to train the American palate to accept them. "The insects will be the solution to feed all those masses, but how do you get insects on the daily table in America?" he said. "In the last twenty years, we grew here in America from iceberg lettuce to baby frisée, so the time is now."

After a few hours, we arrived at a strip mall and parked in front of a drugstore, then walked toward the meeting place, a restaurant, where the *escamoles* were waiting. "OK, let's go," Quenioux said, getting out of the car. "I've got the cash."

The front door to the restaurant was open, and an old man with a drooping moustache was mopping the floor. "Hola, *señor*," Quenioux said. The old man pointed to a Dutch door, which led to the kitchen. Quenioux stuck his head in, and eventually a young woman wearing a dirty chef's coat and a white apron appeared. "You come for the *escamoles?*" she said. "OK, I get for you." She returned a minute later with a plastic shopping bag containing a large ziplock filled with half a kilo of frozen product. Quenioux handed her a hundred-dollar bill.

Getting back in the car, Quenioux opened the bag to examine the goods, a pale orange slush, scattered with clumps of oblong ant babies. "We got the loot!" he squealed.

The Starry Kitchen narrative, with its elements of amateurism, scofflaw pluck, and media savvy, is the kind of restaurant story you hear all the time these days. In 2009, when Thi Tran lost her job in advertising, she asked her Facebook friends what she should do. "Cook, cook, cook," came the reply. Thi is first-generation Chinese, with a natural scowl. She is practical and modest, where her husband, Nguyen, who is Vietnamese-American, is boisterous. He often dresses up in Comic-Con-style costumes for food events, and displays a sign, referring to a spicy tofu dish that is a Starry Kitchen specialty, which reads "Eat My Balls."

Inspired by Kogi—the Korean-barbecue food truck that started in L.A. and set off a national craze—Thi thought Vietnamese tacos might be good, and developed some recipes at home. Three weeks later, Nguyen told her, "We're serving out of our apartment this Sunday," and flyered their three-hundred-unit building in North Hollywood. To him it was normal: like a lot of Asians he knows, he grew up eating in unofficial home restaurants. "In every ethnic neighborhood in L.A. there is someone doing something like this," he said.

Within a few months, their apartment was the No. 1 rated Asian fusion restaurant on Yelp. (Providence, a fantastically expensive restaurant with two Michelin stars, was No. 2.) When the health department confronted Nguyen with the Twitter feed where he shamelessly touted specials and warned him to stop, Thi was unnerved, but Nguyen insisted that the intervention was a blessing. They moved the restaurant, which they had named after a popular Hong Kong cooking show, into a legitimate space in a large corporate plaza, and burnished their creation myth. "It increased our audience," he told me. "We were seedy, and being caught validated that we really *were* underground."

A week after the ant run, I was at Starry Kitchen, watching Quenioux get ready to serve the *escamoles* as an *amuse-bouche*. Nguyen bounded around, talking about his role in securing them. "I called everyone, from Laos, Cambodia, Thailand—all the sources I know got caught," he said. He was thrilled about the air of the forbidden that the dish would confer. "It's going to be a great note to start on—not even the taste, just them knowing it was smuggled and it's ant eggs," he said.

To complement a menu full of Asian flavors—teriyaki rabbit meatballs in miso broth, veal sweetbreads with shishito peppers and yuzu—Quenioux had decided to prepare the *escamoles* with Thai basil and serve them with Sapporo. "These are very spicy," he said, placing an ample green nasturtium leaf on a plate. "I foraged them from my garden this morning." There was a light sheen of sweat on his forehead.

Just before the service, the waiters started to panic. "What am I telling them?" one asked. "I can't just go up to them and say it's ant eggs."

"Tell them it's very exotic, and traditional in Mexico City," Daniel, the sous-chef, said. I went into the dining room and sat down. "This is an *amuse* from the chef," a waiter said, presenting me with the dish, a composition as spare and earthy as a Japanese garden. "It's smuggled-in ant eggs." I rolled the leaf around the tortilla and bit: peppery nasturtium, warm tortilla, and then the light pop of *escamoles* bursting like tiny corn kernels. A whiff of dirt, a sluice of beer, and that was it. They were gone by night's end, but their fresh, succulent sweetness stuck with me. Unexpectedly, I had something new to crave.

Three

BACKDOOR MEN

"I got in 2K live crickets," Brett Ottolenghi, the ostentatiously earnest, honest, perpetually worried young proprietor of Artisanal Foods, a fancy-food purveyor in Las Vegas, wrote me by text message. "Thinking I'd try to cook with them before offering to chefs. But the pen I made isn't working and they are escaping by the hundreds in my house." Five minutes later, he wrote me again. "I think I'll have to live among them. There is no way I can pick up this many. A Chinese chef might help me cook some tomorrow."

Las Vegas is among the top food cities in America, if you go by the number of superexpensive restaurants with famous chefs. Ten of the fifty highest-grossing restaurants in the country are on the Strip, and there are more master sommeliers in Las Vegas than in any other city in the country. Adam Carmer, the casino developer Steve Wynn's first hotel sommelier, described himself to me as "the No. 1 maître d' in town." He says, "Other places, you might have four or five extraordinary restaurants in a state or in a country; here you have four or five in a hotel. For shoes, you go to the mall—that's what the food's like out here." Almost forty million people visited Las Vegas last year. It is one of the places in the world where the outlandish ideas and hyper-precious ingredients of the food avant-garde meet the masses, and Ottolenghi is one of the people making introductions.

Ottolenghi specializes in the small run, the vaguely regulated, the hard to come by, and the about to be banned. He carries Utah clay, fresh Pennsylvania hops, and squid ink from Spain. One of his newest products, which he has yet to place, is *kopi luwak*—coffee beans gathered from civet droppings. The beans, which have an exquisite burnt caramel flavor, are extremely rare and can cost as much as $1,000 a pound. "I have some of the turds," he told me, which makes presentations lively. He often says that he is on a first-name basis with three hundred and seventy chefs in Vegas—the executive chefs and sous-chefs and chefs de cuisine at Jean Georges Steakhouse, Le Cirque, Daniel Boulud, barMASA, and dozens more—by which he may mean that he has forgotten their last names, or, if they are French, is unsure how to pronounce them. To the chefs, he is "the truffle kid"—for his first product, which he started selling online when he was thirteen—or Hamleg, owing to his tendency to walk through casino lobbies carrying the hairy, hoof-on hindquarters of a pig.

Because of its primary identity, as a place to gamble, Las Vegas attracts some of the broadest eaters in the world: high-rolling Asian whales. There are some who say that if the casinos were to stop serving shark-fin soup in the high-limit rooms—where it goes for $100 to $300 a bowl—the city's economy would collapse. But shark fin, a slippery, flavorless textural delight that is the pièce de résistance of formal Chinese banquets, is condemned by many as cruel and unsustainable. Sharks, whose numbers, including that of the "soupfin," have diminished severely, are often de-finned live and then dumped back in the ocean to bleed out, get eaten, or drown. California outlawed shark fin in 2013, and there are efforts under way to ban it in Vegas. This is the kind of crisis that Ottolenghi calls an opportunity.

Among the many impostors in the food business, he hunts for authenticity. Don't get him started on what passes, in most people's minds, for cinnamon: the great majority of it is mislabeled cassia. He gets the real thing from its only source, Sri Lanka. But when it comes to shark fin, inauthenticity is exactly what he's looking for. He has found a company in China that takes tilapia tails—tail, like fin, is cartilage—and makes a faux shark-fin product that is identical in taste, texture, and appearance. There is just one obstacle: the customer. The whales, he says, want the real thing *because* it's rare. His next idea is to use sturgeon tails, which might prove desirable due to their prestigious association with caviar.

Ottolenghi prides himself on the fulfillment of outrageous and obscure demands. He has sourced pink pine nuts for Alessandro Stratta, the chef at Alex and at Stratta, two fine-dining restaurants in Las Vegas. "Just put them in my mailbox," I heard him say to a tortilla-and-chili dealer who had located some in New Mexico. One Chinese New Year, he furnished the buffet at the Bellagio with four hundred pounds of fatted duck breast on less than twenty-four hours' notice. After the authorities forced Guy Savoy, a two-Michelin-star restaurant at Caesars Palace, to remove a popular guinea-hen-in-pig-bladder dish from its menu—the bladder was coming from a non-USDA-approved source—the restaurant turned to Ottolenghi. "They still get tons of requests for it, so they gave me the mission of trying to get domestic pig bladders," he says. He called pig farms and slaughterhouses in four states. "I really exhausted every possibility. There's no way to get a pig bladder in this country—they're all ground up for dog food."

Several years ago, Ludo Lefebvre, the dashing, volatile French chef who invented the pop-up restaurant and became a television star, was cooking at a restaurant in Las Vegas. He asked Ottolenghi for *piment d'Espelette,* a subtle chili pepper. *Piment d'Espelette* is rare; the *zone de l'appellation,* in southwestern France, is only a few thousand acres. In powder form, the pepper can wholesale for $110 a pound. (Paprika is less than $8.) After initially working through an importer, Ottolenghi had decided to become one himself, making him, by his count, the third importer of *piment d'Espelette* to the United States.

That is how he came to spend a drizzly afternoon in the spring of 2010 in the tiny Basque town of Ainhoa, quizzing a young farmer named Claire about her production methods. Claire, who had rosy cheeks and a rippled Gallic nose dotted with moles, explained that they used only *pesticide biologique,* good bugs to eat bad ones. Chickens pecked among white plaster buildings with red tile roofs and peeling black shutters:

Ainhoa's single architectural gesture. Claire invited us into one of the buildings and prepared a pepper tasting. As she swirled the powder in a little stemmed glass, causing it to clink—"Can you hear? It's very dry," she said—she explained the properties she controlled for. The color should be a rich, oxygenated red, and the flavor, ideally, is a balance of fruitiness, toastiness, and *foin,* an aftertaste of hay. A Basque passenger of Columbus's, Claire said, had brought the pepper back from the New World.

The next day, Ottolenghi had a lunch appointment in La Alberca, six hundred kilometers away, at the headquarters of Fermín, the only Spanish producer of Ibérico ham approved by the USDA for sale in the United States. Ottolenghi was the exclusive source for Fermín products in Las Vegas. He woke at eight o'clock, checked the map, and set out optimistically. I had already been traveling with him for a few days and was afraid—of his navigation and of my endurance. Food people either stuff you or starve you. Ottolenghi, an ascetic, is a starver. At home, he often consumes little more than a kefir-and-raw-egg shake in a day. On the first night of our trip, we had stayed in San Sebastián, the Michelin three-star capital of the world, and I found myself alone at dinnertime, eating a grim vegetarian patty in the hotel dining room. Driving to La Alberca, we passed dozens of small towns and scores of restaurants without stopping to eat. I devoured bags of filling-station peanuts and, by the fistful, a loaf of soft gingerbread I had picked up in Ainhoa the night before.

In the late afternoon, we turned off the highway and onto a small road that hugged a mossy stone wall decked with wild red poppies and fried-egg flowers. On the other side was an oak forest. Young bulls bound for the ring relaxed in the shade. It was past four when we arrived in La Alberca, a pork-centric place where the hanging limbs and loins of cured Ibérico pigs serve as decoration for the tapas bars, and outside the church there is a statue of a boar, like a local saint. Just past town, we found the Fermín plant, an elegant structure built in the mid-eighties whose style referred to the area's medieval history: fieldstone facing, held in place by a loose lattice of half-timbers. Raúl Martín, a grand-nephew of the founder, led us down to a basement dining hall with tiled floors and an open fireplace, where Luis, a jug-eared cook with a double chin, was grilling cuts of pig meat: tenderloin, pancetta, ribs, *pluma* ("feather," or loin tip), *presa* (collar), and *secreto,* a cut hidden away between the ribs and the fat. Rich smoke filled the air.

Ibérico meat is unctuous—up to 35 percent fat—and its most luxurious variety, *bellota* (acorn), melts at room temperature. Bellota pigs, which are released into the forest in the fall to hunt for acorns, are so oily that they are known as "olive trees with legs." Last year, Fermín slaughtered only five thousand bellota pigs, for a total of ten thousand hams, ten thousand shoulders. The hams cure for three years; the shoulders, which are bonier, take at least two. Retail shops charge $130 a pound for the ham. Bellota is what sells in Las Vegas.

Martín showed the way to a long wooden table piled with breadbaskets and wine and trays of chorizo and *salsichon.* Javier, a Fermín employee, joined us, and everyone started to gossip about ham, as Luis brought over platter after platter of cooked meat and Ottolenghi stood at an iron *jamonera,* cutting thin slices of bellota for the group.

"We sent today a bellota to the royal palace, for the heads of state of Europe," Javier said. Ottolenghi nodded, and told an equivalent story of Las Vegas aristocracy. Had the Spaniards heard of Cirque du Soleil? Yes, Martín said. "Every Christmas, Guy Laliberté, who started it, buys three bellota legs from Robuchon's L'Atelier," Ottolenghi reported. Then Martín held up a vacuum-packed shank. "This is one of José Andrés's ideas," he said. (The chef is an importer for Fermín.) "It's '*corderico*'—Ibérico-style lamb, fed on acorns and dried. This is the only one in the world."

Early the following morning, we watched the pigs get cleaned, stunned, cut, and hung on hooks from tracks that traced loops on the ceiling. Large men chiseled at them as if they were blocks of stone from which something more aesthetically pleasing could be coaxed. Then Martín showed us the room where the hams were cured—he called it "the bank"—and the breeding farm, so that we could see the Ibéricos alive. They had thick black hides, like toy rhinos, and brayed mournfully as they rutted and fought. A farmworker handed Ottolenghi several acorns of the variety that the bellota gorge on in the forest. Seeing an opportunity to impress his chefs with the depth of his knowledge, he pocketed them. Leaving Fermín, Ottolenghi asked me if I'd ever read *The Jungle*. "It's my favorite book," he said. "It's all about how efficient the meat business is at using every part."

Ottolenghi, a Millennial-generation foodie who grew up watching exotic-food shows on TV, comes from mushroom people. His parents, Arturo and Hannah, seed the logs in their backyard in Gettysburg, Pennsylvania, with shiitakes; morels and chanterelles grow wild. Once, when the family was living in Ohio, before Brett was born and when his brother, Alex, was an infant, Arturo spotted a hardwood forest out the car window. Suspecting that it could be harboring chanterelles, he pulled over and found two solid acres of them. As Arturo tells it, "I picked a few, took them home, and called Chanterelle, in New York, and asked for the owner. I said, 'I know this sounds crazy, but I'm in Ohio and I have some fresh chanterelles—do you want five to ten pounds?' She said, 'Whatever you can ship. Anything I don't use, my friends at Dean & DeLuca will use.' Hannah and I parked Alex in a cradle with a mosquito net over it and packed up as many boxes as we could, took them to the airport, and that same evening all over lower Manhattan people were eating our chanterelles."

On a family trip to San Francisco, when Brett was twelve, he ordered a pasta dish with truffle oil on it. This led to a conversation about the high price of truffles in the United States. At the time, there was only one major importer, Urbani, an old Italian company that still dominates the market. Brett decided to see if he could compete. He was already something of an entrepreneur. In second grade, he sold Pixy Stix and gourmet lollipops at school, in violation of campus rules, and was sent to the principal's office. In seventh, he started importing laser pens from China for eleven dollars and selling them for twenty, and wound up in the principal's office again.

Brett and Arturo started the Truffle Market, an online venture selling truffles that they imported from Italy, in 1998. When *Newsweek* mentioned that their company was selling white truffles for $60 an ounce, compared with Dean & DeLuca's price of $106 for the same amount, business increased tenfold. "I was making thirty percent on it and I thought it was great," Brett says now. "I didn't even know that was a small profit." With perishable products, you have to make a killing; at some point you will inevitably lose a shipment to spoilage or to overeager Customs officials. Brett remembers that Fareed Zakaria placed an order, as did the actor Heath Ledger. Robert Mondavi, the winemaker, began to use the Ottolenghi mushrooms for his truffle parties. But the Ottolenghis' best customer was a young woman in Palm Beach, referred by the manager of the Palm Beach Country Club, who ordered a pound of white truffles a week for the entire season, September through December. She hated truffles, but a business associate of her father's, an oil executive from Houston, liked to fly to Palm Beach for the weekends, and he expected to have a plate of them waiting on his bedside table. He ate them like apples.

In the food business, Brett found youth to be an inconvenience. Rather than present the Truffle Market as a father-son venture, as Arturo had hoped, Brett insisted that his father pose alone for the picture in their first catalog. "To buy a truffle from a guy named Arturo Ottolenghi, that makes sense," Brett says. "Not from Brett, who's thirteen." For a while, he styled himself "J. Brett Ottolenghi" on his business cards. When he expanded the Truffle Market and renamed it Artisanal Foods, in 2008, he used an unsmiling picture of himself, sporting a suit jacket, a three-day beard, and a pair of fake eyeglasses, which he likes to wear for work, particularly when he's meeting a chef for the first time. "I probably have twenty pairs," he says.

Arturo's Italian background was Brett's great good fortune. Arturo's maternal great-great-grandfather had been the Prussian consul general to the Kingdom of the Two Sicilies; he found oil in Indonesia and sold out to John D. Rockefeller in 1900. The Ottolenghis were Italian Jews who converted to Catholicism during the war and donated a set of bronze doors to St. Peter's Basilica. Growing up in New York, Arturo went by the name Milton, but he spent his summers at a large family property in Piedmont, where he developed a taste for white truffles, as well as the language skills that would come in handy when bargaining for them later on his son's behalf. Arturo now runs a business that provides sandpaper to body shops and woodworkers. "I only work with consumables," he says.

For tenth grade, Brett went to St. Andrew's, a boarding school in Delaware. To keep the Truffle Market going, he rented storage space from Arturo and paid his employees to pack and ship. From school, he handled orders and did the bookkeeping. Soon mushroom hunters all over the world were e-mailing him—Serbs and Croats and Chinese, primarily. Someone from Egypt sent him a box of the inexpensive, sandy desert truffles known as *terfez*. Foragers in Oregon sent him white truffles they had found, which he cooked up with scrambled eggs for the whole school. The school cook was his closest friend; they once ordered an alligator, grilled it, and served it in the dining room.

The Croatian truffles were a revelation: the same species as the rarest and most expensive white Italians—*Tuber magnatum*—but not subject to the 100 percent tariff imposed on truffles entering the United States from the European Union. They became the Truffle Market's main product. Brett left St. Andrew's and finished high school at Mercersburg Academy, another boarding school, which was in Pennsylvania and closer to home. While there, he became an importer of Mogu pillows from Japan, and befriended local cheese-makers, who would deliver samples to his dorm room.

Ottolenghi moved to Las Vegas in 2004, to attend UNLV's William F. Harrah College of Hotel Administration. He stored truffles in his room, offending his hallmates with the smell, and kept his cell phone on vibrate while in class, to field orders. Carless, he walked up and down the Strip with a little basket of truffles and a scale, making unannounced visits to chefs at the best restaurants and trying to talk them into buying an expensive luxury ingredient from a baby-faced, bespectacled nineteen-year-old freshman, sweating in his suit.

Storytelling may be the one indispensable skill in food-selling, but the richest histories of ingredients like those that Ottolenghi deals in tend to be suppressed. Ottolenghi once found beautiful *huitlacoche*—corn fungus—on a thirteen-acre farm in Florida. "All my family used to be in the citrus business," the farmer told me when I called. "Then one night it got down to ten degrees. First they went broke, then they got dead. I was Br'er Bear at Disneyworld. Then I was a bartender. Then I got divorced and had to run away from my wife. *Huitlacoche* was my brother's idea. We started doing it together, then we got in a fight and now I'm doing it on my own."

Wild products often come with even more obscure pedigrees.

Huckleberries, fiddleheads, lichens, ramps, ferns, and, of course, mushrooms, are largely unregulated, potentially dangerous, fragile, precious, and scarce. Finding them is a scrounge. Often they represent stolen goods; a great deal of foraging takes place on government and private land, unpermitted. Iso Rabins is a sometime mushroom picker who ran San Francisco's Underground Market—part church bake sale, part faerie bazaar, a place where you could buy DIY rearing-and-grinding mealworm kits—until the health department shut him down. He told me, "Once a chanterelle gets into Rainbow Grocery in San Francisco it has this elitist air of a clean, pure product from the mountains, untouched by man." The truth, he said, is often less savory: tweakers driving dirty pickups into the national forest, mushroom buckets rattling around with the old beer cans. "Meth is a really good drug if you want to forage all the time," Rabins said. "If you want to spend forty-eight hours looking at the ground, meth does a good job." A major West Coast mushroom buyer told me that professional pickers tend to be "feral types." He said he once turned on the news to see a guy he'd been using for a couple of years named a Most Wanted Person.

Commercial foraging is largely subsistence work for marginal people with little connection to the gourmet status of the forest products they are gathering. Sometimes they may not even recognize their yield as edible. One Sunday in the winter of 2012, Belinda and Dan Conne, a couple in their late forties, went with their twenty-five-year-old son, Michael, and their pit bull, Jesse, into the Rogue River–Siskiyou National Forest, a wilderness area outside Gold Beach, Oregon, to pick black trumpets and hedgehogs. The Connes, who did obtain a permit, were amateurs, recent transplants from Oklahoma who had come to Gold Beach in search of work but found little available by the time they arrived in July. They moved into a tent at a campground and eventually into a camper with no electrical or water hookups. Belinda cleaned motel rooms for a few hours a week; Dan, scraggly-haired, tattooed, and missing several of his top teeth, had a back injury and couldn't work.

A neighbor in camp, seeing that they were struggling, taught Michael how to hunt for mushrooms—in addition to the black trumpets and hedgehogs, they found yellow feet, candy caps, and "channies"—which they sold to the local agent for a big mushroom buyer. (The agent they sold to, a Czech forager in his late fifties, pleaded guilty to trespassing in 2006, after being charged with using GPS to poach chanterelles from ranches in Lompoc. His advice to me: Don't get arrested in Santa Barbara County.) For black trumpets, a picker usually gets about five bucks a pound from a buyer, who marks them up 30 percent and sells them to a wholesaler, which sells them for 30 percent more to a retailer, which, depending on the season, doubles or quadruples the price and puts them on the shelves. A typical haul brought the Connes $50, enough to fill their car with gas, buy some propane, and get a few days' worth of groceries. "We did this so we could survive," Belinda told me.

The Connes were having a good day, and, after emptying their buckets into bags in the car, decided to go back out again. Just as they got to a patch of trumpets it started to rain, and the woods grew dark. "We got up on them blacks," Belinda said. "What we did, we were on the trail of the blacks, and we got greedy. We kept picking." When they looked up, they realized they didn't know where they were. "It kept raining harder, getting darker and darker, so we bedded down for the night," she said. Their lean-to collapsed in the storm. In the morning, it was still raining, and the Connes found that they were in the old growth, with no path out. Michael found a fallen tree, rotting and spacious enough for the three of them to sit inside; he hollowed a section of it clean with his knife, and they all crammed in, filling in the chinks with sticks and leaves so they wouldn't get wet. When afternoon came, they pulled large pieces of bark across the opening.

The last thing the Connes had eaten was a batch of peanut butter sandwiches on Sunday afternoon. In the tree, all night, they talked about food. Someone indelicately brought up the Donner Party. They watched big timber ants crawl along the inside of the log. "We thought about poppin' the heads off and eating them that way," Belinda said, adding that the wiggling of a live one would have been too much for her. "That's a last resort. The worms I don't think I could ever do." As for mushrooms, white buttons from the grocery store were the only kind they ate. Dan tried a hedgehog and spat it out; it was his first taste of the delicacy that had lured his family to the woods, and he found it repulsive. "My husband said if we come down to starvin' that we could eat them," Belinda said. His other idea—eat Jesse—was overruled. "Michael and I said we would take one of our legs first," Belinda said. "I would starve to death before I could eat a dog. A squirrel? Yes, I could. But a *dog*?" They placed all their hopes on rescue.

Dan's back hurt so badly that he couldn't move. Michael fell in the creek while collecting water in a ziplock bag and developed hypothermia. The frostbite on his feet turned to trench. Belinda, who also had frostbite, watched her son grow weaker, and was sure that he was going to die. On Thursday, Dan turned to her and said, "Today's the day when they're going to start notifying the next of kin." They listened to the helicopters overhead and tried in vain to signal them with the face of a dead cell phone and the blade of a buck knife. Still, for six days they didn't eat a thing, until—on the day before the search mission would have changed from rescue to recovery—they were spotted and flown to a hospital. Grateful to have escaped with his life, Dan broke his fast with pepperoni sticks and Doritos.

The world Brett operates in, it's a lot of backdoor bullshit and making deals," an old Vegas hand and a friend of Ottolenghi's said. Corruption is rampant. "You'll have a food-and-beverage VP that goes with a certain purveyor because he says, 'I'll sell you crab legs for the buffet and write you a personal check for ten percent of whatever we do. You'll make two hundred and fifty grand because you buy two and a half million in crab.'" Another chef told me about a couple of fast-talking local seafood venders, an Italian who looks Spanish and a Spaniard who looks Italian. "They have very raspy voices, like something out of a scene in a Mafia movie," he said. "They do this bait-and-switch thing, telling you stories, and before you know it there's a thousand pounds of tuna waiting at your back door."

Las Vegas's Butter Man, Clint Arthur, says, "It's very cutthroat." He sells 85-percent-butterfat butter to the chefs at Aureole, Payard, Jean Georges Steakhouse, and Restaurant Guy

Savoy, and once designed an extra-salty butter for David Werly, the executive chef at Le Cirque. "The thing you have to understand is that food is a perishable item; it must be purchased, and someone is going to make money on it. These deals typically last for years, they're worth hundreds of thousands of dollars, and people resort to extreme measures, including sometimes illegal measures, to try to get clients. I've seen high-end chefs in Las Vegas fired for taking money under the table from suppliers."

As the Butter Man, Arthur, who is also the author of a series of inspirational lectures on how to double your income, goes to chef meetings dressed in a button-down shirt in "butter yellow" and a pair of yellow Crocs. Most of the vegetable exotica in town comes from Lee Jones, who has a family farm in Huron, Ohio, where he raises rhubarb "the thickness of three pencil leads," miniature cucumbers with tiny yellow blossoms, and heirloom champagne ice beets, for sorbets. His produce travels by FedEx and is ready to be served within twenty-four hours of harvest. When he comes to Las Vegas himself, he is Farmer Lee, and wears the uniform he has trademarked with the U.S. Attorney General's office: dark blue overalls, white shirt, red bow tie. "It's the authentic real deal," he says. "Colonel Sanders has the white suit and the goatee. Dave Thomas, the founder of Wendy's, always wore a short-sleeve shirt. It gives us an identity."

The city's senior caviar purveyor is Barry Katcher—or Barry Beluga, as he calls himself—who has been selling to the casinos for more than twenty years. His family started in caviar in 1942, when his grandfather and great-uncle emigrated from Russia to Brooklyn. His great-uncle, a cobbler, sold it from a shoeshine box in front of a relative's pharmacy, and came to be known as the Caviar Baron. Caviar Royale, Katcher's company, is, he says, the largest supplier to the hotel-casino industry in the United States. I went to see him—petite and deeply tanned, in late middle age, wearing black down to a pair of platform Skechers—at his retail store, on a stretch of Industrial Road behind Caesars Palace. "Everyone should know where it is," he told me, when I asked for directions. "When the cabs bring customers here to buy liquor I give them a free sandwich." His nickname, he said, originated with a radio personality whose show he used to call in to while making his runs to the airport at 3:30 a.m. "Once, I was sent an illegal shipment of caviar—the guys that got it got it illegally—and I said, 'Hey, I've got seven cars around me with blue markings and their lights on.' It was the FDA. They followed me back here and in front of them I opened twenty tins. It was all live on the air." Katcher sees perfidy everywhere: two-faced purchasing agents, fake beluga, competitors who bribe buyers or—worse—milk him for information and then try to take his customers. "See all these knives in my back?" he said. When I mentioned that Ottolenghi had started representing caviar, he winced and said, "Piece of shit."

The pitch that Ottolenghi makes is for integrity, a posture he communicates with unfashionable brown suits, brown leather shoes, and the fake glasses. "It's a very specific look," he says. "Almost professorial." Being well, if humbly, dressed prevents him from getting stopped by security while sneaking around the back corridors of casinos. "Look like you're supposed to be here," he told me, ineffectually, as we skulked around. Besides, light suits in Las Vegas say VIP host (the slick fixers employed by nightclubs to cater to important customers), which doesn't inspire the trust of chefs. He thinks of himself as an educator and a reformer—teaching chefs about the virtues of the products he is selling, not to mention what is wrong with the wares of his competitors—and prides himself on his bold moves. When he knew that the venerable French chef Joël Robuchon would be in town because one of his restaurants had ordered six of Ottolenghi's bellota hams for a party, he dropped in on him, hoping to present a Spanish caviar that he had recently added to his inventory. "I just gave Chef Robuchon the caviar sample despite not having a meeting," he wrote me in a gleeful text message. "Everyone was looking at me as if I had interrupted the Pope."

Caviar—so dear, so highly controlled, so easily concealed—is the cocaine of food. It comes from the virgin eggs of sturgeon, prehistoric fish of massive proportions. The beluga, or *Huso huso,* is the biggest; it can grow to more than three thousand pounds, and live for a hundred years. The Caspian Sea once teemed with them; in the early nineteenth century, a twenty-four-foot-long female was caught in the Volga estuary.

People have been preserving sturgeon eggs for millennia; for the Phoenicians, they were a food of famine. But by the mid-twentieth century, caviar was a luxury good, an extra-special specialty item. "Even the Russians took part," noted a report on the second Fancy Food Show, in 1956. "They displayed caviar aimed at exciting the palates of capitalists." It takes around fifteen years for a sturgeon to mature. Theocracies and dictators were good beluga stewards, but with the dissolution of the Soviet Union in the 1990s, overfishing and poaching threatened *Huso huso,* along with other sturgeon species prized for their roe, with extinction. "Everyone with a rowboat is out on the Caspian tossing sturgeon into the backs of their boats," a U.S. Customs agent told the *Los Angeles Times* in the late nineties.

In 1998, the Convention on International Trade in Endangered Species (CITES) started setting quotas on the harvesting of wild Caspian caviar. Some years, the amount deemed safe to take was none. In 2005, the U.S. Fish and Wildlife Service banned the importation of beluga, which had recently been added to the endangered species list. Beluga prices spiked, encouraging smugglers and imposters. The less beluga there was, the more "beluga" there was: some of it real, some of it fake, all of it illegal. A Warsaw police officer in charge of an anti-organized-crime unit was arrested at JFK with six accomplices and sixteen suitcases full of undeclared beluga, and special agents from U.S. Fish and Wildlife started to perform DNA tests on incoming caviar shipments, looking for fraud.

The restrictions on caviar have spawned a mini-industry of neologisms based on deep faith in the power of association. Label-imagery, Morris Kushner might have called it. "Beluga," which conjures visions of oligarchs, is the magic word. The largest caviar importer in America, Marky's, which is based in Miami, offers on its website "Prime B Dark Osetra Private Stock Caviar known as Beluga Type Caviar," which is about as meaningful as describing an African elephant as "Dark Gray Special Reserve Animal known as Lion Type Animal." The COO assured me that the company was going to revise its website soon.

"This was written to indicate what others have called it," he said. "There is so much confusion."

One thing, at least, was clear. Before the ban, Marky's aquaculture branch brought fifty-five live *Huso huso* into the United States; when the fish mature in several years the company will have a federally enforced monopoly on beluga in the U.S. market. Another importer has registered the name River Beluga to refer to *Huso dauricus,* a sturgeon native to the Amur River, on the border of Russia and China. *Huso dauricus,* commonly known as kaluga, is a relative of beluga, but not a close one. One distributor I talked to, who deals in *Huso dauricus* raised on a farm in China, said that *his* importer invoices it to him as "beluga hybrid," which is how he represents it to the restaurants he supplies. "The beluga name is what consumers know, but there's no wild beluga on the market," he said. "You have people reaching out, saying, 'What's the next best thing?' You're paying for the scarcity of the species."

In 2000, when the embargo against Iran was loosened, Behroush Sharifi, an Iranian-born, English-educated, American Deadhead with a gigantic beard, decided to start importing from the Middle East. First it was carpets. Then he moved into botanicals: saffron, barberries, and manna from Iran; red hibiscus from Lebanon; mastic, a kind of ancient chewing gum, from Greece. Anointing himself the Saffron King, he trafficked in the ancient, storied, strange, and scarce. His customers were famous New York restaurants like Babbo, Daniel, Jean Georges, WD-50. Around the time he started his business, a friend at the Natural Resources Defense Council (NRDC) asked him for help. The group was petitioning Fish and Wildlife to add beluga to the endangered species list; the agency had missed a deadline to respond and now the NRDC could bring a lawsuit but needed a plaintiff. Sharifi had grown up spending summers on the Caspian, and had flirted with importing Iranian caviar. Helped by his testimony about the devastation of the fishery, beluga was added to the list, clearing the way for the 2005 ban. “Many foodies would be angry that I’d removed something so precious,” he said.

In the absence of wild-caught Caspian caviar, a market for domestic roe, farmed and fished, has opened up. California has been producing caviar since the seventies, when the overthrow of the shah of Iran inspired fears—hopes?—of a shortage; now Petrossian carries it. Paddlefish eggs are coming out of the Ozarks; bowfin roe from the Atchafalaya Swamp gets exported to Moscow. (The FDA allows these products to be called caviar, but purists say that designation belongs only to sturgeon eggs.) On farms, delivery does not always mean death: some aqua-cultivators induce ovulation with synthetic oxytocin—Pitocin, which stimulates uterine contractions, is one—and then “milk” the fish, while others have experimented with cesarean sections. “It’s not lost on me that a lovely unintended consequence of making caviar illegal is that it allows for this emergence, this wonderful domestic product,” Sharifi told me. It is a product he has come to have a special feeling for, now that a new trade embargo has made importing saffron and other Iranian products illegal again. “Principles are one thing but you have to have bread in the bowl,” he told me, explaining that he is now a seller of American caviar.

Ottolenghi’s caviar, from a Mediterranean sturgeon called

Acipenser naccarii, is raised sustainably on a farm in Grenada, and prepared according to a traditional Iranian recipe. I met Philippe Barbier, the recipe master, in Spain: a French Basque with deep-set green eyes, a reddish beard, a yellow front tooth, and unlaced shoes. Driving through the countryside, he said that the culinary potential for farmed caviar was much greater than for the revered beluga, which no one dared serve other than with toast points and riced egg. The lower price of his stuff made it more like any other raw ingredient. "Chefs seem receptive—they're just looking for reassurance that it's a product no one will think they're silly for using," he said. Michel Troisgros, the Michelin three-star chef at Maison Troisgros, in Paris, was using his caviar, he said, to make *payusnaya*, a paste that he formed into a thin sheet and wrapped around a soft-boiled quail egg. "When you cut it, all the yolk is coming out, like a little volcano!" he said. Troisgros had also filled the channels of cooked endive with the caviar and shaped them into black-and-white roses.

After Ottolenghi visited the farm with Barbier, he returned to Las Vegas determined to break into the room-service and private-jet menus of all the big casinos. Hopeful, he went to a major casino and presented the caviar to a team of chefs. They loved it; they especially loved the price. But then one of them asked if Ottolenghi could call it "beluga," as their current supplier was doing. "I told the exec chef what they were doing is illegal in front of 8 chefs and walked out," he wrote me in a text message. The next day, he wrote to me again, saying that he now had all the information he needed to show the casino that its caviar was illegally labeled. "So we should be able to get the business." If all else failed, he had put in a call to the authorities to get his competitor slapped.

Ottolenghi lives in a single-story stucco house he shares with his college roommate, Howie, who actually is a VIP host at Tao, the nightclub made famous by Tiger Woods and, with 1,400 covers on a peak night, one of the top-grossing restaurants in America. When I visited him in 2010, Ottolenghi was getting ready to open a small retail store, near the airport, where he hoped that chefs would shop on their days off. The living room was crowded with cans of Spanish olive oil, French green lentils, hand-kneaded fettuccine, specialty vinegar made by an ornery vintner in Napa, a huge bag of Szechuan peppercorns, and sixteen kinds of salt. In the kitchen cabinets, there were old balsamics and samples of water from all over the world, which Ottolenghi, researching for a special project, had tasted only after a twenty-four-hour fast. His fridge was full of awkward little pancakes of *payusnaya,* which, drawing on the Troisgros example, he was trying to interest his chefs in. Four long chest freezers full of bone-in hams and foie gras lobes lined the garage. A cream-colored 1951 Chevy panel truck, in which Sidney, the Artisanal Foods driver, makes deliveries, was parked out front.

Beside the front door was a small pond, which was home to three sturgeon—pets, Ottolenghi said, that also served as props. Several weeks before, he had bought a fish tank from a pet store, then called his domestic caviar supplier, in California, and asked if they could send him some sturgeon. He started going to chef meetings to pitch the Spanish caviar with one in tow. "He comes in with this fish tank sloshing water to show us what a sturgeon is," Alessandro Stratta told me. "I said, 'I know what a sturgeon is.' Next time, he'll come in here with a pig!" (Stratta placed an order.)

One morning, Ottolenghi went to the airport to pick up Helena Gonzalez, a beautiful twenty-seven-year-old Salvadoran woman whose parents started making foie gras in Sonoma, California, in the mid-eighties, and a better prop by a long shot than a sturgeon in a tank. Her foie gras was one of Ottolenghi's special products: it had the glow that comes from being obscenely delicious, extremely expensive (around $80 a pound), and soon to be unavailable. Foie gras, or "fatty liver," is made by *gavage*, force-feeding corn to ducks or geese until their livers swell to ten times their natural size. Animal-rights activists consider the feeding regimen to be torture, and in 2005 Arnold Schwarzenegger, who was at the time the governor of California, signed legislation to ban the sale and production of foie gras. Sonoma Artisan Foie Gras, the Gonzalezes' company, was the state's one producer. In deference to them, the bill was given a long sunset: they had until July 1, 2012, to invent a method of production that did not involve *gavage*, or close down. It was a rather hopeless proposition. Foie gras has been made the same way since the time of the Pharoahs.

Ottolenghi's first appointment with Gonzalez was at City Center, with Drew Terp, who was then the executive chef at barMASA and Shaboo, a pair of restaurants run by Masayoshi Takayama, whose flagship, Masa, is one of the most expensive restaurants in New York. Wearing a brown suit, a Bic behind his ear, and a pair of glasses tucked into the neckline of his shirt, and carrying a foam cooler loaded with duck breasts and foie gras, Ottolenghi led Gonzalez across the hectic, dimly lit casino floor and around a corner to a fifteen-foot-tall locked door. Beside the locked door was another door, which he tested and found open. He let himself in and sat down to wait for the chef. "It took me forever to find Masa," he said later. "I kept hearing about it. I was, like, 'There's a new really expensive restaurant? How am I not working with them?'"

Eventually, Terp appeared and took Ottolenghi and Gonzalez into the kitchen. "We use Hudson. That's what Chef Masa likes best," Terp, who is tall and fair, with full, rosy cheeks and a curl at his forehead, said. Hudson Valley Foie Gras, which is based in upstate New York, is the largest domestic producer of foie gras, and was Sonoma's primary competitor. "Chef Masa, when he finds something he likes, it's very difficult to get him to use other things." Ottolenghi extracted a big putty-colored lump from the cooler and handed it to Terp, who drew it close to his face and turned it over several times. Ottolenghi ventured that the feed used by Sonoma was, in his opinion, superior—cooked corn, with no added soy protein. Terp shaved off a tiny sliver of the lobe and pressed it into a pan with his index finger. It started to sizzle. "We go through five to six lobes a week," he said. "We do a five-hundred-dollar *omakase* menu, and I'll use half a lobe for a five-top."

Terp removed the piece of seared foie gras with a pair of chopsticks and set it on a cutting board. He tasted it; he liked it;

price, he said, was no object. "I have to run it by Chef Masa," he said. "He's very demanding. I'll have to go through the whole lobe to make sure of the consistency." Ottolenghi asked if he could visit the following week, when the chef was in. "Sure," Terp said. "But it's just him tasting it and saying yes or no. No sales pitch, no talking about sustainability."

Sampling, Ottolenghi not only drops off tidbits but also collects them. The next day, at Andre's, at the Monte Carlo, an old-school fine-dining establishment with a grandfathered-in cigar lounge, custom Limoges china, and wine dating back to the French Revolution, Ottolenghi set to work on the chef, Gary FX LaMorte. Chef was an indoorsy-looking guy, with shiny dark hair. There was a lot Ottolenghi wanted to know: where he had worked before (another French restaurant), where his former colleague had gone (the Caribbean), where he got his rabbit. "I ask because rabbit really interests me," he said. "Rabbit doesn't require USDA approval to slaughter. Anyone can kill one and butcher it in their kitchen and sell it. One day I want to get into that." Picturing Ottolenghi's kitchen, with its view of an algae-covered swimming pool, I shivered. When they got around to the matter at hand, LaMorte mentioned that he needed duck fat for terrines. "We decant the clarified foie fat, chill the terrine, and brush the fat back on for a protective coating, just like you would do at your house in the 1880s or some shit," he said. "You can mix it with cocoa butter. It makes a great salad dressing."

"I want to see more dandelion being used," Ottolenghi said, making me wonder if he had a lead on a patch.

"I like it, but it makes you urinate a lot," LaMorte said.

* * *

For most of Las Vegas's history, food there broke down into three main categories: coffee shop, steak house, and buffet. For high rollers, there were gourmet rooms, with names like the Sultan's Table and the House of Lords, where waiters in tuxedos plated Maine lobster and chateaubriand tableside. Restaurants were a way of fortifying gamblers, to keep them from straying too far from the tables and the slot machines.

The first big chef to come to Las Vegas was Wolfgang Puck, who had opened Spago, in Los Angeles, in the early eighties. The developer Sheldon Gordon approached him with the idea of putting a Spago in the Forum Shops at Caesars Palace, a mall that he planned to build in a parking lot where Formula One races had been held. Puck, who liked to go to Vegas for the fights and already had a branch of Spago in Tokyo, agreed, and the restaurant opened at the beginning of December 1992, when the only thing happening was the rodeo finals. "We had all these people come up to the open kitchen—they'd see the plates and think it was a buffet," Puck recalled. "I said, 'I didn't know they had so many cowboys here. I would've done a rib joint.'"

For the first several weeks, Puck thought he'd made a terrible mistake, and drank himself to sleep every night with a bottle of wine in front of the TV. Then New Year's came, the shows resumed, and the Consumer Electronics convention came to town. Spago had lines out the door. Steve Wynn started hanging out at the bar, and so did the Molaskys, big local developers. Puck would see customers from the L.A. Spago at the fights—Arnold Schwarzenegger, Jack Nicholson, Tony Danza—and bring them back to Spago afterward. Before long, the Vegas location was outperforming L.A.'s. "People started hearing the numbers we were doing at Spago," David Robins, the restaurant's chef, who moved to Las Vegas to help with the opening, told me. "I'd get calls saying, 'Did you really do a million this month?' I'd say, 'Actually, it was one-point-two.'"

In the late nineties, while getting ready to open the Bellagio, a $1.6-billion resort on the site of the old Dunes casino, Steve Wynn, mindful of Puck's success, decided that the property needed to be a dining destination. He sent a team of consultants out to recruit celebrity chefs, and when the Bellagio opened, in 1998, it housed world-class restaurants by Sirio Maccioni, Michael Mina, Julian Serrano, Todd English, and Jean-Georges Vongerichten. Soon every big casino had a roster of star chefs. Joël Robuchon came out of retirement to open two restaurants at the MGM Grand in 2005; in 2009, Pierre Gagnaire, a three-star Michelin chef in Paris, opened his first restaurant in the United States, at the Mandarin Oriental hotel at City Center.

From the beginning, the problem with haute cuisine in Las Vegas was ingredients. All you could get were frozen proteins and overstock produce. When Puck first arrived, he told me, "I went to visit a fish guy, who took me into a thirty-thousand-square-foot freezer. I said, 'No, no. That's not who we are. We want fresh tuna and salmon.'" He had his chefs drive a van to the Santa Monica Farmers Market for fruit and vegetables. As more and more high-level chefs arrived, a culture developed of what one chef called "FedEx cuisine." Claude Le Tohic, the executive chef at Robuchon, who won the 2010 James Beard

Award for best chef in the Southwest, gets his butter and his cheese overnighted from France. According to Julian Serrano, it is easier to get good ingredients in Las Vegas than in San Francisco, where he used to work, because the airport there often gets fogged in, whereas in Las Vegas the weather is almost always clear, and a plane lands every three minutes at McCarran Field.

Paul Bartolotta, the chef at Bartolotta at Wynn, a complex that Steve Wynn opened in 2005, is perhaps the most extreme example. The concept of his restaurant—simple preparations of fish and crustaceans at exorbitant prices—depends on seafood being flown in as often as five times a week from the Mediterranean, in coolers equipped with microchips to monitor the temperature throughout the voyage. He has no patience with concerns about sustainability. "Las Vegas is a pilot project to see if man can live on the moon," he says. "There's nothing local—our water comes from somewhere else, our electricity comes from somewhere else." Fishermen have sent him texts in the middle of the night from their boats in the Adriatic, with pictures of themselves holding fresh-caught specimens and messages like "Want this fish?" On one such occasion, the fish was an eighteen-pound ombrina; when it arrived at the restaurant, forty-eight hours later, Bartolotta walked it onto the floor and offered it to a party of golfers as the main course in a tasting menu they had ordered. He took it back to the kitchen, sprinkled some salt and pepper on it, tied up the tail so it would fit in the oven, and within ninety minutes the golfers were eating it. Their bill came to nearly $5,000, before wine.

Another local feature is the wildly variable demand. Olivier Dubreuil, the executive chef at the Venetian and the Palazzo, which together command nearly two million square feet of convention space, says that he sometimes serves eighty thousand people one day and twenty thousand the next. "I can use five hundred *magrets* and then never use them again," he says. "I can use sixty pounds of foie gras in three days." Even in the age of cutbacks, the pharmaceutical companies still spend handsomely. When Tylenol comes to town, he told me, food budgets soar.

Vegas may be the one food town left in America where the ego of the customer still trumps the ego of the chef. If a big player wants a cheese pizza, he gets a cheese pizza, even at a formal French restaurant like Alex. I heard a story about a Korean high roller who travels twice a year to Wynn with an entourage of twenty-five and plays six-figure hands of baccarat. One night he tried Bartolotta and loved it so much that he arranged to bring his whole group back the following night. Only this time he was in the mood for a roast-beef dinner. So what did Bartolotta do? He went out and found some beef to roast. Bradley Ogden recently bought from Ottolenghi some 1890 balsamic vinegar in tiny bottles that looked as if they should hold perfume; they cost $350 apiece and would most likely be served to high rollers, after supper, on mother-of-pearl spoons. "Vegas is the entertainment capital of the world," David Robins, of Spago, says. "We want to treat customers with respect, and we want to take all their money."

A relative of mine who lived in Buffalo and went by the name Shorty Plumb used to run booze across the border to Canada in the back of a pickup truck loaded with horse manure, and never got caught. Truffle cheats follow that same rule of thumb: you hide the good stuff in with the shit. The sums of money involved can be vast. White truffles from Italy cost up to $4,500 a pound wholesale; black ones, $800. Claude Le Tohic, Robuchon's executive chef, told me that when truffles are in season he goes through ten or twelve pounds of black ones and five pounds of white a week. He sometimes offers a six-course truffle tasting menu, which includes a truffle tart, and serves a truffle–foie dish topped with edible gold.

For an importer, the temptation to con can be strong. Some will stash a box of truffles deep inside a container load of something boring, like lettuce, to dodge the import tax. Others route their paperwork through places not within the bounds of the EU. For years, Ottolenghi says, all the European truffle companies were based in San Marino, a tiny independent republic in northern Italy, which was exempt; now most run their paperwork through Croatia. Another common trick, this one played on chefs, is to add a few worthless Chinese truffles to a box of black Italians; the color is indistinguishable, and the Chinese truffles take on the aroma of the more expensive ones. A chef would have to know the subtleties of truffle morphology to pick out the impostors, or isolate each truffle under a bell jar and smell it again after waiting fifteen minutes. Ottolenghi finds the chicanery infuriating; crooks serve as a good foil for virtue, but they make for tough competition in the marketplace. "Basically, selling truffles, you're a smuggler," he says.

I asked Joseph Magnano, the young, tattooed West Coast representative for Sabatino Tartufi, a large importer based in Umbria, about the business. At the time, he was the top truffle seller in Las Vegas, and he saw it as a magnet for come-latelies. "Every distributor in Las Vegas at one point or another will try to get in on it, try to get on my coattails," he said, agitated, between sales calls at the Wynn. He had on a black wool cap and carried a small cooler full of truffles. "But they don't know how to sell truffle. They don't *care* to know about truffle."

I asked if there was a lot of fraud. "Oh, a hundred percent," he said. "I'm not saying that *we* do it, but I'm saying it's there, especially during black winter–truffle season, because it's at the same time as Chinese truffle season. Chef will never know the difference if he doesn't know truffle. You *can* identify them, they have a different hardness, the flavor's different, they taste more rubbery, they're not as clean, the veins are skinnier, it's just not a good product. You can tell, if you know truffle." A Chinese truffle, Magnano said, smells like burned drip coffee, while a bad white truffle tastes like a greasy Lay's potato chip. But he dismissed Ottolenghi's priggishness. "It's not that the business has no ethics—it's a business," he said scornfully. "If you don't move product, you don't live."

A few years ago, Ottolenghi sent a letter to his chefs, announcing that, after twelve years, he was scaling down his truffle business, "because the only way to succeed selling truffles in Las Vegas is to have lower ethics and cheat more than your competitors." He went on to say that saffron, "a once noble spice," was going the same way, and claimed that not a single restaurant in Las Vegas was using pure product. Most of the saffron on the market—sold for $85 an ounce—was, he said, a hash of crocus parts dyed with red food coloring. He, on the other hand, was personally importing saffron directly from Spain. The letter served as an announcement that his fresh shipment had arrived and that he would be offering it for $145 an ounce.

While in Spain, Ottolenghi went to see Pina, his saffron source in La Mancha. "Saffron is the second product I started selling, after truffles," he told me. "Light products do well on the Internet." Pina has a lab where it analyzes competitors' saffron to suss out fakes, and Ottolenghi thought that this would be a selling point to chefs: they'd give him a one-gram sample of whatever they were using, he'd pay to have it tested at Pina, and if it turned out to be dyed the chefs would promise to buy from him. "I know I'm going to win that bet," he said.

After he got home, Ottolenghi was back on his beat, going from chef to chef, a brown leather satchel slung over his shoulder, hand-selling his goods: 100-percent-pure saffron; vanilla bean from Papua New Guinea; and a variety of salts, including one that had been smoked over a Chardonnay cask. It was 116 degrees, and, to his embarrassment, he couldn't wear a suit. Furthermore, his sturgeon had died, and Chef Robuchon had said no to the Spanish caviar. But SW Steakhouse had just ordered a kilo, for $1,500; barMASA was using the foie gras; and RM Seafood, Rick Moonen's sustainable fish restaurant at Mandalay Bay, had picked up both.

At midday, Ottolenghi trudged into the Rio, an old casino that houses the purchasing department for all the Harrah's properties in Las Vegas. He wound his way past giant carnival masks and fixated smokers staring at the slots, and through an unmarked door to the loading dock, where crates of plucked chickens sat next to plastic bags of precooked chili. In a windowless office off the dock, he sat down to make a pitch to a senior buyer. "I'm trying to convince everyone to switch to real saffron," Ottolenghi said. "It's terrible. There's more cheating going on in saffron than almost any other product." He pulled a jar from his satchel, and took off the top. A heady, tobacco-like aroma filled the room. He held up a piece, bright red, like a shrunken coral. "The fake ones, you put them in water, the water will turn orange-red from dye," he said. The buyer pushed a pair of glasses up onto his forehead. "Interesting," he said flatly. "Never knew that." Ottolenghi leaned in, and suggested that he could do a demonstration for the chefs, soaking the saffron from their stockrooms in water to show them what they really had: flavorless flower bits and food coloring. The buyer agreed, and Ottolenghi packed up his wares and said good-bye. But, rather than leaving, he started walking down the hall, popping his head into other buyers' offices, just to introduce himself and say hello and see if they might like to take a sniff of his vanilla from Papua New Guinea, which was the same species and just as good, based on his research, as the prized Tahitian stuff, and a bargain by comparison.

Ottolenghi has attended the Fancy Food Show since he was eight. (The minimum age is eighteen.) I went for the first time in 2012, to the winter show in San Francisco. Before long, I ran into Ruth Reichl, the former editor of *Gourmet* who had become the director of Gilt Taste, an ever-changing online market for everything from golden-roe bottarga to gluten-free pound cake. Reichl, an experienced showgoer, was reminiscing about weird, off-putting products past, like Gourm-Egg, a tube of extrudable hard-boiled eggs, for salad bars and restaurants. This time around, the novelties were throwbacks: "ancient grains," chia seeds, camote flour—subsistence fare from the early days of agriculture.

At Culinary Collective, a sophisticated Washington-based importer with a line of pre-Columbian flours and grains, Betsy Power was talking up *kañiwa*, a hearty, high-protein grain that grows in the Andean *altiplano,* which she had recently placed in some Whole Foods stores in Northern California. Power extolled *kañiwa*'s earthy, nutty flavor and its plumping ratio, comparing it favorably to its sometimes bitter-tasting cousin, quinoa. "People had started growing quinoa, due to the Western influence in the market," she said. "*Kañiwa* was out of favor. They were growing it for animals"—a sure sign that it was poised for exploitation by the wealthiest eaters. The rise of Bolivian quinoa, though, served as a warning: embraced by Americans as a high-brow carb, its price nearly tripled in five years, making it unaffordable to the poor Bolivians who once made it a staple of their diets but now relied on less-expensive processed foods.

"The caviar flows like glue at the show," Julia Child once joked. When an attractive Korean woman wearing a T-shirt that read "I'm Probiotic" walked by, I followed her back to her booth in search of something to eat. "Probiotics is the buzzword," she said, spearing some red-hot kimchi on a toothpick and handing it to me. "The American palate is beginning to understand what live food means. Pasteurized and dead things are part of the old food system." Her card promised well-being to those who consumed "the Champagne of Pickles."

I found Stewart Reich, Max Ries's great-nephew, taking

meetings on a tartan-covered café chair at the lavish Walkers Shortbread booth. Behind him, imposing wooden display cases were filled with cookie tins, down-lit like handbags at Hermès. Walkers was a success story—an obscure Scottish cookie discovered in the seventies by two guys from the Bronx as they traveled through Europe looking for products to import. They placed an order and figured that if the cookies didn't sell, they would give them away. At the time, Walkers was only in two or three countries; now it's a $200-million-a-year business, with a presence in eighty countries.

There were lots of things like that at the show: food givens that the old hands could trace back to their uncertain beginnings. "Balsamic vinegar is in everything now," Reich mused. "Not that long ago it was only available from Dean & DeLuca." Mario Foah, the panettone guy, had Reich beat on that; he later told me that he was one of the first to import it, in the early eighties, before anybody knew what it was. "I went to somebody's home in Milan and they made a risotto with balsamic vinegar. I said, 'What's *this* stuff?'" he recalled. He bottled it in a special straw-wrapped container, presented it at the Fancy Food Show, and dazzled the food press. "That was the year balsamic vinegar took off," he said.

At the next booth over were the remains of Reese, which Max Ries sold to Pet Milk in the mid-sixties. (He died at home on Lake Shore Drive in Chicago, in 1984.) Reese is currently owned by a distributors' consortium called World Finer Foods, which also represents Bonne Maman preserves, McCann's Irish Oatmeal, and Panda licorice. According to the consortium, Reese is still the country's top-selling brand of artichokes, water chestnuts, hearts of palm, and wine vinegar. The wall of Reese products looked like the contents of a mid-century bomb shelter: capers, anchovy fillets, asparagus spears, packed in glass and labeled with idealized pictures of the contents.

When I ran into Ottolenghi, he was wearing his blue blazer and khakis and had just come from a meeting in Seattle with some importers of *wagyu,* extra-fatty Japanese beef; a nearly three-year ban on imports, due to hoof-and-mouth, was soon to be lifted. After that, he had stopped at the Monterey Bay Aquarium to investigate the potential of selling sea urchins from the last sustainable population, off the coast of British Columbia. Here at the show he was excited about some vinegar made from rotten bananas. "I don't know who I'm going to sell it to—but someone!" he said. He spent a long time looking at the Cinco Jotas ham—an Ibérico even more expensive than Fermín, which was making its U.S. debut.

Then Ottolenghi saw something else, something slick and sleek and new, with a great story. It was Ian Purkayastha, a nineteen-year-old truffle merchant from Arkansas who had skipped college and was now the U.S. distributor for an esteemed Italian line, selling to Per Se, Daniel, and Jean Georges. (A few months later, he launched a new company, which specializes in wild edibles, like milkweed, pine bud, and Queen Anne's lace.) He was trim and confident, with heavy dark eyebrows, and was wearing what appeared to be an Armani suit. Ottolenghi checked him out, and offered his impartial assessment. Purkayastha was the genuine article. He said, "He's younger, and he sells *way* more truffles than I do."

PART II

DOWN THE RABBIT HOLE

Four

THE RAWESOME THREE

Neophilia and neophobia—loving and fearing the new—are conflicting impulses that arise simultaneously in infants around the time that they attain mobility: babies put everything in their mouths and start to reject the unfamiliar. That's about where I was with unusual food, the crawling stage, when I heard about Rawesome, an expensive, all-cash, members-only specialty store devoted to radically unprocessed food, run out of a lot in Venice, California. Rawesome was based on the topsy-turvy idea that "safe" food was food procured outside official channels. Its members strained the boundaries of food adventuring to the point of reckless abandon—and did so with an attitude of extreme finickiness, in the name of protecting their health.

Rawesome attracted a clientele of health-seekers, yoginis, celebrities, and the seriously ill. The store, which advertised itself with a sign that read "Rawesome Foods—Raw and Organic—Out of the Ordinary and Downright Extraordinary," carried provisions that were otherwise inaccessible: unheated honey from the Bolivian highlands (outside the fallout range of the A-bomb tests), sun-dried cashews from Bali, raw cow colostrum, goat whey, and camel milk from a dairy selling it for "craft use." Cheese came in unmarked tubs—often lacking dates or labels—and in the meat cooler there were jars containing raw bison kidneys, spleen, hearts, and testicles, which customers often sliced open and ate on the spot. "We had some real vampires going through there," a former Rawesome worker, who lived for a time in a shipping container on the lot, said. "Everyone wanted to suck the cow's udder." Liv Tyler and Mandy Moore shopped there occasionally. Mariel Hemingway was a regular, as were Peta Wilson and Vincent Gallo. Fred Segal, the boutique owner, ordered a box of food every week, and John Cusack's personal chef, Rawesome workers said, was forbidden to shop anywhere else.

James Stewart, Rawesome's owner, a robust man in his mid-sixties with a beachcomber's moustache and a wardrobe of Hawaiian shirts, had been in the food business a long time. As a teenager in the mid-sixties, Stewart told me, he moved from New York to California with his mother and sisters, who became famous Hollywood groupies; one of them, Reine, had a baby with Peter Tork of the Monkees. Stewart lived across from the Whiskey and got a job at HELP (Health, Education, Love, Peace), one of the city's first health-food stores, where he was introduced to the teachings of Yogi Bhajan, a Sikh who brought kundalini to the United States, and started wearing a turban. He grew sprouts, which he sold to supermarkets, and worked for the Beach Boys at their store, Radiant Radish. One of Stewart's companies, an organic produce business, was called Green Energy. "I figured it was just green coming out of the ground, turning into money," he told me. "It was a cycle." For his ability to source shade-dried manuka raisins and dried persimmons—rarities in the seventies—he earned the nickname Mr. Exotic. By the time he opened Rawesome, he said, half the products he stocked could be found at regular health food stores and farmers' markets; the other half, the "unique products," he called them, were illegal.

Early one morning in the summer of 2011, as one of the coconut juicers—known around Rawesome for their stoned demeanor and their unsocialized way of wearing mud masks in public—started extracting the day's supply, there was a knock at the gate. Outside, more than a dozen agents from the FDA, the county health department, and the Franchise Tax Board had assembled, in raid jackets and tactical vests; armed LAPD officers provided security. Stewart was arrested and put in handcuffs. He had $9,000 in his pocket, because he'd been planning to go downtown to pick up merchandise. His fruit money was entered into evidence. Over the next several hours, a crowd of about a hundred Rawesome members gathered to watch as agents loaded produce onto a flatbed truck. When the agents dumped some eight hundred gallons of raw dairy down the kitchen drain, members wept.

At its core, Rawesome was a raw-milk business. For more than a year, it had been the subject of a nine-agency investigation, in which undercover agents infiltrated the network of dairy dealers supplying the club. Count 3, Overt Act 12 of the felony complaint for arrest warrant: "'Deb' is in beige colored Ford van. . . . When 'Customer Ward\Kennedy' asks for his order, 'Deb' searches through five ice coolers in the back of the van and pulls out the water-soaked order: six unlabeled containers of raw dairy products." The operatives, among them the feared California Department of Food and Agriculture investigator Scarlett Treviso—code-named La Rue—mingled with customers and, using what Stewart's lawyer said were "purse cams and pole cams," photographed Rawesome's cooler, dry-goods trailer, and open-air produce market. They also took pictures of members coming and going through a corrugated metal gate. What they saw there shocked them, including, according to the complaint, membership agreements that said, "'As a member, I completely reject and refuse all governmental standards . . . any governmental sanitation standards for food storage and display' and I am 'out of the jurisdiction of any governmental department and its regulations.'" An undercover source told me, "It was one of the two most extreme communities I've ever worked in. The other was animal rights."

The day of the bust, the police also went to Santa Paula, sixty miles away, to hit Healthy Family Farms, a small operation that supplied the club with poultry, eggs, and, for a time, raw goat products from a forty-head herd that Rawesome boarded there. The farmer, Sharon Palmer, a single parent who manages the farm with her three teenagers, was arrested. A fifty-nine-year-old graphic designer named Eugenie Victoria Bloch, a Rawesome member who helped sell Palmer's products at farmers' markets, was also arrested, outside her home in Los Angeles.

Stewart, Palmer, and Bloch, who came to be known as the

Rawesome Three, were charged with felony counts of conspiracy; Stewart and Palmer were charged with an additional two felonies, for running an unlicensed milk plant and processing milk products without pasteurization, and with various misdemeanors, including counts of poor sanitation and improper labeling. (All three pleaded not guilty to all the charges.) The tax-board data indicated that Rawesome was generating more than $500,000 a year in income, yet neither the business nor the proprietor had filed state tax returns. Stewart's bail was set at $123,000, with the stipulation, common in drug cases, that he be held until the court could ascertain that the bail was not "feloniously obtained"—high stakes for a grocer. For his defense, he hired Ajna Sharma-Wilson, at the time an attorney at one of the top marijuana-defense firms in Los Angeles. The analogy was plain: raw milk was the new pot, only harder to get.

Paranoia and defiance rippled through the Rawesome community after the raid. At a screening of *Farmageddon*, a documentary about small producers victimized by national and state food-safety laws, which concludes with absurd footage of an earlier raid on Rawesome, in 2010—agents, guns drawn, stalking among crates of fruits and vegetables—Stewart, in a white palm-tree shirt unbuttoned to his sternum, said that he was not at liberty to talk about some of what he had learned from the discovery. A big, mustachioed man, hunkered down in his chair, cautioned him to be even more circumspect. In a thick accent, he said, "Are you aware that there is possibly an informer sitting amongst us right now?"

Sharma-Wilson tossed her long dark hair. "I invite an informer to hear this," she said. "Our forefathers drank straight from a cow." She went on, "This is a guerilla war. This all started with the Pure Food and Drugs Act of 1906. The FDA actually stated recently that 'There is no "deeply rooted" historical tradition of unfettered access to foods of all kinds.'"

At a hearing in October 2011, thirty supporters wearing white T-shirts that read "Raw Milk Heals" gathered outside the courtroom. Many were baffled by what had befallen their neighborhood market. "Rawesome was an intelligent local food ecosystem. It was alive, and it was regulating itself on a level so far beyond what the USDA or the FDA means when it says 'food safety,'" Camilla Griggers, who teaches English at a nearby college, said. "That we would be dragged through the court system on a food-safety issue is so laughable. Rawesome was a gourmet club par excellence of the best food you could get anywhere in the world."

Never mind the immersion circulators and the hydrocolloids, refined American cuisine has a regressive side, wrapped up in nostalgia for an idealized past. Raw milk stirs the hedonism of food lovers in a special way. After relying for years on milk smuggled from California and Utah, Ottolenghi, in Las Vegas, is trying to build Nevada's first raw-milk dairy. Because raw milk is not heated or homogenized and often comes from animals raised on pasture, it tends to be richer and sweeter and, sometimes, to retain a whiff of the farm—the slightly discomfiting flavor known to connoisseurs as "cow butt." To chefs, it is almost mystical. "Pasteurization strips away layers of complexity, layers of aromatics," Daniel Patterson, who has used raw milk to make custard and eggless ice cream at Coi, his two-Michelin-star restaurant in San Francisco, said. "At the beginning of spring, the milk is at its sweetest. The cows are getting a lot of herbs that are really verdant and green, and the milk has a higher fat content." It is not just the flavor, though, it's what it represents: something unprocessed, sentimental, pure. "Raw milk is a primary touchstone of that sort of agrarian, old-fashioned way of life," Patterson said.

Another highly regarded California chef told me he had helped a nearby farmer buy three cows from a breed carefully picked for the character of its milk and set up a small herd share, an agreement of uncertain legality whereby consumers own a percentage of a herd and are entitled to an allotment of milk. The farmer insisted on cash payments, no paper trail. "Only recently have they allowed receipts to go through my bookkeeper, but even now we don't say what it's for," the chef told me. "We say 'cow services.'" He uses the raw cream to make butter, ice cream, and a *cajeta*—Mexican caramel—that he describes as "haunting." He said, "Dairy is the single most delicate and sensitive indicator of *terroir* I have encountered. When you take milk or cream and pasteurize it and homogenize it, you've killed the originality."

Naturally, I wanted to try it. When I went to the chef's restaurant, though, I thought it wise to pass the butter up. I had just found out that I was pregnant. Milk, being rich in protein and low in acid, is one of the best growth mediums on the planet. Bacteria love it. Unpasteurized milk can carry salmonella, campylobacter, and *E. coli* O157:H7, the strain that came to public attention in the nineties, when four children died after eating contaminated meat at Jack in the Box. Listeria—which can cause miscarriage, premature birth, and newborn death—has been traced to *queso fresco*–style raw-milk cheeses, sometimes known as "bathtub cheese," a reference to unsanitary home-production methods. The USDA fact sheet for consumers that I found online offered unambiguous advice. If you want to avoid listeriosis, it said, "Do not drink raw (unpasteurized) milk."

Only a small fraction of the population—between 1 and 3 percent—drinks raw milk, and fewer than 200 cases of outbreak-related foodborne illness are attributed to it each year. Still, its popularity is rising, and regulators, puzzled by the raw-milk phenomenon, are growing concerned. A recent CDC study reported that raw dairy was 150 times more likely than pasteurized to cause an outbreak. Tanya Roberts, a retired risk assessor for the USDA who specializes in *E. coli* O157:H7, told me, "I would never drink it. It's *loaded* with pathogens!" The FDA "strongly advises against the consumption of raw milk," maintaining that there is no nutritional advantage and a great health risk; John Sheehan, the agency's director of dairy food safety, has likened it to "playing Russian roulette with your health."

The government's real objection to raw milk is that they think people are playing Russian roulette with their *children's* health. Pasteurization was introduced to the American dairy industry to solve a children's-health crisis. By the mid-nineteenth century, most of the milk available in cities was supplied by "swill dairies," stables built alongside distilleries, where cows were fed macerated grain left over from the production of whiskey. The spent grains boosted milk production temporarily but left the cows—confined to dirty, crowded pens—malnourished and prone to disease. In 1858, *The New York Times* published an editorial titled "How We Poison Our Children," decrying the "bluish, white compound of true milk, pus and dirty water" and blaming swill milk for eight thousand infant deaths in the city the previous year. "The article which had borne from the beginning of the world a reputation for wholesomeness was in reality a deadly poison," the *Times* said. The state of milk was "intolerable to civilized society."

Four years later, Louis Pasteur came up with a heat treatment to kill bacteria in wine, and his method was soon applied to milk. When Nathan Straus, a philanthropist and later a co-owner of Macy's, set up depots where poor families could get pasteurized milk at discounted prices, the number of deaths among New York City babies dropped precipitously. What began as an argument for treating milk produced under unsanitary conditions became an argument for treating all milk. Speaking at the Pasteur Institute in 1905, the director of the depots read a statement from Straus saying, "It is milk—raw milk, diseased milk—which is responsible for the largest percentage of sickness in the world. . . . I hold that the only safe rule is—Pasteurize the entire milk supply and make it a function of the municipality."

Others, believing that pasteurization should only be a last resort, argued for dairies to be inspected rigorously and held to strict hygienic standards. Though a number of states set up "medical milk commissions" to oversee a dairy certification process, pasteurization, the more efficient and fool-proof approach, won out. Raw-milk sales are now illegal in eleven states and permitted in a number of others exclusively through herd-share agreements and on-farm sales; in four states, raw milk can be sold only as pet food.

Since 1987, when Ralph Nader's Public Citizen organization sued the Department of Health and Human Services to prohibit interstate commerce in raw milk, it has been a crime to transport it for sale across state lines. The resulting underground market is by definition unregulated; consumers must take it on faith that the milk is clean, something that, without testing, even the farmer can't know for sure. Good standards for inspection and proper labeling could significantly reduce the likelihood of outbreaks, but for now the two sides—those who call for unfettered access and those who completely oppose it—are deadlocked. "The conversation needs to start with really solid facts about the incidence of bacteria in raw milk," Jo Robinson, an investigative journalist who runs the website Eat Wild, says. "We're not doing enough to reduce those risks."

More than a hundred years ago, Ukrainian scientist Elie Metchnikoff, who was the deputy director at the Pasteur Institute laboratory in Paris, identified the health benefits of bacteria associated with fermentation. (He won the Nobel Prize and is considered the founder of the field of probiotics.) Rawesome extended this idea to all bacteria, claiming that a disease-resistant gut must be populated with the kinds of microorganisms most people strenuously avoid. In order to shop there, you had to sign an agreement saying that you preferred your food to "contain microbes, including but not limited to salmonella, E. coli, campylobacter, listeria, gangrene and parasites" and liked your eggs "completely unrefrigerated and unwashed from the chicken and covered with bacteria and poultry feces." Members not only rejected government food-safety standards as inapplicable to their nutritional requirements; they found them to be dangerous, because they allow for food to be treated with radiation and antibacterial chemicals. In the 2010 raid on Rawesome, the California Department of Food and Agriculture took samples of cheese made by a dairy in Missouri and found that they tested positive for trace amounts of listeria. "We told them we threw it out, but I don't think we did," a former USDA employee who worked at Rawesome for two years told me. "Listeria really didn't matter."

Suspicion of technology runs deep in the raw-milk movement. In the 1930s, a Cleveland dentist named Weston A. Price traveled around the world studying isolated populations experiencing their first exposure to "the displacing foods of modern commerce." In *Nutrition and Physical Degeneration,* which has become a central text for the movement, he wrote that people who ate unprocessed, indigenous foods had strong teeth, regular bone structure, and overall good health, whereas those who had adopted an American diet—refined sugar, white flour, pasteurized and skim milk, and hydrogenated oils—had cavities, facial deformities, and other problems, which they passed along to their children.

Advocates of raw milk hold that pasteurization kills enzymes that make food digestible and bacteria that contribute to a healthy immune system. Drinking raw milk, they say, confers numerous health benefits—vitality, digestive vigor, strong teeth, clear skin—and even has the power to treat serious ailments, such as diabetes, cancer, and autism. Sally Fallon Morell, the founder of an advocacy group informed by Price's work, recommends feeding raw milk to infants. (A pamphlet from her organization entitled "Homemade Raw Milk Formula for Babies, and Raw Milk for Toddlers & Children," equates breast milk with unpasteurized cow's milk, claiming that both contain "active biological systems that naturally protect the milk itself—and the infant who drinks it—from infection.") Carola Caldwell, a registered nurse who drove several hours from Lake Arrowhead to shop at Rawesome, overrode years of medical training to feed her son raw milk and meat. She told me that the diet had cured him of extreme allergies, chemical sensitivity, and moodiness. "Within three weeks of starting raw food, he became a different child," she said.

There has been little science to support these claims. The closest thing to an objective body of data appeared in 2011, with the publication of a large-sample study linking children's consumption of unheated "farm milk" to reduced rates of asthma and allergies. The researchers, based in Europe, where raw milk is more widely accepted, determined that whey protein was the protective element, but they stopped short of advising people to consume raw milk, because of the risk of pathogens. The next step, they wrote, would be to develop "ways of processing and preserving a safe and preventive milk."

Raw milk has always been legal in California, but the preponderance of regulation has made it hard to come by. In the late nineties, not long after James Stewart started selling raw milk, the state's largest provider shut down its raw operation, leaving, by Stewart's count, eight licensed raw-milk cows. As he searched for new supplies, he heard from Mark McAfee, a former paramedic who had inherited his grandparents' farm, in Fresno. "I called up James and said, 'I've got two hundred and fifty cows here, all certified organic or on grass,'" McAfee told me. "He says, 'I'll be there in three hours.'" According to McAfee, Stewart singlehandedly rebuilt the market for raw milk in Southern California, and introduced him to the nutritionist Aajonus Vonderplanitz, a former *General Hospital* actor who claims to have cured himself of multiple cancers by eating a diet of raw meat, eggs, and milk, and sharply restricting his water intake. Vonderplanitz, who calls his approach the Primal Diet, says that for a treat he bleeds meat into raw milk: "Tastes like ice cream!" Vonderplanitz became an investor in the farm, and his followers became McAfee's customers. Organic Pastures is now, by McAfee's estimation, the largest raw dairy in the world, with 430 cows. It produces 2,400 gallons of milk a day, which retails for $16 a gallon.

One chilly November day, I drove out to Organic Pastures with McAfee, an energetic, trim man who was wearing a thick parka and clean blue jeans. The first time I had seen him, at a rally before one of Stewart's court appearances, he was drawing battle lines from a podium. "Look at the frickin' enemy. Remember who they are: Monsanto, Tyson, Cargill, the FDA," he said into a microphone. "In ignorance, our great-grandparents traded freedom for safety."

Now, in the car, McAfee continued his narrative of struggle. "When people start drinking raw milk, it's like this awakening," he said. "It's a phenomenally transforming immune-system food that is largely oppressed, suppressed, ignored, vilified, hated by processors and those that are involved with the structure of the American Dairy Association," he said. "It's a massive food fight."

That day, McAfee was waiting for the state to lift a month-long embargo on his milk. For the second time in five years, Organic Pastures had been implicated in an outbreak of *E. coli* O157:H7. Five young children had fallen ill; three were hospitalized and treated for hemolytic uremic syndrome, which can lead to kidney failure. The same strain had been found in his calving pen, and he had instituted new safety procedures at the farm. Still, the embargo was costing him $150,000 a week, and he felt that the state was punishing him intentionally. The recall had driven the price of raw milk in some stores up to $40 a gallon, with priority going to mothers. "We've been trying to keep the peace with all of our consumers," he told me.

McAfee pulled into the farm and stopped beside a village of neat trailers: an office, a retail store, and a creamery, where hundreds of bottles stood waiting to be sent out. He talked with a manager, and said grimly, "It looks like we won't be getting released today." We drove down an unpaved road, past McAfee's house, a large Mediterranean spread with a pool, a pair of pet goats, and a hangar where he keeps a plane. In the dairy barn, a row of cows with steaming, swollen undercarriages lined up to be milked. Workers hosed them down—manure is a major potential source of pathogens—then stripped their teats with iodine. The state requires frequent testing, and McAfee takes expensive precautions to keep the milk clean. But, he said, "Manure is the carrier of the beneficial bacteria found in raw milk. The whole pasteurization community does not understand that at all."

Most milk on the market comes from animals fed a diet containing corn and soy—typically genetically modified—rather than grass, the food they evolved to digest. Since 2004, milk has been legally identified as an allergen; the FDA and the CDC both cite it first, before shellfish, nuts, and wheat, on their lists of top allergens. Perhaps as a consequence, in recent years people have been drinking less of it, instead choosing alternatives like soy, almond, and rice milk. At the same time, prices for feed and fuel have escalated, and many dairies have gone out of business. There has been a spate of dairyman suicides, several of them in California. But, since McAfee's previous *E. coli* recall, in 2006, when six children got sick after drinking his products, Organic Pastures has grown steadily. McAfee is doing far better than most of his pasteurizing counterparts; the company, he says, sold $9.6 million worth of milk products in 2012.

One winter morning, with a heavy fog lying over Los Angeles, the Dairy Fairy, a Rawesome member who quietly assumed Stewart's procurement responsibilities after the bust, got in her car and headed for the drop. Every week, she takes orders from the Rawesome diaspora for raw dairy, sauerkraut, and meat, most of it transported from Amish country in truck space rented from a large produce operation. To compensate her for her time, she is given a box of groceries, which is meaningful, since she works freelance, and she and her boyfriend spend about $500 a week on food. (Their dog eats raw, too.)

At first, the drop had gone down in public parks across the city, but the Dairy Fairy had decided that was too risky. One day, at a convenience store, she noticed a man selling cars off the lot. "I was like, That's kind of shady," she said. "So I went and talked to the owner. He said, 'I'm from Egypt—I love raw milk!' I trade him milk for us to park our truck here." The beauty of the location, she said, is that trucks come and go all day long; no one notices the milk truck, unmarked and inconspicuous, parked in a corner of the lot.

The truck was waiting when she arrived. A young couple popped out of the cab; the woman had a pixie cut and was wearing knee-high yellow-and-black athletic socks from a CrossFit gym. The man helped the Dairy Fairy unload from her trunk two cases of black-market raw butter, made with cream from a nonfat-yogurt operation in New England, priced at $16 a pound. "This stuff is sacred!" the Dairy Fairy said. The butter-maker, she said, demanded that they rendezvous in strange spots to make the handoff: cash up front for butter. The last time, it had been at LAX. This time, she had had to meet him by the side of the road in Pasadena.

As the sun burned through the fog, the former members of Rawesome started to arrive: skinny women on bicycles, old ladies with tote bags, a CPA in a shiny black BMW SUV. Vincent Gallo—pink sunglasses, lumberjack shirt, moccasins—came for his box, which included goat yogurt made by someone who used to work at Rawesome. "I go up in the mountains and get the raw goat milk," the yogurt-maker said. "I actually have to sign a waiver saying I won't bring anyone up there or say who they are. They are top secret." Business was good, he said. "I'm selling a *ton* of colostrum."

An attractive woman with flowing hair opened her box and drank from a quart of milk. "I love how the eggs were so full of poo last week," she said, with a thick milk moustache. "I got some really pooey ones and I was like, Yeah!" Eating this way, she told me later, made her feel free—liberated from the oppression of modern life, especially that of refrigeration—though it hampered her in certain ways, too. Restaurant meals were impossible: she had to bring her own raw ground bison meat, which she wrapped in prosciutto and smeared with raw butter she carried with her in a mason jar. She just had one thing to tell me: she hoped I wasn't eating yogurt from the grocery store. "That stuff is *so* bad for you," she said.

A few weeks later, the Dairy Fairy called me. She'd had an uncomfortable conversation with the butter-maker, who runs a successful gourmet business and sees no advantage in exposing his dealings in contraband dairy. "He said, 'You were the drug dealer! The drug dealer does not talk to the media!'"

To many in the national food-freedom movement, raw milk is the test case. Two years ago, the Farm-to-Consumer Legal Defense Fund, a nonprofit legal organization that helps raw-milk farmers, sued the FDA to lift the ban on interstate sales. (The suit was dismissed.) In responding, the FDA asserted, "There is no absolute right to consume or feed children any particular food." Statements like this stoke anxiety about the government's intentions. "Raw milk is just symbolic of this attitude of government regulators that they are the ones that make the decisions about what foods we can have," David Gumpert, an advocate-journalist who writes a blog called *The Complete Patient,* says. "You have this trend now toward irradiation. It's not required, but it's been sanctioned by the FDA. The next step may be for the FDA to require that all spinach *has* to be irradiated."

In recent years, the FDA has raided Amish and Mennonite farms that supply unpasteurized dairy products to out-of-state food clubs; in 2011, a farmer in Pennsylvania was driven out of business. The raid at Rawesome appeared to be an escalation of a strategy that raw-milkers think aims to kill the business entirely. Mike Adams, the editor of the website Natural News, compared undercover regulating agents to the East German Stasi, and warned of reprisals. "I believe we are very close to entering the age of a shooting war between farmers and the F.D.A.," he wrote. "I would encourage the F.D.A. agents who are no doubt reading this to strongly consider: Is your war against raw milk worth risking your life?"

"How far down the rabbit hole do you want to go?" Ajna Sharma-Wilson, the lawyer, asked me. Several months after the raid, she and Stewart and a group of his supporters converged at a hotel in Las Vegas, to attend the Constitutional Sheriffs and Peace Officers Association convention, an event put on by Richard Mack, a former sheriff from Arizona who successfully challenged a provision of the Brady Bill before the Supreme Court and was running for Congress as a Republican from Texas. I met them there. Mack, who told me that he'd spoken at "more

Tea Party events than Sarah Palin," had drawn a hundred sheriffs, from across the country, who feel that the federal government is infringing on individual rights. He had invited the raw-milkers, he told me, because he wanted to educate both the sheriffs and the lawbreakers. "I want them to call their sheriff," he said. "I want their sheriff to protect them from the FDA."

Among the booths—Gun Owners of America, the John Birch Society, anti-income-tax proponents selling a CD called *The Politics of Jesus*—was a table piled with raw cheeses and fresh produce. The vegetables had come from a sustainable Nevada farm that had recently become a food-freedom darling when a health inspector showed up at a "farm to table" dinner and made the farmer pour bleach on the vegetables, maintaining that, because she could not determine how long ago they had been cut, they were unfit even for pigs.

At the table were several Raw Milk Freedom Riders, mothers who practice civil disobedience by crossing state lines with raw milk. Their splashiest protest so far has been a raw-milk-and-cookie sit-in on the steps of the FDA, in Silver Spring, Maryland. One of them had a seven-month-old baby on her hip. Sheriff Mack, an imposing figure in cowboy boots, a turquoise shirt, and a loosened teal-colored tie, kept throwing his arm around her and joking that he was going to arrest her for feeding her baby unpasteurized breast milk.

The mother was around my age and lived outside Washington, D.C.; she had started drinking raw milk when pregnant with her second baby. (This one was her fifth.) I asked her if she wanted to walk around and check out the booths. I kept looking for signs of the culture clash between the raw-milkers and the antigovernment extremists, but I couldn't get purchase. The raw-milkers claimed to be on board with everything, from putting a stop to roadside sobriety tests to ending seat-belt laws. Apparently, wanting the government out of their food colored everything for them.

Aside from the Freedom Riders' farm table, the only other food booth belonged to Freeze Dry Guy, a company that sells "freeze-dried foods for uncertainties." Preppers, as the community of apocalypse-ready food-hoarders is known, take food self-sufficiency to an extreme. Freeze Dry Guy's pitch was Store What You Eat—the idea being that if you're a big meat-eater, you're not going to want to add adjusting to a vegan diet to your list of problems when catastrophe strikes. Germans starved after World War II, the marketing material said, because they considered corn to be pig food. "These were not stupid people. They just had strong prejudices about what they would not eat. . . . Ever had monkey's brains, goat's eyes or grubs? Ever try to make an 18 month old child eat Brussels sprouts? Good luck! What if that were all you had?"

The Freedom Rider stared at a huge can of freeze-dried "Oriental-style spicy chicken": monkey's brains to her. Finally, a wedge issue! "Wow," she said, as she read down the list of industrial and GMO ingredients. "Wow."

At lunchtime, a buffet was set up in the middle of the room, with cold cuts, pasta salad, and bags of chips. Sheriff Mack loaded up a plate. "I grew up absolutely hating milk," he told me. "I would gag on it! Now when I drink their milk, maybe it tastes better to me because it's freedom milk. It just has a little rebellious flavor in it. To me, it's the new civil rights. It's Rosa Parks."

Mack wandered over to the farm booth and asked one of the women there if she had eaten. "We brought our food, 'cause this is genetically modified," she said, pointing at the bag of popcorn in his hand. Someone poured Mack a glass of milk, and he turned to face the roomful of sheriffs—old fellows, mostly, with holstered handguns at their hips. The raw-milkers cheered as Mack took a big, showy sip and called out, "Freedom milk! Freedom milk! Freedom milk!"

That night, Stewart's supporters threw an "ice-cream speakeasy" for the sheriffs in one of the hotel rooms. There was uncured sausage and raw cheese made by an Amish farmer currently fighting charges in Wisconsin. The raw milk was flowing, as was the cold-pressed hibiscus juice, sweetened with raw honey.

"I heard you won't touch anything raw," a goat farmer from Utah said, looking at me pityingly. In a small seating area, Stewart arranged tangerines, carob pods, and Satsuma mandarins on platters. Along one wall was a giant freezer filled with raw-milk ice cream: cherry from the Dairy Fairy, and chocolate and vanilla that Sharma-Wilson and the woman who loved dirty eggs had made in their hotel room that afternoon. "I sniffed every egg," the woman said, meaning to reassure.

The romance of the small farmer is a powerful thing in the American food marketplace. The reality can be jarring. Sharon Palmer, who had taken up farming after a career in business, sought to connect Healthy Family Farms to this story, describing it as a "sustainable, pasture-based farm," where all the animals—chickens, ducks, Cornish game hens, lambs, cows, milk-fed pigs—are raised from birth and harvested by hand. When she was arrested in August 2011, she again positioned herself as part of a larger narrative, telling the *Ventura County Star*, "It's not just about me. It's happening all over the country. I am very, very hopeful that this will become apparent that this is government abuse."

But just because a farm is small does not mean that the farmer always makes good decisions about how he raises the food you eat. A community that resists labeling and inspection as government intrusion puts itself at the mercy of its suppliers. (One longtime customer complained to me of buying rancid pork from Rawesome in an undated package, but he also used the occasion to brag that his gut microflora were strong enough to handle it.) Although Rawesome is held up by those who mourn it as a paradigm of intimate, enlightened consumership, its members may have known less about the origins of their food than they thought. A few years ago, a splinter group led by Aajonus Vonderplanitz began to question the integrity of Healthy Family Farms, claiming that the chicken and the eggs were outsourced and contained high levels of mercury and sodium. (Palmer and Stewart admitted to briefly selling eggs from another farm, but dispute the lab tests.) The former USDA employee who worked at Rawesome said that she was furious to discover that the chickens she believed to be exclusively pasture-fed were in fact finished on corn. "There's no such thing as non-GMO corn feed!" she said.

From the Dairy Fairy, I bought a pound of sacred butter and some milk in a plain, lightly sweating plastic gallon jug—no date, no label. It was yellowish, with a thick mantle of cream. I was tempted, but I didn't dare. It came all the way from Pennsylvania, and, visions of Amish country notwithstanding, I had no clue what that farm looked like. I poured my husband a glass. "It coats your mouth, almost like drinking half-and-half," he said, pronouncing it delicious. Five minutes later, he said the taste was still with him: a gamey, sweet-hay-manure flavor that intensified when he stepped outside.

The butter stayed in the fridge until I got word of a Primal Diet potluck hosted by Vonderplanitz at a condominium in Marina del Rey. Etiquette required that I bring something from Vonderplanitz's recipe book—"Nuts over Meat" (raw lamb on a pile of zucchini, covered in fresh nut butter), say, or a flask of "Power Drink" (raw liver, thyroid, testis or ovary, lung, brain, adrenal gland; raw milk; red onions). I took the butter instead, placing it on the counter in the kitchen, next to room-temperature oysters, raw chicken chunks, strips of raw red bison, cut fruit bobbing in cream, and a few open jars of raw milk. The whole room stank: warm, bilious, inescapably animal, like a nursery full of neglected babies surrounded by panting carnivores.

Vonderplanitz sat on a deep couch, among leopard-print pillows and faux-fur throws, surrounded by three young acolytes. Double-height windows looked out on the beach. He told me about his clients who thrived on raw food during their pregnancies. "It's so good for your baby," he said, and invited me to eat. "You have to pick it up by your hand, real primitive, cannibal-like," he said, widening his pale blue eyes and smiling to show his strong teeth. "Thank you," I said, but didn't move from the couch. He introduced me to his friends, two heavy-browed bodybuilding brothers in their twenties and the nineteen-year-old girlfriend of one of them, who was a personal trainer. They told me that, on Vonderplanitz's recommendation, they had started eating rotting meat, though it was sometimes hard to do. "When the beef is green, you're like, 'Uhhhhhh,'" the young woman said. "My dad was pissed, like, 'What are you doing? You're going to be sick.'"

Vonderplanitz specifies using the highest-quality meat, and the young folk complained of the expense. The older brother said that when he couldn't afford gourmet meat, he ate spoiled meat from the regular supermarket. I let that sink in for a second: these middle-class kids were deliberately eating like the survivors of an apocalypse. It seemed to me they'd cherry-picked a losing combination, though—the modern convenience of cheap conventional beef with the caveman's limitation of eating it raw.

"What could be healthier than eating something completely unprocessed?" the older brother said.

"Like the cavemen did," the young woman said.

"Animals don't cook their food. They can survive anything. Humans on a cooked diet are weaker."

Vonderplanitz turned to me. He was bothered by the fact that I hadn't helped myself to the buffet. "Are you in any way connected with any government agency?" he asked. I reassured him, breathing through my mouth, that I was not, and got out of there before I embarrassed myself by throwing up all over the faux fur.

* * *

Not long after that, I had a dream the egg lady asked me how much grocery-store yogurt I was eating and I lied. I was sick of people telling me what to eat and what not to eat; I had come to my own conclusion about it and wanted to be left alone. In my irritation, I began to appreciate how maddening it must be for someone who believes that raw milk is saving her own or her child's life to be told she can't have it. Imagine if the annoying people interfering with the very private decision of what I ought to eat to stay healthy represented the federal government. No wonder the raw-milkers took refuge in the suffocating, self-enclosed world of the like-minded. It felt safe to them.

In the end, the Rawesome Three never went to trial for their alleged milk crimes. Stewart, who had spent time in jail on a related matter after failing to make bail, pleaded guilty to two misdemeanors, for processing raw goat milk at Healthy Family Farms and for operating a food facility—the Rawesome lot—without a permit; he was sentenced to 253 days in county jail, but credited for time served. In a separate case, he also pleaded guilty to two counts of felony tax evasion, and was given a suspended sentence of sixteen months in jail, and required to pay some $325,000 in restitution to the Franchise Tax Board. Palmer pleaded to a single misdemeanor, for having her dairy in an "insanitary condition" on the day of the raid. She had to pay a fine and perform forty hours of community service. Bloch, who took a misdemeanor for improperly labeling food, paid a hundred-dollar fine. All the rest of the charges were dismissed.

You can buy raw meat at the grocery store and feed it to your kids and no one can stop you. But milk has exceptional emotional power. Be it human or cow, it is the first food to which we are exposed, making it unlike other products, both for consumers, who associate it with basic nourishment, and for regulators, who see its oversight as a grave responsibility. Michele Jay-Russell, of the Western Institute for Food Safety & Security at U.C. Davis, told me, "From a public-health perspective, milk has fallen into the category of water. Providing a clean milk and water supply is fundamental to what the government sees as its job." But she acknowledges the frustration of consumers who can't get a product that they feel they need. "The crux of the conundrum is: Why shouldn't it be their choice?"

Five

DOUBLE DARE

The Food and Drug Administration was the great achievement of the pure-food movement, and a centerpiece of Progressive Era reform. Harvey W. Wiley, known in bureaucratic history as the Father of the FDA, started his career in Washington in 1883, as chief chemist at the Department of Agriculture, which at that time was tasked not with meat inspection but with boosting the country's agricultural output. His office was founded to verify the uniqueness of fertilizer formulas for those seeking patents. Six feet tall, and more than two hundred pounds, with, a biographer noted, "only a suggestion of a paunch to testify to his fondness for the pleasures of the table," Wiley was an outspoken and controversial crusader for unadulterated, properly labeled food.

Unlike today, when diners seek adventure, eating in the nineteenth century, especially for the poor, was an act of inadvertent daring. Rapid urbanization had cut people off from the sources of their food; mass production was changing that food's very character. Refrigeration was limited. Chicanery and fraud were common. Unscrupulous and ignorant producers, trying to stretch shelf life or save on ingredients, put ashes in bread and formaldehyde in milk; chemical preservatives like borax, a laundry booster, were routinely added to perishable foods to mask or defer spoilage.

Born in a log cabin in Indiana to a family that grew almost all their own food and traded milk and butter for whatever they could not make themselves, Wiley lamented the industrialization of the food system. "In the good old days preceding and immediately following the War between the States, there was little need of protection of the people from impure, adulterated and misbranded foods and drugs," he wrote in a memoir. "The great bulk of the people raised most of what they ate." Processed foods appalled him; he advocated a "natural" diet composed mainly of whole grains, fruits, and vegetables.

In Wiley's time, the food avant-garde was made up of reformers calling on the federal government, which did not yet have a significant role in regulating the food supply, to establish a safe, standardized American diet. In 1902, at the beginning of Theodore Roosevelt's first term, Wiley asked Congress for $5,000 to conduct experiments on commonly used chemical preservatives. With the money, he built a kitchen and a dining hall in the basement of the Bureau of Chemistry, an imposing brick building on what is now Independence Avenue. Then he recruited from the Department of Agriculture a small band of men, choice specimens aged eighteen to twenty-nine, including a sprinter from Yale and former captain of a high-school cadet regiment, who were willing to test his belief that preservatives were harmful to human health.

Three times a day, Wiley's "boys" assembled to eat food prepared for them by Perry, a civil service cook previously employed by the queen of Bavaria. The menu was designed by Wiley, who, the press noted, "has some original ideas about feeding human beings." The food was administered in precise doses, weighed out by chemists in lab coats, lending the enterprise a theatrical aura of science; in spite of occasional pleas of hunger, no more than the exact amount Wiley had calculated would nourish a fit young man was given. More significant, the food was "pure": fresh roast beef, pork, chicken, and turkey; eggs, milk, and cream from dairies personally inspected by Wiley; seasonal fruits and vegetables, or high-quality canned goods preserved by heat sterilization only.

Into this food, Wiley slipped the suspected toxins. To test the effects of borax, he contaminated the milk and butter with boric acid and borate of soda, two varieties commonly added to meat and dairy products. (Perry asked for a raise: borax was a trickier ingredient than the salt he used to season the queen's meals.) When the men learned to taste borax and started avoiding the tainted foods, Wiley resorted to giving them the borax in capsule form. In an adjacent laboratory, their "secreta" were analyzed by government chemists.

After a month or so, some of the subjects began to feel nauseous and depressed and to complain of headaches. Two retired from the squad. Wiley had to navigate a delicate matter of public opinion, describing the men's reactions to borax as unpleasant enough to demonstrate its harmfulness, without making it seem as if he had endangered them. When one of the dropouts died, several years later, of tuberculosis, his mother blamed the Poison Squad, a claim Wiley dismissed as absurd. He did, however, conclude that borax, taken in small doses over a couple of months, or in large doses over a short time, caused many of his subjects to become "ill and unfit for duty."

The experiments made Wiley famous. "It is getting so bad that people point to me on the street and say, 'There goes the man that runs Uncle Sam's cooking school,'" Wiley told *The Chicago Daily Tribune*. "It's getting unbearable. The other night, walking down the aisle of a theater on my way to my seat, people nudged one another, pointed me out, and said, 'There goes Borax.'" (That might have been wishful thinking: most people called him *Old* Borax.) As the experiments continued, his extreme eaters were likewise turned into figures of fun, captured in songs and skits: "Thus all the 'deadlies' we double-dare / to put us beneath the sod; / We're death-immunes and we're proud as proud—/ Hooray for the Pizen Squad!" The men contributed to the caricature, divulging all kinds of details to reporters—for a practical joke, one had dosed his squad-mate with quinine found in the lab—and giving themselves the slogan "Only the brave dare eat the fare." Colleagues began to accuse Wiley of practicing "yellow chemistry."

In spite of Wiley's well-publicized experiments and the efforts of numerous women's groups around the country calling for a federal law, a comprehensive pure-food bill proved elusive.

Wiley later wrote that "There seemed to be an understanding between the two Houses that when one passed a bill for the repression of food adulteration the other would see that it suffered a lingering death." Then, in 1904, Upton Sinclair, a struggling novelist with a toddler and an ailing wife, went to Chicago on assignment for the socialist paper *Appeal to Reason*. His purpose was to write about the mistreatment of immigrant workers in the stockyards and the abuses of the Beef Trust, the six firms that dominated the American meatpacking trade. Wearing old clothes and carrying a lunch pail, he spent seven weeks wandering around the plants and talking to the men and women who worked there.

Sinclair fictionalized his findings—lightly, he said—and published them serially, taking his readers on a tour through what he called the "spoiled-meat industry." His allegations were shocking: he told of putrid hams refreshed with chemicals and sausages made from meat that sat on the floor with rat droppings and poison. The processers, he wrote, used "everything about the hog except the squeal"—a culinary boast today, then taken as evidence of corporate avarice—and labeled the scraps under whatever name would sell. Lamb and mutton were actually goat, and the recipe for "potted chicken" called for tripe, pork fat, beef suet, beef hearts, and veal bits. (Speaking to *The New York Times* later, Sinclair supplied additional ingredients: "the meat of unborn calves and cows' udders.") The industry, he said, favored tubercular cows—they fattened efficiently—and when European distributors sent back sausages too moldy to sell, the packers would remake them for the home market, using borax to hide the spoilage.

Sinclair's central figuration was that just as cattle and swine were chopped up, ground down, and exploited in every conceivable way in the great factories of Packingtown so, too, was the human labor force. His most shocking contention brought the metaphor to life. In the steamy, ill-lit cooking rooms, he wrote, workers sometimes fell into the vats, where, forgotten, they would stew "till all but the bones of them had gone out to the world as Durham's Pure Leaf Lard!" A poster for the movie version of his story that appeared several years later showed a cameo of a man falling backward into a vat, wisps of vapor reaching for him like hungry ghosts.

After being turned down by numerous publishers who thought its claims too sensational, *The Jungle* was accepted by Doubleday, Page—which sent a lawyer to Chicago to assess its validity—and came out in early 1906. That winter and spring, the papers were full of Sinclair's revelations. Here was an explanation for the tinned meat, so disgusting that a general referred to it as "embalmed beef," which had sickened many soldiers, including those in Roosevelt's command, during the Spanish-American War. Defenders of the Beef Trust resorted to embarrassingly weak arguments. "In Vats, But Not In Lard" ran the headline of a *Chicago Daily Tribune* story intended to debunk Sinclair. The deck was less than reassuring: "Bodies of Father and Son Who Lost Their Lives in Tank in 1897 or 1898 Probably Were Pulled Out and Not 'Canned.'"

Americans, naturally, were repulsed by the notion that they might be at worst unwitting cannibals, and at best rat-eaters. The country was only 130 years old; the Donner Party tragedy, in which a group of Midwesterners seeking a better life in

California got trapped in the Sierra Nevada mountains and resorted to eating their dead, had happened a mere sixty years before. Appetite was a site of colonial anxiety: Were Americans going to be savages or gentlemen? Would the country's wilderness make its new citizens wild? Civilization itself seemed to be at stake. "There can be no more important public issue than the wholesomeness of the people's food," *The New York Times* said. Sales of prepared meats dropped steeply—or so said the packers, whose best political leverage lay in claiming vast economic repercussions. President Roosevelt read *The Jungle* and ordered a special investigation; his agents found no proof of tinned human but issued a report saying they'd seen men climbing over heaps of meat in dirty boots and relieving themselves on the killing beds. "In a word, we saw meat shoveled from filthy wooden floors, piled on tables rarely washed, pushed from room to room in rotten box carts, in all of which processes it was in the way of gathering dirt, splinters, floor filth, and the expectoration of tuberculous and other diseased workers." According to Roosevelt, the crisis demanded "immediate, thorough-going, and radical enlargement of the powers of the government."

In the two days before *The Jungle* was published, Harvey W. Wiley, flanked by assistants carrying what *The New York Times* described as "numerous multi-colored bottles, which contain poisonous substances of various kinds," testified before a congressional committee on behalf of the latest pure-food bill. When the congressmen asked him about naturally occurring instances of the additives he tested—the benzoic acid inherent in cranberries, for instance—he laid out a personal philosophy of food and culture. "Assuming that the food of man, as prepared by the Creator and modified by the cook, is the normal food of man, any change in the food which adds a burden to any of the organs or any change which diminishes their normal functional activity, must be hurtful."

With the momentum generated by *The Jungle,* the Pure Food and Drugs Act, also known as "Dr. Wiley's Law," passed, on the same day as the Meat Inspection Act, which required pre- and postmortem inspection of animals, as well as inspection of all meat products, with special attention given to the rendering process. Together, the laws gave broad new responsibilities to the Department of Agriculture and began to establish an American standard for edibility. Dr. Wiley's Law made it a crime to adulterate or misbrand any food or drug sold in the country. Food was considered adulterated "if it contain any added poisonous or other added deleterious ingredient which may render such article injurious to health," and misbranded if it was deceptively labeled, not in its original container, or failed to disclose certain ingredients, including cocaine, heroin, and cannabis. The Bureau of Chemistry, guided by Wiley, endorsed old-fashioned smoke, salt, vinegar, and sugar, while coming out against chemical preservatives. Food Inspection Decision 76, the first ruling from the USDA after the passage of Dr. Wiley's Law, banned borax.

Eventually, Wiley's influence diminished—he made the mistake of condemning saccharine in front of Roosevelt, whose doctor administered it to him daily—but he continued to decry preservatives. "[M]odern housewives are veritable Lucrezia

Borgias, handing out poison from the ice box, from the broiler and the skillet, and the little tins of dinner she buys when breathlessly rushing home after her exciting bridge games at the club," he said. "The average ice box is a charnel house, which not only holds death, but spreads it." His obsession with labeling, too, was unallayed. Toward the end of his career in government, he sued Coca-Cola—he was anticaffeine—because although the drink no longer contained cocaine, its name suggested otherwise.

What is normal when it comes to what people eat? When a congressman pressed the point with Wiley, saying, "Who is to define normal food; there is a great difference of opinion about that," Wiley, the first gatekeeper of the American food supply, simply said, "I will admit that." To him, normal was the food of his rural Midwestern childhood. In 1907, he published "Foods and their Adulteration," a reference book based on his Poison Squad work, in which he denounced the "sophistication of food articles" as a crime against humanity. Intended for the ambitious housewife, the book outlines chemistry experiments that can be performed at home to detect the presence of unwanted additives and preservatives. But it is also a work of taxonomy, reflecting the cultural biases of the United States in that moment. Under the heading "Animals Whose Flesh Is Edible," he acknowledges that every animal on the planet has at one time or another been food for someone, before stating that "in a civilized community, however, except in times of disaster and dire necessity, certain classes of animals only furnish the principal meat food." He limited the list of civilized proteins to cattle, sheep, and swine. Goat flesh was rarely eaten, he wrote, "and horse meat scarcely at all."

Wiley insisted that he wasn't trying to tell Americans what to put in their mouths. "It is not for me to tell my neighbor what he shall eat," he said once. "Anything under heaven that I may be pleased to do I want the privilege of doing, even if it is eating limburger cheese." But he represented an era determined to codify our way of eating. The prescriptive attitude and the drive toward conformity were general. One of Wiley's supporters in calling for a ban on chemical preservatives was a Chicago magazine with an upper-middle-class readership called *What to Eat*. In 1906, the year of the Pure Food and Drugs Act, it relaunched under the no less sweeping but more official-sounding title, *National Food*.

The Bureau of Chemistry eventually split off from the USDA and became the Food and Drug Administration. It is responsible for policing the food supply, with the exception of meat and eggs, which are under USDA jurisdiction. "We do the cheese pizzas, USDA does the pepperoni," an FDA historian told me. Wiley wanted to return food to its natural state, and the food system to its earlier intimacy. But since his time, the sophistication of food articles has accelerated in ways he could never have imagined. The aversion to the industrialized food system that coalesced with Sinclair's novel did not lead to the system's dismantling but to its fortification, and the safety net designed to guarantee food purity is now, to some, an emblem of food corruption.

The deeper into the foodie world I ate, the more aware I became of its reactionary tilt. Though the public has embraced it as a mainstream hobby, foodie-ism is a counterculture. Its shared values are a love of the special, sub rosa, small-batch, and handmade and a loathing of homogeneity, mass production, and uniformity. Among foodies, the FDA, the USDA, and the local health department are often viewed as misguided. One need look no further, foodies say, than the slop sanctioned by the government—meat treated with antimicrobials, hormones, and antibiotics; plants grown from genetically modified seeds—to see why regulations should be ignored. For instance, the USDA approved a process called "pH enhancement," whereby beef trimmings are exposed to food-grade ammonia gas to kill pathogens (primarily *E. coli* O157:H7), resulting in a product called Lean Finely Textured Beef (LFTB), which gets mixed with ground beef. Not only has USDA approved the process, but it also distributes ground beef containing LFTB—which goes by the nickname "pink slime"—through the school-lunch program.

In foodies' disdain for the rules, there is a note of snobbery: What could the feds possibly tell *them* about food? "The regulations are designed for larger-scale businesses, not for small-scale producers," Sarah Weiner, the founder of the Good Food Awards, told me. Her organization honors "tasty, authentic, responsible" traditional foods like pickles, preserves, and charcuterie. "It makes it really hard to have a food culture."

In 2011, the Food Safety Modernization Act, the most significant revision of federal pure-foods regulation in decades, was signed into law. A response to a rash of food outbreaks that killed dozens of people across the country—salmonella in peanut butter, *E. coli* in spinach, listeria in cantaloupe—it gives the government recall powers and sets standards for safe production and handling of fruits and vegetables, even for small businesses. Some worry that it will mean the end of family farms and farmers markets, or at least prove onerous to them. In an interview with *Mother Jones,* the Portland chef Naomi Pomeroy encapsulated the frustration. "The only reason that we even need to worry about food safety is because large companies and corporations have ruined our food supply," she said.

The intellectual heirs of Wiley's pure-foodists, ironically, are the very same people trying to shield their ways of eating from the purview of regulators. "The reason there's a food-rights movement is because more and more people are afraid of the food that's available in the public system," David Gumpert, who blogs at *The Complete Patient,* said. "They want to be able to access their food privately." Stranger still, the movement's most prominent political supporter is the libertarian former congressman Ron Paul, whose 2011 *Family Cookbook* opens with a recipe that calls for Double Stuf Oreos, Cool Whip, and instant chocolate pudding.

Appetites are hard to legislate, and people usually end up doing what they want to do. The year Sinclair wrote *The Jungle,* he got his first summer cold. It was the beginning of a series of ailments that led him to John Harvey Kellogg's Battle Creek Sanitarium, which promoted vegetarianism, and to the writings of Horace Fletcher, "The Great Masticator," who prescribed chewing your food extra thoroughly. After that, he followed Elie Metchnikoff, the Nobel Prize winner based at the Pasteur Institute. When these programs failed Sinclair, he tried fasting. After twelve days, he broke the fast with a milk diet—two gallons a day, warmed—recommended by the fitness guru Bernarr Macfadden, who had altered the spelling of his first name so that it would sound like the roar of a lion. Then Sinclair went raw, subsisting mostly on fruits and nuts. He felt amazing: he threw away his laxatives and went bareheaded in the rain. In his free time, the man whose affect friends had previously described as "spiritual" found himself doing chin-ups and standing on his head.

Fruits and nuts and milk-cleanses, though, were not food for thought. He could jump around and never got colds but found that the diets weren't conducive to what he called "brain work." (He referred to himself as a "brain worker.") Trying to write a novel while eating raw, he lost twelve pounds in sixteen days; after six weeks, he'd lost twenty. Eventually, he discovered the work of Dr. James Salisbury, an early advocate of low-carb eating and the inventor of the Salisbury steak. (Salisbury steak, according to the USDA, must be at least 65 percent meat—beef, pork, cow heart—and the rest can consist of varying amounts of bread crumbs, flour, fungi, vegetables, liquids, and binders.) After several years as a committed vegetarian, Sinclair heeded Salisbury's advice, and adopted a diet of broiled beef and hot water, relieved by periods of fasting. At first he was repulsed by meat; he couldn't stand the thought or smell of it. But he came around. "I am sorry to have to say that it"—the Salisbury system—"seems to be a good one," he wrote in a book about his dietary adventures that was published in 1913. "Sorry, because the vegetarian way of life is so obviously the cleaner and more humane and more convenient. But it seems to me that I am able to do more work and harder work with my mind while eating beefsteaks than under any other *regime*; and while this continues to be the case there will be one less vegetarian in the world."

Six

HAUTE CUISINE

For six months after our border run, Quenioux had been thinking about that pot-smoked chocolate. In his mind, he had begun to build a menu around it, with a theme, medicinal herbs, that would also reveal the yet-unknown flavors of the Chinese markets and apothecaries in the San Gabriel Valley. After a long search, he found his hostess, an elegant, dark-eyed woman with a blameless putty-colored ranch house in the hills above Encino, surrounded by overbuilt mansions on small lots and defended by a large electric gate.

On the day of the first site meeting with Quenioux and the Starry Kitchen team, she opened the door in yoga pants and a black Izod sweater, dark hair pulled back in a black headband. She had designed the kitchen at her house herself, with two ovens and a long dining table extending from a center island,

and a picture window framing a stand of birds-of-paradise and a view of the San Gabriel Mountains. Now her sixteen-year-old son had taken over and was using it to make pickles and ice cream and his current fixation, coffee. He prepared himself a cup in a vacuum siphon while drip brewed for her guests.

Sitting down at the kitchen table, she put on her glasses and opened a laptop. It was time to plan the party. How many people should come? Would it be too cold, in early April, to grill outside? Her husband appeared at the door that led to the patio and pool. His shirt was untucked; he was coming from the gym in the pool house, where there was a sauna and a Viagra clock. "You guys take your meeting and have fun!" he said, rushing past us into the house.

They talked about timing and dress code. The hostess mentioned that she didn't want her name disclosed and that the faces in the photographs should be blurred. "No social media," Nguyen said, a violation of his business strategy and personal philosophy, but sensible under the circumstances. "Are the kids going to come?" Quenioux asked the hostess. She and her son looked at each other. "He wants to, but . . ." she said. "They'll stay in the kitchen with us," Quenioux said reassuringly. They agreed: no smoking. "Smoking is so cliché and gross," Quenioux said. "Let's keep it about the food," she said.

"I'm a foodie girl," she said. "It's the circles I run in. For me, that's the whole thing." She just hadn't yet figured out how to tell her husband, a straight arrow, that the culinary event they were hosting, with food by one of their favorite chefs, was already being widely discussed as the Weed Dinner.

* * *

One afternoon, I met Quenioux at a neat white clapboard house, where he lives among collections of china bric-a-brac and intoxicating European perfumes. He wore a yellow-brown-and-green-striped ski cap and a pair of red Converse. We took my car, a station wagon—his is a silver convertible, and too small—picked up Daniel, and headed east. Quenioux had been researching Chinese medicinal herbs and was getting excited. "Some are dangerous—fatal, actually—and some have a very distinct taste," he said. "We need to gather the actual product."

Quenioux has been shopping in the SGV for years. "There I find *everything* we need for the cooking we do—sea urchin, yuzu, green tea powder," he told me once. "I can get two pounds of duck legs, no problem. I defy you to find me that on the Westside. Or some fresh blood, or a live squab—even live frogs." He gets alligator at the Hong Kong Supermarket and swears by the chicken testicles from a Taiwanese-American chain called 99 Ranch, which he refers to as "white kidneys" on his menus. "If you want to buy a pound of top round at six p.m. on Thanksgiving Day, you can go to the Chinese," he says. When he needs black-fleshed Silkie Bantam chickens, he pops out to the Chinese-Vietnamese grocery store Shun Fat, branches of which have replaced Targets and Vons and Ralphs, and which, because of the meat selection—far more inclusive than Wiley's "civilized" array—is known to some as the Dead Pet Store.

"God created a huge palate, and it's there to be picked up," he said in the car. "There is a flavor I love, that so few people do: bitterness!" He described a dessert composed of a beer fruit roll-up, beer taffy, and hops crème caramel, finished with Italian white truffles and served with truffle-barley ice cream and beer nuts. Tasting individual components, the kitchen staff puckered their lips and complained; the diners, eating the whole, loved it.

"My thing is opening up new tastes," Quenioux said. Sweet coxcombs—poached in simple syrup and grenadine to give them the bounce and flavor of a red gummy bear, and served on top of vol-au-vent filled with orange *crème pâtissière*—he counts among his great discoveries. Then there was rabbit tartare. "Nobody's ever done something like that," he told me. "To the foodie person, to eat raw rabbit is new. You develop a new taste in your palate, so it's exciting for people. Rabbit is very lean but it's full of gelatin. When it's raw it smacks." He mixed it with yuzu, chilies, and olive oil, rolled it into a ball, and tossed it in white truffle powder. "It was really so fricking good." Lately, Quenioux has been focused on ingredients like okra, sea cucumbers, cactus, and raw egg white, whose slippery textures are difficult for Americans. "I want to teach people to appreciate it," he said. "There's so much about slimy that is good."

When we arrived at Wing Hop Fung, a huge Chinese apothecary in a Monterey Park shopping mall, the Trans were waiting, Thi in gray surgical scrubs, Nguyen eating some kind of doughnut from a restaurant in the mall. She knew Wing Hop Fung's selection well: she brings her parents there to shop whenever they are visiting from Texas. She handed out a list of ingredients, including aphrodisiacs, longevity tonics, diuretics, sedatives, red bird's nest, and something called dodder, to remedy male impotence.

"The smell!" Quenioux exclaimed as we walked in, passing an impressive wine and spirits department—$2,000 bottles of Latour and Château Lafite; 1953 Macallan—on the way to a wall of bins filled with astragalus, peony root, and cordyceps, a mushroom whose common name is caterpillar fungus, due to its way of invading larvae and replacing the animal tissue with its own. (In Hong Kong, Thi said, it is steamed and served with meat.) The range of items was astonishing. Most of them did not register to me as food. There were dried fish maws, yellow as dead toenails, and deer tendons, hoof on: seasoning for congee. Quenioux held up a package of Hangzhou chrysanthemum that looked like a brick of hash. "Oooh that smells good," he said. Thi pointed them to the wolfberries, shrunken red sacs. "Twenty splashes of that for sexual vitality," Thi said. "It's good with wood pigeon." Quenioux swooned over the dung-like Chinese truffles—"A hint of chicory," he said, huffing—before stopping at a bin filled with dried apricot kernels. He scooped up a handful and let them slip through his fingers. "There's a north one and a south one," Thi said. "You can't use that much of the north one because it becomes poisonous." The menu, they decided, would have to come with a disclaimer. No pregnant women, Thi said. I looked away.

The back wall of the store was devoted to dried seahorses. Sold in $500 kits for making soup, they looked like they belonged at a crafting fair. Behind a counter, framed, was an $8,000 piece of ginseng from the Blue Ridge Mountains. Under the counter were trays of Catskills ginseng, for $1,899 an ounce. Appalachian ginseng-hunters? The mind reeled. "The older it gets the more expensive it is," Thi said. Barrels of cheap, young stuff ($280 a pound, from Wisconsin) were scattered about the floor.

"Can we do, like, ginseng gelée with an aspic, in a consommé? Or start a soup with it?" Quenioux said.

On the way home, Quenioux continued to imagine the dishes he might make. "We have to think about ginseng, longan berries, the celery-scented thing, that risotto-like grain, the bird's nest," he said. "If I smell something, I can mix the flavors in my head."

The culinary avant-garde and the marijuana underworld have lately become intimates. Increasingly, their equipment is interchangeable. Over the years, the Chicago chef Grant Achatz has experimented extensively with scent. Achatz, whose restaurant Alinea has three Michelin stars, is trained in molecular gastronomy, the steaming-beaker approach to cooking used by Ferran Adrià at El Bulli in Catalonia, where Achatz worked briefly. Borrowing chemical stabilizers, thickeners, and gels from industrial food manufacturing, molecular gastronomy—also known as Modernist cooking—seeks to subvert the diner's expectations delightfully, using all five senses. Achatz is the most romantic of the molecular gastronomists. A Pre-Raphaelite among Dadaists, he once put dry ice in a vase with charred garlic, rosemary, thyme, and black pepper: cookout fog. Another time, he leaned hot stones against a live tomato stalk, to conjure the quintessential summer smell of walking in the garden in the morning and brushing up against tomato leaves. In 2005, right before he opened Alinea, one of his investors suggested he check out the Volcano, which he had seen while traveling in Amsterdam.

The Volcano is a squat metal cone-shaped heater with a filling chamber for "plant material," a digital panel displaying the precise temperature, and a large plastic balloon to capture the plant's vapor. Its traditional use involves fitting a mouthpiece to the air balloon and inhaling. The Volcano's manual recommends using it with chamomile and lemon balm. "We could see it would have the ability to pump out a lot of scent and vapor and capture it," Nick Kokonas, Achatz's business partner, told me. "It worked perfectly, from a culinary—and from a theatrical and emotional—perspective."

In the years since, Achatz has vaporized grass, oak leaves, and hay. "My favorite is to trick people into thinking they're eating something that's not edible," he says, such as, for instance, venison with leather aroma. His signature vapor is lavender, which he serves in a plastic balloon covered in Irish linen, under a bowl of yuzu pudding, ham *nage,* and gooseberry coulis. Before presenting the dish, the waiter punctures the bag of lavender air with a syringe in a four-by-four grid, so that the weight of the bowl releases the scent. At Alinea, Achatz's molecular cocktail lounge, the bartenders use it for the Rob Roy, which comes to the table in a plastic bag filled with lavender air. As the waiter cuts it open with scissors, it looks and smells like a new-age spa treatment. (I had a virgin one; the toasted-lavender smoke formed a film over the flavor of the deep red juice—the smell of a glamorous grandmother, covering up her snuck cigarette with eau de toilette.) When the Alinea cookbook came out, the Volcano was listed on the equipment page, along with agricultural syringes, a paint-stripping heat gun, and a refractometer for measuring sugar content in Brix. The four Volcanos in the Alinea kitchen are named John, Paul, George, and Ringo.

U.S. Customs prohibits the importation of anything used primarily as drug paraphernalia. A few years after Achatz's discovery, Customs launched an inquiry into the Volcano, which is made by Storz & Bickel, a German company. Adam Schoenfeld, who imported and marketed it, was at the time in his twenties and had recently graduated from The Evergreen State College in Olympia, Washington. "I flew around the world, I did this, I did that, I went to Thailand, I discovered the Volcano, I ate lots of cool food, I designed my own curriculum around travel and business," he told me. When Adam, whose father is the New York restaurateur and dumpling impresario Ed Schoenfeld (Chinatown Brasserie, Shun Lee, RedFarm), found out that Achatz had a Volcano in his kitchen, he sensed an opportunity. He sent vaporizers to technically experimental chefs like Wylie Dufresne, Dave Arnold, and the pastry-maker Johnny Iuzzini. "It was about expanding the usage," Schoenfeld said. Customs eventually relented, determining that the Volcano could be used as "a device to aid in a method used in modern cooking called 'molecular gastronomy.'"

"The Volcano is a multipurpose vaporization device," Schoenfeld told me one day. We were in his apartment, a walk-up in the flower district in Manhattan. He was pale and damp-palmed, with tortoise-shell glasses and purple-and-black Adidas sneakers. I sat by the window so that I could breathe. "The premise is that you use heat to gently extract the flavors, essential oils, and aromatic compounds," he said. "You can vaporize oils, plant materials. It is not sold for marijuana." Nevertheless, he has learned that when sending to restaurants he ought to send two if he hopes the Volcano to be used in the kitchen. "Almost inevitably, one makes it back to someone's living room," he said. Kokonas said there had never been an issue of theft at Alinea. "Using the Volcano is not a rock-and-roll-TV-chef thing," he said. "It's a Michelin-three-star-chef thing."

Representatives from Storz & Bickel have done demonstrations at the National Restaurant Association Show, in Chicago, and at the Fancy Food Show in San Francisco, where they trapped cinnamon-and-clove-scented vapor under a glass cloche and served it with tangerine slices. "It was a holiday scent," the representative told me. "Like spicy cookies." He was just getting used to the expectations of his new milieu; someone let him know he needed to wear a white coat and maybe a hat. Last year, Storz & Bickel made a presentation at Mandy Aftel's house in Berkeley. Aftel, a Berkeley perfume-maker who lives behind Chez Panisse in a bungalow permeated with the restaurant's kitchen smells, recently released a line of essential oils for chefs. To the presentation, she invited the chef Daniel Patterson and the food writer Harold McGee, and they vaporized marjoram—which had unexpected bubblegum notes—and bacon.

The laboratory equipment firm PolyScience started making culinary equipment a decade ago because Philip Preston, the company's president, is a foodie. Working with the chef de cuisine at Charlie Trotter's, a pioneering Chicago restaurant that recently closed after twenty-five years, he developed an immersion circulator that became the industry standard for *sous-vide,* a way of cooking meat slowly at a low temperature in a water bath. Then he made the Anti-Griddle freezing plate for Achatz. PolyScience also makes the Smoking Gun, a handheld tool with a chamber for burning aromatic woodchips and a tube with a nozzle attachment. Preston, who invented it, says that, in spite of appearances, the idea came not from a misspent youth but from seeing a keyboard cleaner at a computer store. "I'd been keen on adding cold smoke flavor," he said. "I thought, if I unscrewed this bit and screwed this bit, I could turn it into a smoker." When he got home, he pulled the screen out of a faucet and made a bowl out of a plumbing fixture, and sent the prototype to Dufresne, who cold-smoked lettuce with it. "Then everyone wanted one," Preston said. "Grant, Wylie, Jean-Georges, the Voltaggio brothers, Thomas Keller—you'd be hard-pressed to find a really high-end chef not using it." He went on, "It's one of those things that people look at and say, 'Oh, yeah, I know what else you could do with that.'"

The Smoking Gun costs $99.95 at Williams-Sonoma; Preston says together they sell ten thousand a year. To accomplish the pot-smoked chocolate course at Quenioux's dinner, Daniel and Nguyen went looking for something like it. At a head shop in the wholesale district, they found a poor-man's version, for fifteen bucks. It was disguised, no doubt to deceive Customs, as a vacuum for cleaning a computer keyboard.

As the technologies of Modernist cooking make their way into home kitchens, everyday American cooking is becoming more precise, complex, and refined. Products previously used for making paints, plastics, and cosmetics are becoming familiar ingredients, much as, two hundred years ago, cornstarch migrated from the laundry to the larder. "You'd be amazed how many people are using lecithin"—an emulsifier used in industrial food production—"at home to thicken sauces," chef Will Goldfarb says. Goldfarb, an alumnus of El Bulli, the molecular gastronomy restaurant in Catalonia, has a website, Willpowder, where he sells high-tech cooking ingredients. "Meat glue has become pretty normal," Goldfarb says. "We get a lot of questions from viewers of the Food Network."

This extends to people who are cooking pot at home. Not long ago, I talked to a couple, let's call them Josh and Amanda. She went to cooking school in New York and interned at a three-star restaurant there. He was a fan of *Weeds*. When they lost their jobs in 2008, they thought they'd try making edibles out of their house in Los Angeles. Their idea was to produce fruit-candy-flavored THC-laced strips, similar to Listerine breath strips. "I was looking for a way to infuse oils and turn them into a stabilized solid," Josh said. "I don't have a chemistry background, so we went down a cooking road. We came at it from a molecular perspective."

Josh had given Amanda the Alinea cookbook for Christmas. Flipping through recipes for soy bubbles and smoke gel, they found one for "Spice Aroma Strips." The recipe called for Pure-Cote B790, a "film-forming" starch manufactured by Grain Processing Corporation, which makes corn-based products for the pharmaceutical, personal care, and food industries. Pure-Cote lends a sheen to the surface of snacks and cereals and prevents chocolates from scuffing; it also constitutes the skin on some softgel capsules. At the time, the home-cook market for industrial food chemicals was just emerging, and Josh found himself cajoling big companies accustomed to ton orders into sending him one-pound samples. When they got their hands on some Pure-Cote, they found the results too brittle—glassy rather than pliant. Josh read that the chef Sean Brock, in Charleston, was experimenting with Ultra-Tex 3, which, according to the chemical company that makes it, is a "high performance cold water swelling modified food starch." Pretending he was writing a cookbook, he corresponded with Brock, who led him to Ultra-Tex 8, which yields a pliant, paper-thin product. It became the secret ingredient of their "Medi-strips."

A few years later, Josh and Amanda were both employed again, and they quit the business. Only a couple of close friends ever knew that they had turned the apartment above theirs into a grow house and candy kitchen, where, in addition to the strips they produced all-natural, organic, psychoactive fruit leather with produce from the Santa Monica Farmers Market. Spherification being a fundamental move in molecular gastronomy, they briefly considered making pot caviar, but were daunted by the stabilization and packaging challenge. No one knew about the disposable cell phones, the Russian gangsters, or the middle-of-the-night runs down the alleys in their neighborhood, dumping roots and leaves in other people's waste bins. They had become an ambitious, confident culinary team; they laughed when they read the recipe for fruit leather in Nathan Myhrvold's *Modernist Cuisine*, a six-volume set that aims to be the OED of molecular gastronomy. "We had cranked out a lot more of it than they had," Josh told me. "Their approach was a bit basic." For dinner parties now they serve deconstructed piña coladas with coconut strips, minus the THC, and make pineapple glass from Pure-Cote. The first time they ate at the Bazaar, a José Andrés restaurant in Los Angeles known for its effortfully whimsical take on molecular gastronomy (liquid mozzarella, cotton candy foie gras), it was with the proceeds of their molecular edibles business.

Cannabis has been used around the world for millennia. Chinese herbalists prescribed it for absentmindedness, and rich Romans ate roasted marijuana seeds for dessert. In the mid-1950s, Alice B. Toklas included a friend's recipe for hash fudge in her cookbook; it was slyly recommended as something fun to serve to your bridge group or at a chapter meeting of the Daughters of the American Revolution. "In Morocco it is thought to be good for warding off the common cold in damp winter weather and is, indeed, more effective if taken with large quantities of hot mint tea," the recipe read. "Euphoria and brilliant storms of laughter; ecstatic reveries and extensions of one's personality on several simultaneous planes are to be complacently expected." As for sourcing, *Cannabis sativa* grows wild as a weed throughout Europe, Asia, and Africa; in the Americas, the closely related *Cannabis indica,* "while often discouraged . . . has been observed even in city window boxes."

In California, marijuana has an ambiguous legal status. The state condones medicinal use, while the federal government prohibits it outright. To get fresh leaves for a cannabis pesto, Quenioux went to a neighbor in Highland Park who has a little patch. For the rest of the applications, he sent his sous-chef, Daniel, to buy an ounce of high-quality custom-hybridized marijuana from a grow house with a white picket fence in suburban Pomona. It was the equivalent of going to the farm to meet the people who grow your mache, rather than buying it at Whole Foods.

After the trip to the apothecary, the team gathered again, at Starry Kitchen, to plan the menu. Thi had put together a list of possible dishes. "So let's go over this," Quenioux said. "Does the osmanthus have any medicinal properties?" he asked, looking at a description of a cake made with osmanthus and chestnut powder. Thi said it was good for digestion and headaches.

"I should ask my employees, 'cause they buy a lot of it—they all have medicinal cards—but how much *is* weed right now?" Nguyen asked. Daniel said his source would sell to him for $350 an ounce. "The higher potency lets off a better flavor," he said. "The lesser stuff tastes like dirt." The leaves, which are far less potent, would be good for salads and garnishes; the buds could be dehydrated and ground down to powders.

Quenioux proposed beef culotte with cannabis in place of rosemary, another sappy, resinous herb. "The whole idea is to really try to do a breakthrough," he said. "Bringing cannabis and all those medicinal herbs from the apothecary side into food."

"The fifth course will be ribs," he went on. Ginger, wolfberries, sesame oil. He suggested confiting it in duck fat. "Oh, but it's twenty-two dollars a pound," he sighed. He glanced over his right shoulder to a fountain where some ducks were swimming. Thi mentioned that they sometimes wandered into the restaurant. "Shit, you should have closed the door!" he said. "Maybe we can grab them at night."

* * *

To the matter of taste: an experimental distiller I spoke to who once, after hours, ran a couple of loads of marijuana through his still to satisfy his curiosity, said, "It's a cross between hop tones—that floral, slightly skunky aroma—along with deep, musky sage tones." He distilled it into brandy—the THC, which has an aggressive, tarry flavor, separated out—and tasted it: earthy base notes. "Then I put the sample away in the hope that someday the entire country comes to its senses," he said. His tests with straight infusions yielded more dramatic results. He drank some with friends from Chez Panisse and, he says, "I found myself stuck to the floor ten minutes later. My math was way off."

"Very vegetal, very green and bright, with just a little bit of bitterness," a bartender who used to make drinks at Momofuku Ssäm Bar, a buzzy restaurant in New York's East Village run by the Korean-American chef David Chang, told me. The bartender, who doesn't serve his concoctions to the public, uses a rapid-infusion technique to make a smoky marijuana-mescal, double charging a canister of mescal and marijuana with nitrous. The first charge dissolves the gas into the mescal; the second forces the mescal to permeate the bud. When the canister is opened, releasing the pressure, the enhanced alcohol seeps back out of the plant. He's got a friend who pairs marijuana with gin and chartreuse for a lighter profile. "It's being done all over the country," he told me. "It's so illegal on so many levels that no one talks about it openly."

As with insect cuisine, marijuana edibles have traditionally been designed to bury the flavor, hence all the cheap chocolate. Among the avant-garde, the emphasis is on revealing its taste. T., a trained cook who several years ago started Tastebud, a pot-confectionary business with his then girlfriend, a pastry chef, uses high-grade E. Guittard chocolate to complement the earthiness of the marijuana, along with butter that sometimes costs more than the weed. "Berries and herbs have an affinity," he told me, a principle he uses to guide the hard-candy flavors. (His assessment: cherry is delicious, sour apple's hideous.) "A pastry chef who had worked at El Bulli tasted my raspberry bars and went on and on about them, how the cannabis meshes with the butter, and the pastry's flakiness," he told me. "To get praise from someone who worked at El Bulli—a *Spaniard*—that was amazing." At the moment, T., who specializes in caramel "potcorn," is trying to source mushroom popcorn—the round-popping variety that is the industry standard for caramel corn—that is non-GMO. The idea is to add an organic, GMO-free label to his packaging for the food-conscious customer.

To Quenioux, marijuana has a piney scent, with hints of kumquat. "I would compare the leaves to vetiver," he said. Daniel detects grapefruit notes. "We wanted to showcase the flavor rather than mask it," he told me. To capture the essence of cannabis in butter and in coconut oil, he fine-ground it in a coffee grinder and passed it through a sieve, reserving the crystals. Then he employed the classic ratio outlined in the recipe for "Space Butter": a pound of fat to an ounce of bud. He cooked it slowly for half an hour in a bain-marie, carefully controlling the temperature, just as if he was making clarified butter for the restaurant.

"It reminds me of Almond Joy," Daniel said, opening the jar of coconut oil, which was a pale, greasy green. It was late afternoon at Starry Kitchen, a few weeks before the dinner, and it was time to test the dishes. The day before, Nguyen had announced that Jonathan Gold would be attending. The restaurant was officially closed, but the kitchen, a tight galley equipped only with a few electric burners and a high-power toaster oven, was full of volunteers. Daniel took two large spoonfuls of the oil, melted it in a pan, and added monkfish cheeks. Suddenly the kitchen smelled of a Jamaican beach: pot smoke and Bain de Soleil. Quenioux dumped a container of pesto made from sorrel, spinach, garlic, and fresh marijuana leaves into a pot of congee, turning it grass-green, and spooned it into bowls. I tried a bite—rich and nutty with a light medicinal taste—and spat it in the trash. The cooks lined up. "You guys are going to have to let us know a few hours from now if you feel really stoned," Quenioux said. "You have to eat the whole thing."

The morning of the dinner, Quenioux walked into Starry Kitchen with a plastic tub filled with carefully washed marijuana leaves separated by layers of paper towel. He had just clipped them from his friend's patch. "Where's my soup?" he said, and dumped a twelve-gallon bin into a pot on the Cook-Tek induction oven. "I always said I would never do consommé in this kitchen, *ever*. But I got pushed." This one was made in the European way, with a *clarif* of wild boar, partridge, carrots, leeks, egg white, and onion, and, for the purposes of experimentation, ginseng (a blood-cleanser, in Chinese medicine) and

Angelica sinesis (a woodsy, licorice-scented stalk, which is traditionally used as a uterine tonic). "These tastes are not recognized in people's brains," he said. "They haven't developed the taste for it, and so we added kaffir and galangal to get people happy."

Quenioux poured a handful of apricot kernels from the Chinese apothecary into a saucepan and covered them with consommé. They would confer a fresh, almondy flavor, but too many, Thi warned, might induce vomiting. "Date! I need date!" he said, and dropped nine red jujubes (for anemia) into the pan. The potential legal entanglements of the night ahead nagged at him. Nguyen, he said, had become nervous enough to get a medical marijuana card the day before, from "Doc 420," a pot doctor with her own bikini calendar. "I say, 'Well, Nguyen, are you concerned? Should I be concerned about something?'" Quenioux muttered, adding chunks of papaya to the soup.

A security guard with a walkie-talkie poked his head in the restaurant door, and everyone in the kitchen froze. A tall cook with glasses and a goatee, who was roasting a tray of partridge skins in cannabis butter, crouched down and peered through the pass-through. Daniel glanced up from a sheet of pastry he was basting, also with cannabis butter. Quenioux composed himself and went to talk to the guard. A moment later, he returned, giggling: someone had dumped trash in the wrong bin.

Quenioux melted more coconut oil on the stove, filling the kitchen with a rank, dizzying smell, and put a bowl of it on the counter. Out came the tapioca maltodextrin, a powder for making powder. He added it to the oil bit by bit, and slowly the substance in the bowl clumped. Passed through a fine sieve, it turned into a fluffy, flaky heap—pot snow, at room temperature.

Daniel spooned it up and tasted it. "That's sexy," he pronounced. "That's fucking cool." Over the snow, he shook a little jar: the reserved crystals. "You have to treat it like a lady," he said, tossing it gently with a fork.

That evening, it was clear and windy in Encino. A film of pollen swirled in the pool, and the birds-of-paradise bobbed like oil derricks. The hostess had on a black dress and straw-soled wedge sandals. Her husband, who had clients in from China, had decided to entertain them at the country club instead. In the kitchen, an Irish bartender, red-bearded and thin, with pointy shoes, stood at the stove stirring a cauldron of garam masala, ginger, cardamom, hashish, and milk, which he was going to serve with dark rum. "I used to do this in Ireland as a kid," he said. "I'd take butter and hashish on a spoon and heat it up and dump it in yogurt." He opened a jar of vodka, which he had infused with marijuana using a PolyScience Smoking Gun and then mixed with a marijuana-vanilla tincture. He called the drink a Medicated Gibson. To me it smelled exactly like Dorm Room Couch.

Daniel checked the time on his phone. Instead of a picture of a girlfriend or a pet, the background image was a lobe of foie, searing in a pan. Soon the guests, shuttled by minivan, for security reasons, from the parking lot of a nearby Gelson's supermarket, started to arrive: foodies in their twenties; a porn editor; a prominent libertarian attorney and his wife, a Broadway producer; a Cal Tech neuroscientist in his seventies who had never tried marijuana before. "There's Jonathan Gold!" said a twenty-five-year-old Yelper sitting at my table. Alex and Alex, a young married couple—she a student of applied physics, he a tunneling engineer—stared at him over their *pêche* lambic, before he-Alex summoned the nerve to go meet him. "He's a really big fan," his wife said.

Nguyen came out from the kitchen. "Mr. J. Gold, you are not special here!" he announced to the room, proving that, in fact, he was. "You get to sit down and eat like everyone else." He went on to describe his idea of a plausible legal loophole. "Technically, you are here for a $150 gift and you can stay for dinner," he said.

"As a lawyer, is this legal?" someone asked the libertarian attorney. "No," he said, and smiled. He went on, "Free minds and free markets. The government says you can't eat the kinds of ingredients you want at a dinner like this, and we think you should be able to."

The soup came out—clear and musky, with a sweet, strong almond-extract flavor from the apricot kernels, and a suggestion of slipperiness from some nameko mushrooms. When the monkfish congee was served, the hostess took a delicate bite. "It's a little tingly," she said. "Otherwise it's *delicious*."

"I'd describe it as billowy," her tablemate said.

The atmosphere was billowy, too, the guests high on the promise of getting high—but not actually, some complained, getting all that high. The neuroscientist said he felt sleepy, like he had drunk a bottle of beer. A woman in a green beret scratched her back with a fork. But everyone perked up for dessert. Quenioux had scrapped the osmanthus cake in favor of an osmanthus panna cotta—creamy, with the light, floral sweetness of elderflower—which was served with rhubarb gelée and blood-orange sorbet. The plate was decorated with kumquats, tomatoes, an asparagus spear, a swish of frozen cream, and the pot snow. "What an extraordinary druggy joke!" an art historian with a pierced brow said. "It tastes like cannabis, but it looks like cocaine." On the way out, Quenioux handed each guest the "gift" that had inspired the meal, a glass apothecary jar containing two truffles and a gasp of marijuana smoke.

Food, in the foodie movement, is often treated like a controlled substance. With the Weed Dinner, Quenioux took the conceit a step further, but that was not even his point. All he wanted was to investigate a virgin flavor. He left the dinner with several dishes and ingredients to add to his repertoire: the congee and the osmanthus panna cotta, the marijuana powder, the apricot kernels. "These were phenomenal," he said. He recently made "dust" from the kernels, and served it on a dish of duck gizzards, hearts, and tongues. He told me he has no qualms about serving pot food in a more public forum, like at a pop-up. Quenioux is the avant-garde of the avant-garde; consistently, though, his peculiar fixations—ants, hearts, stolen flowers, hare—have become part of the culinary vocabulary. "I want to appreciate the marijuana, and the Chinese herbs, as a culinary device," he said. "In ten years, marijuana will be the new oregano."

PART III

DISCOMFORT FOOD

Seven

GUTS

In the early 1940s, Maurice C. Dreicer, born on the Upper East Side of Manhattan, heir to a jewelry fortune, embarked on a quest to find the perfect steak. The meat, he determined, had to come from a happy, corn-fed, four-year-old steer. It should be cut to a two-pound steak—less than that he considered an hors d'oeuvre—at least three inches thick, and aged for four to six weeks. It should be cooked to 120 degrees—a temperature he called "extra blood-rare"—over charcoal, and be served, without seasoning, on oak not porcelain.

Dreicer's restaurant ritual was extreme. He prowled cities with a pair of binoculars fitted with a camera, which he used to photograph diners through restaurant windows, and he devised his own system of merit: to restaurants that served good steak he awarded a silver butter knife; those with "superlatively fine steak" got one in gold. When his food was served, he produced from his pockets or from the black doctor's case he sometimes carried with him a scale to weigh a raw steak, a ruler to measure its thickness, a magnifying glass to inspect the marbling, a thermometer to verify the temperature, and a silver butter knife; meat that did not yield to it would get sent back. Sometimes he brought a homemade device with two probes and a dial, which he claimed tested acidity. In later years, he added a pair of white gloves and a monocle. Waiters often thought he was from the health department. He committed wholly to the role; once, in San Francisco, he visited twenty-three restaurants in one night, tasting the specialties of every house.

His rules for consumption were, as you might expect, specific. Steak, he believed, was best eaten after an appetizer of shrimp cocktail (he mixed his own sauce from a quarter of a lemon, a teaspoon of French mustard powder, a dab of English mustard, a touch of hot sauce, and three turns of a pepper mill). Tomatoes were the only acceptable accompaniment. And, if possible, steak should be eaten alone. "Women talk too much. A steak eater should not be distracted, so he can receive the utmost enjoyment from the steak," he said. "The only way to enjoy a steak is to concentrate on it, and exclude everything else from your mind."

By 1949, Dreicer claimed to have already eaten steak in a thousand restaurants. By 1969, he had spent more than $600,000 on the project. A decade later, the restaurant count was ten thousand, in eighty-two countries. A manuscript, "My 27-Year Search for the Perfect Steak—Still Looking," at last materialized, but failed to find a publisher. Evidence suggests that Dreicer did not want his quest to end. By the late sixties, he and his "traveling secretary"—a young woman named Brigitte, who spoke English, French, German, and some Spanish; acted as his chauffeur, as he did not drive; and at some point became his wife—had relocated from New York to the Canary Islands. They spent months on end visiting fine hotels and eating delicacies, grading charts in hand. She kept thin by limiting the amount of liquid she consumed. He was the kind of man who lit his cigar with two matches at once to intensify the flavor. He once joked that if he ever did find the perfect steak, he'd be out of a job.

The figure of the modern gourmet was still taking shape in Dreicer's time. A 1961 *Los Angeles Times* piece on the emerging business posed the question "But who is a gourmet?" and said, "No clear portrait has yet been drawn." The reporter then cited Max Ries, of Reese Finer Foods, who told her that the "average gourmet customer" was forty to fifty-five years old, of moderate earning power, and preferred "to entertain at home with cocktail parties, little dinners or backyard barbecues. And for the most part these fancy food shoppers do their own cooking." What was noteworthy was that American gourmets did not employ cooks.

A student of restaurants, Dreicer longed to professionalize his obsession—and argued before the tax court that his deductions, far in excess of his earnings, did not constitute a lifestyle but culinary research. The twentieth century didn't know what to make of him. Newspapers identified him as a "professional gourmet" or as a "gastronomical authority" or as a "fellow of infinite zest and tireless intake." The tax court, which ruled against him, referred to his "epicurism" and called his manuscript a "sybaritic swan song." He was an amateur expert, a food-nerd savant, in a world that did not yet recognize this category of being. Today, we know exactly what to call him: America's first foodie.

Steak was the lingua franca of mid-century American dining and the common denominator Dreicer thought would allow him to compare the quality of food in different regions of the country and around the world. Beef consumption in this country hit its peak in the seventies. Since then, it has declined nearly forty pounds per capita a year. In the past five years, while still eating much more meat than any other country in the world, we have also cut back on chicken and pork. As meat has become a less important part of the American diet, the rituals around eating it have grown increasingly primitive. The white gloves have come off; contemporary foodies want an unmediated experience.

"It's not Bacchanalian, it's Caligulan!" the woman to my left exclaimed one night at Totoraku, an invitation-only, all-beef restaurant in Los Angeles, as course after course of raw beef came to the table. She was a member of a dining group that calls itself the Hedonists. On my right, another Hedonist, a Totoraku regular who had invited me along, was photographing each dish with a macrolens and macroflash. I felt obliged to gulp down as much raw beef throat as I could, and made sure that I was seen doing it.

In its first issue, in 2007, *Meatpaper*, a San Francisco journal devoted to exploring meat as a metaphor, identified a *"fleischgeist"*:

a "growing cultural trend of meat consciousness, a new curiosity about not just what's inside that hotdog, but how it got there, and what it means to be eating it." One of *Meatpaper*'s founders told me that at their early public events people almost came to blows over access to corn dogs. "I'm still wrapping my mind around what happened," she said. "There was a certain kind of urgency and aggressiveness around consumption. It was a savage meat party—frenzied and visceral." She meant "visceral" literally: to a striking degree, the meat movement is about organs.

More than other kinds of foods, meat forces a confrontation with our animal natures. In his classic 1941 paper on disgust, the Hungarian-born psychiatrist Andras Angyal observed that, because it comes from a dead animal, one would expect meat to be universally repulsive, yet almost every culture on earth has found ways of accommodating it psychologically. In America, extracting the muscle and selling it apart from the animal has been very effective. "Beefsteak does not involve for us the meaning that it is part of a dead animal," Angyal writes. Cooking is another essential part of the transformation—raw meat evokes the animal more perfectly, and is therefore unappealing to many. But some animals, no matter how you slice or cook them, never make the leap from dead body to food. "This failure is best shown by the fact that in any given culture only the meat of a limited variety of animals is eaten, while that of many others is avoided as disgusting," he writes. The disgusting proposition of the *fleischgeist* is to remind the eater at every turn that the thing on his plate once lived, and to suggest that just about any animal is fair game.

Offal—the parts that "fall off" when you hang a piece of

meat—generally occupies a dubious space in modern Anglo food culture. In *Charcuterie and French Pork Cookery,* the English food expert Jane Grigson wrote, "Before the war I remember hearing '*Ai* never eat Offal', spoken with emphasis and pride, a brave flicker of light in a crude waste of offal-gobblers, yet another pea felt through twenty mattresses. War shortages taught better sense. Nutritive values were proclaimed and prejudices fell, at least as far as kidneys, liver and hearts went."

In 1995, Fergus Henderson opened St. John, in London, an expensive restaurant for offal-gobblers, which made offcuts fashionable. Henderson, who thinks eating should involve what he calls a "hands-on grappling with bones," has become a hero to certain American chefs. In addition to marrow bones, he serves pluck: the heart, lungs, windpipe, liver, and intestines. According to Anthony Bourdain, Henderson's cookbook *The Whole Beast: Nose to Tail Eating* is "a cult masterpiece . . . a historic document that flew in the face of accepted culinary doctrine . . . [a] proud proclamation of the true glories of pork, offal, and the neglected bits of animals we love to eat." In the book, Henderson comes across as a nutty old nanny, blood-spattered glasses askew, clucking away about fat chunks and blood, and about how "soothing" and "reassuring" innards are. He applauds the "amazing ducky quality of Duck Hearts on Toast."

"Fergus's little book influenced an entire generation of cooks to think outside steaks and chops," Tom Mylan, who runs The Meat Hook, a butcher shop in Brooklyn, told me. Diners were drawn to its realness, the antithesis of foam. "What is more authentic than eating heart and marrow bones?" he said. "It made for an experience exclusively based on adventurousness. Only certain people could muster up the courage. Serving offal is one of the very few authentic experiences where people are going to respond with their full attention. Either you have their fascination or their complete disgust and revulsion."

A year into the declared *fleischgeist,* Animal opened. A small, spare restaurant decorated with a framed lamb's skull and a Muppets lunchbox, in an old Jewish district of Los Angeles, it celebrates the indelicate, messy, uncivilized side of meat. At first, until the din of meat-eating grew deafening, it had no soundproofing. There are still no tablecloths, no centerpieces, and no candles; it is a restaurant broken down, blowing it out before the demolition crew arrives. Animal's co-owners and co-chefs, Jon Shook and Vinny Dotolo, are in their thirties and used to have a show on Food Network called *Two Dudes Catering.* They cook an elevated version of what Gold calls "Boy Food": loco moco—a Hawaiian surfer meal, which they make from artisanal Anson Mills rice, a Niman Ranch beef patty, a quail egg, a slab of Spam, and (historically) a brick of foie—and poutine, covered with cheddar and an oxtail topping that has the texture of chaw. The place invites transgression—in fact, it commits it alongside you. Its landlord, next door, is Schwartz Bakery, and the lease stipulates that, for competitive reasons, the chefs cannot advertise as kosher. Schwartz has nothing to fear. Animal uses three kinds of bacon and manages to incorporate pork into just about everything, including the bar of dense dark-chocolate mousse that is its signature dessert, and which customers often order with a glass of milk. Shook's parents are

Lubavitchers. Shook and Dotolo embraced whole-animal cookery with gusto. Grappling with the product in its least-processed form appealed to them on an aesthetic level; the economics of using every part spoke to their thrift. Nate Appleman, a proponent of offcuts and charcuterie, who by his mid-twenties was part owner of a restaurant in San Francisco, says that the only way he could afford to serve the same meat as Thomas Keller—the highly esteemed chef at The French Laundry, in the Napa Valley, and at Per Se, in New York, considered among the finest restaurants in the country—was to buy the entire beast and cook it all. Shook and Dotolo have served lamb tongue ravioli, lamb heart *paprikás*, deviled lamb kidneys, veal brains *à la grénobloise.* "What they do at Animal is use the cuts nobody wants," Appleman says. "They're really pushing the limits. They had a dish on the menu that was thirty duck hearts in curry. It was hard even for me to get through."

Dotolo—five feet six and broody, with glasses, a multicolored sleeve tattoo, and a three-day beard—is the primary architect of the menu, and he is uncompromising about his food fantasies. He has sometimes served fruit whole, without utensils, so that the customers will have the pleasure of feeling juice run down their chins. "I had this weird thing last night," Dotolo told me once. "I was, like, eating tofu and I was, like, thinking about how much it reminded me of, like, bone marrow and, like, brains and, like, that weird texture—like, soft, a little bit gelatinous. But the flavor of tofu is, like, so *yelchth.* I'll think about that now for, like, maybe a year before I think about something to do with it. I think it'd be fuckin' hilarious to do tofu at Animal, just because it throws people off so much." He thought for a second, and said, "Maybe you do tofu with meat."

One day, Dotolo got his hands on a whole lamb from a local purveyor. "I can't say who, 'cause it's not approved, but it's fuckin' good," he said. "It's all fed on apples and pears and lettuces." Shook butchered it in the kitchen. They prepared the liver with roasted butternut squash and sage brown butter, and the leg with green-garlic tzatziki, farro, and rutabaga greens. "Now I just have two tenderloins and a neck to use," Shook said. They served the brain to the chef de cuisine at the Beverly Hills branch of Thomas Keller's bistro Bouchon when he came in to eat one night. "I cut the skull open—whack!—with an ax," Dotolo recalled. "Most guys use a band saw."

The following afternoon, seven frozen pigs' heads arrived from Niman Ranch, and in the morning they went into a brine. They were for head cheese, which Shook and Dotolo were taking to a food festival in South Beach. In the afternoon, Shook, who is small and voluble, and wears boots with his shorts, opened the walk-in cooler and checked on the heads. One, in a pot, was already cooked; it was for the restaurant. "I was talking to my friend Tandy Wilson, at City House, in Nashville. I was, like, 'Man, your head cheese stays so fuckin' moist,'" Shook said. "We got real wasted and he said, 'Boy, the trick is to cook the head and leave it in the pot overnight.' So we tried it and it worked amazing."

In the kitchen, Dotolo stood over the cooked head—cartilaginous, magenta, baring its teeth—and rooted persistently around the cheek and neck for the prime bits. "We're partially professionally trained chefs, partially self-trained," he said, removing a delicate layer of skin, like a pink satin blanket, and tossing it into a garbage can. Then he tore a hunk of flesh from the jaw and shredded it with his fingers. "It's a pretty meticulous job," he said. "Some people don't see the worth in it. I think of it as the transformation of something you would never eat into something really tasty."

The food lovers of South Beach were, if not delighted, at least challenged. It was broadening by force. Shook said that everyone kept saying, "Head cheese? What's head cheese? Is that like blue cheese?" One woman, when Shook finally had a chance to explain, spat it out on the table and said, "Oh my fucking God, I've been kosher for thirty-two years." Shook giggled, recollecting. "Not anymore, you ain't!"

Before Animal, there was Incanto, in San Francisco, the first American restaurant devoted to Fergus Henderson's beliefs and a more puritanical expression of the whole-animal proposition. Incanto began as a traditional Italian place owned by Mark Pastore, a mild-mannered and reasonable man, who is extreme only when it comes to Dante: he has a special room at the restaurant where he displays a bust of Beatrice, and he sometimes dresses up as Dante for Halloween. In 2002, when Incanto had been open for a year, Pastore partnered with the chef Chris Cosentino. Now the walls of the main dining room are decorated with antique butchers' tools—splitting cleaver, bone saw, sausage stuffer, lard bucket—and the references to

Dante tend to come in shouted form and refer to the nine circles of his Hell, to which inattentive employees may be condemned.

Cosentino is forty, hyper and exhausted, with a small, pursed mouth, a sharp nose, and spiky dark hair. He wears thick-framed rectangular glasses and a stirrup of facial hair that makes it look as if his jaw could come unhinged, like a ventriloquist's dummy's. Under stress, he gets blinky and pissed. His coffee order is a Quattro. The first time I met him, he was sitting at the counter at Pigg, his new restaurant in downtown L.A., where, alongside products from Boccalone, his cured-meats business ("Tasty Salted Pig Parts" is its motto), he serves Fermín's acorn-chomping *jamon de bellota—crudo.* Serving raw pork is cocky, a frank challenge to American sensibilities, and an inversion of Angyalian disgust: what should repel is presented as attractive. Cosentino dares you to eat it.

The official opening was a few days away and Cosentino was tweaking the dishes. "Layer a little bit more ear in there," he told a cook behind the sneeze guard, who was preparing ear slices with a side of brain aioli, which Cosentino calls "brainaise." "Make it look like a sandwich of ears."

He turned to me. "What do you think the culture of texture is in the United States?"

"Crunchy?" I suggested.

"Correct. What do you think the culture of texture is in Asia?"

"I think there's more slime," I said, picturing the chicken feet—bones half-enrobed in silky, fatty, gathered skin—that were my first encounter with it-is-what-it-is Asian presentation.

"Jiggly—soft—unctuous. *That's* why offal isn't very popular in this country. There's nothing crispy—unless we make it crispy." He described frying the ears and pairing them with pickled peppers, mint, and red onion. He said he expected to go through 150 pounds of pig ears a week.

Upset by the amount of waste in the meat industry, Cosentino started serving the parts Americans no longer wanted to eat: spleens and blood and sperm; lungs, lips, and livers. Embedded in his dishes are sermons on how properly to treat an animal: he serves pig's snout with escargot and watercress, because pigs in nature like to eat the snails and vegetation found near streams; he pairs wheatgrass pasta with cow stomach and intestine, because cows ought to eat grass. A few years ago, he said in an interview with *Meatpaper* that the one meat he finds too extreme is *balut,* the Filipino unhatched chick—a whole animal, eaten whole. "It was difficult, but I tried it," he said, rating it "pretty gnarly." But he believes that meat-eating should be hard. Bringing people face-to-face with the reality of what they are eating makes them more conscious of their choices, and sometimes they respond by ordering the vegetarian entrée. For a while, he eliminated butter and made his pastry chef use suet for pork-fat cookies and lard caramels. He imitated a pastry chef, whining, "I don't want to make suet pudding. That sounds nasty." Then, playing himself, he barked, "Shut up! Make fucking suet pudding."

He went on, "They call me a barbarian. They say I'm meat jihad. I just think we need to look at food in the U.S. with a more open mind." To avoid becoming a hypocrite, he takes his kitchen crew to slaughter an animal every year. Once he killed a heifer named Bertha so big that, even after she was divided between two cars, the weight of her popped his hubcaps off.

Not long after becoming the chef at Incanto, Cosentino instituted an annual Head to Tail dinner, two nights of extreme offal, prix fixe, that allow him to explore the outer boundaries of decency, manners, and taste. The second year, Fergus Henderson showed up. "That was fucking daunting," Cosentino says. "This is the first time I've cooked for Fergus. I'd met him, I'd eaten in his restaurant, I'd staged in his restaurant, but I'd never cooked for Fergus." He served a shaved tripe salad, pig's-brain prosciutto, and lamb heart. The final savory course, before a chocolate blood pudding, was a braised pig head with grilled liver and large intestine—a dish that had to go in the oven two courses before it was time to serve it, so that it could caramelize. After Cosentino fired it, John Relihan, the young cook responsible for it, approached him and said sheepishly, "Uh, chef, I, uh, didn't put the, uh, head in the oven." The dining room was full. "Now I'm backed up on what to me is the grandfather of it all. We're shitting the bed on Fergus's table," Cosentino says. Five minutes passed, and no food emerged, so Cosentino leaned through the window into the kitchen and bellowed, "John Relihan, you will give me head! You will give me head *now*! You will give me *fucking head*!" When he turned around, the whole dining room was silently staring at him.

Benjamin Ford, a chef who serves a variety of domestic hams and a whole-pig dinner at his place, Ford's Filling Station, in Culver City, says he always tries to get a woman to read over his menu and make sure it's not too alienating. Cosentino, apparently, takes no such precautions. When Anthony Bourdain filmed *No Reservations* at a Head to Tail, the menu included raw venison heart on a brioche made with pig skin; a goose-intestine soup Cosentino called "anal-ini," because, he says, "it looked like a little goose asshole"; and a dish he named "Big Brain, Little Brain": cow's brains and testicles. For dessert, he made a doughnut filled with pork-liver-chocolate ganache and served espresso brewed with pig's blood. He heated the blood until it coagulated, then strained it out, leaving behind a metallic flavor familiar to anyone who's ever been punched in the nose. Cosentino is one to force a joke. One of the dishes he is proudest of involved asparagus (a diuretic), lamb kidney (a filter), and a bright yellow lemon vinaigrette, which he turned into a fluid gel with agar and sprinkled around the plate's edge, like drops on the rim of the bowl.

Cosentino's mission is to bring the offcuts associated with poverty cooking into the realm of fine dining. For a long time, he ignored foie gras: too luxurious. But in the years following the passage of the ban in California in 2005, foie gras—fatty, foreign, soft, *femme*—took on a different aspect. Soon to be forbidden, it became a totem of food-world machismo, the unlikely *über* organ meat. One chef had "foie gras" tattooed across his knuckles. Cosentino vowed to protest to the end, right up to the enforcement date. The ban, which prohibits the sale of any product of a force-fed bird, may incidentally eliminate magret (the fatted breast), most duck prosciutto, tongue, heart, fat, testicles, and down feathers. Cosentino saw foie gras as a whole-animal issue: the duck, paragon of exploitability, was being placed off-limits. "The duck is the pig of the air," he said. "You can use everything."

* * *

In the spring of 2012, I went to San Francisco to watch Cosentino get ready for the last Head to Tail that could include foie gras. It was two days before the event, and already the atmosphere at the restaurant was wistful and charged, like a high-school graduation party. Cosentino had on a T-shirt that said "Stop Tofu Abuse. Eat Foie Gras" and a dark blue apron with white stripes. The previous day, his pastry chef had all but cut her finger off with an immersion blender, so he had taken over making the dessert: foie gras panna cotta with shavings from a frozen maple-cured foie gras torchon. The dish required forty-eight lobes, the yield of forty-eight ducks. But now he had to worry about that night's regular dinner service.

When the host arrived, Cosentino called him over. "Hey, listen," he said. "We've got a VIP tonight. Vinny Dotolo is coming in. He's the owner of Animal. Death and destruction comes upon him."

Cosentino put on his chef's coat and went into the kitchen. Like a pagan altar before a battle, it smelled of cooking meat—a nearly extinct pleasure, now that everyone west of the Hudson cooks *sous-vide*. (It's strictly regulated in New York City.) There was a digital clock, with seconds, on the wall, in the middle of a death's-head mural that resembled the flag of a motorcycle gang. "Shut up and cook," it read. In the walk-in cooler, a pig hung from a hook and hay-brined beef tendons were splayed on a rack like wet noodles. There was a bucket of foie gras, steeping in milk; a layer of orange-yellow fat had formed on the surface.

Cosentino opened a box of lamb spleens, which were being pressed. "Oh, dude! See how dense and firm they are?" he said. He poked one, grayish, greenish pink, and expressed a drool of blood. He opened another container, this one full of lambs' heads, green-flecked with marinade, and still in possession of their cold, blue eyes. "Vinny Dotolo from Animal is coming in," he said. "I'm going to make him cry."

Manfred Wrembel, the chef de cuisine, a small, handsome man with a neat beard and cropped hair, appeared at his side. "We could do sweetbreads!" he said, bouncing a little on his toes. "We could confit the potatoes in tallow." He swung a bucket of duck fat enticingly.

"I'm going to fuckin' destroy them," Cosentino said again. "I think he's with his wife, though, so I don't know." Then he remembered that he had three mahi-mahi humps. "Do two on the board and one for him. That hump is going to be fatty, fatty, fatty, fatty, fatty. It's a cool set-up." He went back into the kitchen, rubbed his eye, and tasted a chunk of duck heart from a hotel pan full of gizzards, livers, and hearts.

"Good, eh?" Manfred said. "Disgustingly good?"

Cosentino started picking out the choicest bits for Dotolo. "I'm going to do best-part-of-duck risotto for him," he said. "With duck egg instead of cheese. Pain and suffering is coming."

A few hours later, Dotolo and his wife, Sarah Hendler, were seated at a corner table at Incanto. Hendler is slim and precise, with fair skin and a skeptical aspect. Her role in the Animal universe has been to try to erase in the public consciousness and hide from her parents Dotolo and Shook's reputation as stoners, enshrined in their reality show and in an early feature story about them in which their friends were depicted sticking cocktail picks up their noses and one friend tried to catch the "awful fountain" of his own urine in his mouth. She represents civilization, and she tries valiantly to hold the line.

"I like very specific things," Hendler said. "I like pasta." Before her was a plate of sea urchin and beef tendons and a plate of lamb kidneys. "We didn't order it," she said. She looked at the kidneys. "Am I going to like it?" she asked Dotolo.

"No, but you should try it."

"We went to Per Se and the waiter was shocked that I don't eat tripe or *uni,* and I'm married to this guy!"

"My favorite dish at Per Se was the tripe," he said apologetically.

Cosentino came over with the mahi hump, and Hendler gently remarked that they might have too much food already.

"I'm going light, are you kiddin'?" Cosentino said. "This is easy." He told them about the foie dessert he was working on.

At the mention of foie gras, Dotolo grew glum. Animal, he said, sold thirty orders of maple-sausage-foie-and-biscuits every night, and went through $400,000 worth of foie a year. Later, Shook told me he found the ban absurd. Like the food-freedom contingent, he considered the government's standards far beneath his own. "I think the foie gras I'm serving here is better than the chicken they're serving in the elementary schools, and the ground beef with the pink slime."

"I'm inspired by it," Dotolo said at Incanto. His first transformative food moment was walking into Michelle Bernstein's kitchen at The Strand, in South Beach, and smelling foie gras searing in a pan. "I was like, '*Wow,*'" he said.

"I don't like foie gras," Hendler said. "I finally tried the loco moco." She shrugged.

Foie gras, Dotolo said, was only the beginning of the vegan predation. "We believe that what will be next is caviar, sea urchin, and then line-caught fish," he said: the low-hanging fruit, unbacked by corporate lobbyists. "They'll never fuckin' touch the beef industry."

"Bone marrow," Hendler said. "That's another thing I don't eat. It's the consistency."

Cosentino and Dotolo bemoaned the scarcity of high-quality offal in the U.S. "All innards end up in commodity—it's so stupid!" Dotolo said. "We say, 'You kill all these cows, where are the hearts?'"

"Hamburger," Cosentino said.

"Dog food," Dotolo replied.

"It's a dirty, fuckin' nasty business," Cosentino said. "The offal goes as payment to the slaughterhouses. They bulk it up." After much searching, he said, he had found a source for green tripe—intestine stained from a diet of grass and left in its natural state. "White tripe is bleached with Clorox," he said. "Doesn't it say on the bottle, 'Don't Drink?' I'd give you a bag to take home but it's still frozen."

"I'm not a tripe person," Hendler said. "I'm a nice Jewish girl from New York City."

By 5:30 on the night of the Head to Tail, there was a line out the door. The theme of the night, chalked on the specials board, was "Respecting the Right to Choose the Meat We Eat!"

"And people don't like offal," Cosentino said smugly. "They think it's gross." Harold McGee, the food writer, was one of the first to arrive. He has helped Cosentino with technical problems over the years, such as how to pasteurize blood without causing it to coagulate and lose its color. He sat at the bar with a friend, and when the *amuse-bouche* arrived—whipped calves' brains and toast—he tapped his temple and nodded. I struggled with the brains—not with the creamy, mild taste, but with the idea of them. For me, they were, as Claude Lévi-Strauss might have said, "bad to think." The reference felt too pointed, too much of a put-down of bovine intelligence—as if the highest possible use for this young brain was to feed mine.

A few seats down sat the Dapper Diner, a heavy Asian fellow with a side part, who was wearing a lavender shirt, a striped periwinkle bow tie, a maroon vest, a silk handkerchief in the pocket of a brown sport coat, and a thumb ring. He was tweeting a picture of the menu. "I just tweet," he said. "I don't write." (His bio on Twitter, which I looked up later, reads: "I eat. My 4 basic food groups are foie gras, sweetbread, truffle, & pork belly.") It was his second Head to Tail. "Last year, he did bone marrow éclair," he said, a huge smile breaking over his congenial face. "I love offal. Other places are doing it, but not as much as here. You see sweetbreads and liver showing up more and more, but here they've been playing with it longer."

The first course was homemade rigatoni—purple from Chianti, bitter from endive—served with a venison liver sauce and the first fava beans of spring. "This is me taking it back," Cosentino had explained to the waitstaff earlier. "'I ate his liver with fava beans and a nice Chianti'—because for years when we started doing this menu they called me Hannibal Lecter." The sauce was peppery and greasy, like bits left in a pan.

Out came a fishy, deep puttanesca with a kick. In place of noodles, Cosentino used strips of pig skin, and he had named the dish "Porca Puttana!"—a nasty thing to say in Italian.

Cosentino's wife, Tatiana, a formidable blond woman who is his partner in the cured-meats business, was also dining at the bar with a friend. "Pig whore?" she said when she saw him. "That just rolls off the tongue?" He kissed her on the cheek. "Pussy pasta?" he ventured. "It's unctuous and gelatinous and we are a country of crunchy. It's an experiment in gooey, icky, sticky textures."

Tatiana said that Cosentino no longer felt so alone. Pig ears and tripe had practically become clichés. "Now everyone's doing it," she said. "Beef heart is gateway offal. It sounds scary but it tastes like a sirloin."

After we had eaten the head, feet, heart, and spleen of a lamb, puffed beef tendons, and some oysters, it was time for dessert. The waitress delivered a shallow bowl containing a molded cream-colored panna cotta, golden popcorn, and pink flakes of shaved torchon, with strawberries on the side. The little animal-rearing lesson—and sick joke—was that the panna cotta was covered with popcorn (duck food) popped in foie fat and covered with foie-enriched caramel: extreme *gavage*, cannibal-style.

"I missed most of that, what did she say?" Tatiana's friend asked after the waitress had finished describing the dish.

"She said, 'Foie, foie, foie, maple, foie,'" Tatiana said.

* * *

One day, sitting at a Guatemalan bakery in a nondescript, mid-central-nowhere part of Los Angeles, wearing a T-shirt showing an octopus next to a bottle of soy sauce, Jonathan Gold said, "When I was an editor at the *LA Weekly*, in the mid-eighties, there was a woman who worked there and was in a lesbian meat collective. She first approached me because she thought I might have a line on where to get some lungs—which I didn't, because they're not allowed. There's too much surface area for the USDA to inspect and they're too prone to infection. But I always loved the idea of twenty women getting excited because Tuesday was going to be spleen day." Gold's colleague was ahead of her time; twenty-five years later, he said, women had finally started getting into meat. "There's a whole sanguinary thing going on that's beautiful," he said. "If women can take charge of their own sexuality, why not take charge of their own carnivorousness?"

It seemed to me that Abby Abanes, the founder of a thousand-member Meetup dining group called Pleasure Palate, had done it. Abanes is in her mid-forties, shy, with frizzy dark hair and a face dotted with small moles. She was born in the Philippines and moved to L.A. when she was five; she lives with her mother in the San Gabriel Valley. Several years ago, she decided she needed more friends and a hobby; partly inspired by Gold, she became a foodie. The first time I met her, on a bus down to Tijuana for forty-eight hours of binge eating, she was wearing an oversize T-shirt with a butcher's diagram of a pig on it. Hers was an utterly normal life, perverted by food. Since I, too, was on the bus and took part in the binge, I suppose that the same thing was happening to my life. All I lacked was the food-themed clothes.

As the first to cover the Kogi truck and a participant in the first "tasting" at Umami Burger, when it was just a BYOB one-off on lower La Brea Avenue, Abanes has achieved a modest foodie celebrity. She maintains eighty-three Pinterest boards, including Anchovies/Sardines, Bacon Love!, Avocado, Banana and/or Peanut Butter, Durian, Oxtail, Snickerdoodles, Cute Food, and Spam. When her group gathers, three or four nights a week, everybody knows the rules. "Don't eat yet!" one of them told me. "We're all like vampires over the corpse while Abby takes pictures."

One cold, clear winter morning, I went with Abanes on a Pleasure Palate outing to the San Gabriel Valley: a bunch of ladies, down to eat weird stuff. The last to arrive was Cecilia Fabulich. She pulled up in a metallic beige Prius with the license plate "DINE LA." A competitive cook, who once won the Judges' Trophy at the Grilled Cheese Invitational, Fabulich told me that Pleasure Palate members pride themselves on discovering restaurants. "We like to dig out new places. It gets really—" She thrust her elbows back fiercely. "Sometimes I write on *Chowhound,* and I have felt that Jonathan Gold kind of stalks us on there."

As we stood in the parking lot, someone passed around a small foam tray of preserved eggs from 99 Ranch. Bisected, they were like sulfurous planets, with rings of amber-colored jelly and rotten green paste, and a sludgy gray-green center. I speared one with a toothpick and put it close to my face. It reeked of a urinal. I moved it toward my mouth, but some force field repelled it, and I could not get it in. This was supposed to be the warm-up; I was glued to the bench. I secreted the egg in a napkin and put it in my pocket.

We introduced ourselves by naming the most outlandish food we'd ever eaten: *balut*; Korean fermented bean soup; *nattō* ("fermented soybeans—the more you stir it the slimier it gets"); "*balut*, blood soup, or the little worms I had in Mexico"; "the goose intestine I ate Wednesday night"; "I think I've had cat meat once." After learning that one of the women was a nurse, I decided to stick close to her. At different restaurants around the mall, we ate jellyfish, stinky tofu, and insect snacks. At a place that served steamed pig intestine and pig's-blood soup, I leaned across the table and murmured in the nurse's direction. "Are there issues about food safety?"

"If it's an infected pig, sure," she said brightly. "I've had patients who've gotten really sick." *Infected pig*: not the words you want to hear when you sit down to lunch. I turned my attention to the crinkly, golden intestine, which looked suddenly friendly.

Leaving the mall, we walked a few blocks to Nature Pagoda, a health-food restaurant with a B rating, run by the owner of a Chinese apothecary. The waitress brought two cracked white tureens to the table. One held soft-shell turtle in a broth as dark and dank as tank water. The meat was tough, like turkey, but the soup was delicately flavored with ginseng and astragalus; goji berries and gobo root bobbed on the surface. In the second was ox penis. "For the first time, I'm scared," a woman named

Emilie said. She had been to medical school and had worked in the urology department at UCLA. From an herbaceous, pond-like bullion thick with sticks and ruffles of black fungus, she spooned a piece of penis. "That's the corpus cavernosum," she said—the collagenous structure that fills with blood to create an erection. At the end was a hole, the urethra. Emilie explored it with her chopstick. "That's a big hmmmmm," she said.

"It tastes like tendon," Fabulich said. "It needs Tabasco." Gold, writing to me once about some boiled ox penis *he* had eaten, had used just one apt word: *chewy*. I overcame the urge to spit it out.

Our final destination was a cute Hong Kong–style dessert shop called Tasty. Girls with long ponytails, wearing knee-high socks and fur-trimmed coats, sat in booths decorated with big pink paper camellias. After a few minutes, a waitress wearing a yellow apron appliquéd with daisies brought a glass parfait dish to the table. It contained layers of black rice, coconut milk, mango, and a translucent pulpy substance with the fragrant flavor of lychee. That was *hasma,* frog fallopian tubes. At the end of the day, Abanes said, "I'm more of an oxtail kinda girl."

Eight

OFF MENU

Conscientious foodie-ism works only if you know what you are eating. A few years ago, Dave Arnold, the genial, mop-haired food pioneer who at the time ran the Culinary Technology Department at the International Culinary Center, published a piece in *Popular Science* called "Why I Eat Lion and Other Exotic Meats." "As the food revolution continues to gain traction, our ancestral lust for robust, unusual meats is starting to spark and reawaken," he wrote, and provided recipes for *sous-vide* yak, bear, and lion steak ("57°C for 24 hours. Tastes like pork but richer"). Later, he was horrified to discover that his source—the owner of Czimer's, outside Chicago, which supplies much of the beaver, bear, and lion served in America—had pleaded guilty several years before to illegally selling numerous endangered tigers, including two Bengals, and an endangered black spotted leopard from the Funky Monkey

Animal Park, in Crete, Illinois. The meat, unloaded from a van into a back building, sometimes late at night, was, needless to say, not inspected by the USDA; according to the plea agreement, one of the animals, a liger—a lion-tiger cross—was shot and killed in a trailer in the parking lot. Czimer's sold much of this illegal meat as "lion."

The conflict between foodies' embrace of novelty and the conservative impulses of animal-rights and environmental groups is growing starker. If you are a Gold, though, the struggle is just another form of sibling rivalry. When Jonathan Gold got back from Korea, in the fall of 2008, he published a piece about eating whale in Ulsan, a port city in the south. "I am surprised to discover that the whale is delicious, leaner than beef, with a rich, mineral taste and a haunting, almost waxy aftertaste that I can't quite place," he wrote. "I am already anticipating the nasty glare I will inevitably get from my marine-scientist brother, Mark, who as the leader of Heal the Bay has dedicated his life to pretty much the opposite of this. I swear: I'll never eat whale again."

Mark responded, on the *LA Weekly*'s Letters page: "Bro—now you've crossed the line. For far too long, you have been chowing down on every marine critter I've spent my life protecting, from shark's fin soup to live prawns to bluefin to wild-caught sturgeon (largely freshwater). What did I do to you in our childhood to justify this ichthyocide?

"Now you're on to whale meat. This time you've crossed the line. IT IS ON!"

In the summer of 2009, I went fishing in Iceland and—local custom—bit the dorsal fin off the first salmon I caught and swallowed it. I got through it, with the help of a cook who cut the fin three-quarters of the way across for me, and a slug of vodka. A few days later, in Reykjavík, some of my fishing friends took me to a sleek Icelandic-Japanese restaurant. They ordered whale and invited me to try it. The truth is that it didn't occur to me to say no; yes had generally been my reflexive answer to a food challenge. The whale—I didn't know enough to ask what kind—came to the table. It was unappetizingly red, with an oily flavor that recalled the smell of a burnt wick in a hurricane lamp. My friends spent the rest of the meal talking about the high mercury content of the meat and the polarizing politics of the hunt. It all tasted like brain damage to me.

Several months later, The Hump, a Santa Monica sushi bar with a reputation for catering to thrill-seekers, was accused of serving an endangered species of whale to undercover vegan activists. The sting operation was orchestrated by Charles Hambleton, one of the producers of *The Cove,* a documentary about the dolphin hunt in the former whaling town of Taiji, Japan. Hambleton is a soft-spoken man in his late forties, with a distracted, trembly affect he ascribes to all the tuna he ate on location: he and the film's director, Louis Psihoyos, both got severe mercury poisoning.

Hambleton, whose father worked for Pan Am, grew up all over the world. As a child in Moscow at the height of the Cold War, he was forced to eat caviar sandwiches because peanut butter cost too much. Living in Antigua as a dive instructor and a treasure hunter, he ate whale with the old fishermen, and has no regrets about it. (His ethical line is that he won't eat factory-farmed meat.) When I met him recently, at a coffee shop in Los

Angeles, he was wearing a skull ring, a memento from his work as a pirate-trainer on all four Pirates of the Caribbean movies. On *The Cove*, he planned the covert missions, setting up blinds for filming the dolphin hunt, and dummy blinds to trip up the local police. When I asked him what had prepared him for the job, he said, "I was good at creative problem-solving, long hours, nasty conditions." I pressed him, and he rattled off his lawyer's phone number from memory.

In a couple of days, Hambleton said, he'd be leaving for western China with Psihoyos and the six-person Pirates of the Caribbean prosthetics crew, who had designed him a new face, with a broadened nose, darkened skin, and brown contact lenses, as well as a head of straight dark hair. Disguised as a Chinese-American buyer, he was going to film at an exotic-meat market in Wuhan, where tigers and dolphin heads are said to be sold openly, and use the footage for a television show about environmental crime-solving. Psihoyos would probably have to sit in a wheelchair to conceal his height. The prosthetics took six hours to apply and had to be worn overnight. Hambleton showed me a picture: shades of Mickey Rooney.

He told me he had heard about The Hump's secret menu from a source at Sea Shepherd, a renegade anti-whaling organization. The notion that Santa Monica, one of the most environmentally progressive communities in America, might be the site of such a blatant violation of national and international protections was alarming. Here was an opportunity, he thought, to carry on the mission of *The Cove*, with potentially more sensational results. Hambleton recruited Crystal Galbraith, a slender twenty-six-year-old *Cove* groupie with bleached blond hair and a mole under her right eye, who, he hoped, could lure the chefs into his trap.

Galbraith had read *Skinny Bitch* in college. "I was a normal eater at lunch and by dinner I was vegan," she told me. One night in the fall of 2009, she put on her best dress, a knee-grazing, tight-fitting black number by The Row, and set out to save the animals. At an apartment in Santa Monica, Hambleton removed a snap from her Guess purse and sewed a spy camera in its place. Galbraith brought along a Chinese friend who was fluent in Japanese. They settled on a backstory: they'd just taken jobs in Japan and wanted to acquaint themselves with the culture by eating the most exotic food possible. "I thought, 'This will be scary and I don't know how I'll feel, but there's no other option but to leave with a sample of whale meat,'" Galbraith told me. Her friend, Galbraith said, wasn't vegan, nor was she an animal activist. She was in it for the free sushi.

Not all that long ago, the U.S. government tried to convince people that whales, whose oil was used to light lamps, lubricate transmissions, and make margarine, were edible. In 1918, at a gathering at the American Museum of Natural History in New York described by *The New York Times* as "a conservation luncheon," the chef from Delmonico's served humpback pot-au-feu and whale planked à la Vancouver. The diners, "men prominent in scientific, business, and professional spheres," praised it: so like venison! Given its cheapness, they "were almost unanimously in favor of having whale meat substituted for beefsteak and urged its immediate adoption as a feature of the national war diet." Again, in 1943, the *Times* reported, "Whales, those greatest of mammals whose pastures comprise seven seas, will be hunted for their flesh, which will be used to help fill the gap in the nation's meat supply." The Department of the Interior gave reassurances that the meat was "wholesome when properly handled and it does not have the fishy taste which makes seal meat almost unpalatable."

Over the next several decades, the popular conception of whales began to shift, from floating oil factories to noble, cerebral beings. In 1970, Roger Payne, a marine biologist, published *Songs of the Humpback Whale,* a recording of humpback music he and his wife made from a sailboat: groaning whales, creaking rigging. Whales, it seemed, were more than beasts; they had culture. Other researchers, inspired by the findings, reported other varieties of advanced social behavior: humpbacks making bubble nets to trap their prey; sperm whales nursing for as long as thirteen years; and male killer whales living with their mothers into adulthood. Much remained mysterious, particularly about the baleen whales, which are too big to study in aquariums, but it was easy to make inferences from their large brains, complex neural pathways, and the behavior of their clever smaller relatives, the dolphins.

After centuries of increasingly high-tech hunting, several whale species were nearly extinct, and the American public began to view killing cetaceans for any reason as both an ecological and an ethical tragedy. Eating them, which in spite of the government's efforts never caught on here, suddenly struck people as barbaric. "We think these animals should be protected because they're really evolved," Diana Reiss, a leading cetacean researcher and the author of *The Dolphin in the Mirror: Exploring Dolphin Minds and Saving Dolphin Lives*, told me. "They share many of the things we do—social complexity, tool use, social awareness. They should have a right not to be killed." A collection of overlapping regulations was put in place to reflect this special consideration. In 1972, Congress passed the Marine Mammal Protection Act, making it illegal to kill whales, dolphins, and porpoises, regardless of population numbers, and banning their import, export, and sale; the Endangered Species Act of 1973 outlawed the hunt, harassment, or capture of vulnerable populations. Violations of these laws can lead to imprisonment and hundreds of thousands of dollars in fines. The 1973 Convention on International Trade in Endangered Species (CITES) regulates international trade of all whales and dolphins. In addition, since 1986 the International Whaling Commission has imposed a worldwide moratorium on commercial whaling.

The Hump was singularly well located, overlooking the runway at the Santa Monica Airport, a great place to watch rattling vintage planes and featherweight experimental aircraft take off and land. It served things few others could or would: blowfish, which contains a deadly toxin and can be fatal if improperly prepared; *keiji*, superfatty salmon babies which, before they are sexually mature, follow the adult fish to the rivers, where they are harvested. (One in ten thousand salmon caught is *keiji*, and the price can be as high as $150 a pound.) A sign on the door read "Warning! This sushi bar does prepare live sea food in full view, at the counter." It was routine to see a chef take out a live eel and drive a spike through its brain, and serve it seconds later. Live lobster was cut in half and presented with the tail meat draped over the carapace, and the head, still moving, beside it on a bed of ice. Eddie Lin, who writes an adventure-eating blog called *Deep End Dining* and frequented The Hump, said, "The effect of it is the animal is watching you eat it."

Brian Vidor, the restaurant's owner, is tall, with bushy white hair and the warm but slightly furtive manner of someone who has spent too much time in camp. In the seventies, he worked as a guide in the safari park at Great Adventure in New Jersey. Then Chipperfield's, a British circus-and-carnival company, hired him to go to the Sudan to capture white rhino calves, elephants, hartebeests, and topi for a zoo in Prague. They scouted for the animals from the air, in a small plane called a Piper Super Cub, and rounded them up with trucks, darting the mothers with tranquilizers so they would not stampede when the hunters took their young.

After that, Vidor took a job with a company called International Animal Exchange building a safari park—baboons, giraffes, rhinos, elephants, tigers—in Miyazaki, Japan. For the next fifteen or so years, he traveled all over Asia, building zoos. In Taipei, he drank snake blood in Snake Alley and tried his first insect: a Jerusalem cricket, fried with garlic and red pepper, served with beer. In Singapore, he had scorpions on toast. By the early nineties, he had become a flight instructor. Landing at the Santa Monica Airport, he noticed a "For Lease" sign, and decided to become a restaurateur, re-creating his favorite Asian street foods at a restaurant called Typhoon, where part of the menu was devoted to edible insects. Several years later, he opened The Hump upstairs for the customers who had graduated to a more morally complex and expensive confrontation with omnivorousness.

Whale consumption occupies a special place in the Japanese conscience. In *Tsukiji,* a book about the Tokyo fish market, Theodore Bestor, a professor of anthropology and Japanese studies at Harvard, writes that whales are the object of "ritual concern," mourned in special Buddhist services called *kuyo*. Etymologically considered fish—*kujira*, the word in Japanese, means "major fish"—whales were exempt from Buddhist prohibitions against eating meat. (Catholics, historically, saw the issue similarly, and allowed whale on Fridays.) After the war, when there were food shortages, it became an important source of protein; General MacArthur encouraged fishermen to convert their boats to whalers. Canned whale, mostly less-desirable sperm whale, became the Spam of mid-century Japan, remembered fondly by some aging Japanese, reviled by others as something they ate only in desperation.

But subsistence whaling, a limited, coastal phenomenon, has little in common with Japanese whaling today, which takes place on both the coast and the open seas, including in an area of the Southern Ocean designated a sanctuary by the International Whaling Commission in 1994. Under a research exemption from the moratorium, the Japanese take about a thousand whales a year, including sei whales, which have been listed as endangered since the seventies. To outsiders, their reasons can appear tenuous. Originally, government scientists justified the hunt by saying it was unavoidable: in order to collect the tissue necessary for DNA analysis—a tool for understanding stock structure—the whales had to be killed. Now that it is possible to biopsy living whales, they say that they need to examine their stomach contents for proper ecosystem management. The hunt, which is accomplished by firing an exploding harpoon at the whale, is considered by many to be inherently inhumane. In any case, U.S. scientists have a hard time finding anything useful in the Japanese data, because the whalers go only where they know the whales to be, and they do not carry scientific observers aboard.

Japanese pro-whaling politicians and organizations insist that whale stocks are healthy, and characterize the opposition as "culinary imperialism." The government spends copiously to support the hunt—reportedly some $45 million in 2011, including funds intended for tsunami relief—though it struggles to find a market for the meat, which, according to the terms of the research exemption, it is obligated not to waste. In 2008, the government sold ten tons of whale at a discount to schools in Yokohama for Traditional School Lunch Week. Homey, old-fashioned, and not particularly prestigious, the meat nonetheless commands a high price at specialty all-whale restaurants, where everything from tongues to testicles are served. The tastier tail and belly cuts of the rarer baleen whales are sometimes available at fancy sushi bars. But a poll conducted by the International Fund for Animal Welfare in early 2013 showed that only 10 percent of Japanese had eaten whale in the previous year.

How to explain a circular, propped-up, ecologically dubious, economically precarious industry—other than to say that's what happens when governments get too involved with the food business? Subterfuge. "The whale industry has nothing to do with whales," Casson Trenor, a former Sea Shepherd activist who in 2008 started what he believes to have been the world's first sustainable sushi bar, Tataki, in San Francisco. (Now you can eat sustainable sushi in Boise.) "It has to do with drawing a line in the sand about national sovereignty and resource management," he said. "The idea of other countries being able to determine what can and can't be taken from the ocean is anathema to the Japanese." To this way of thinking, Japan has created a baffle to distract Western conservation groups from the fishery it truly wants to shield from interference: bluefin.

When they got to the restaurant, Galbraith chose a seat facing away from the bar and placed the purse with the camera in it on the table. On the chair next to her, she put her friend's purse, which had a gallon-size ziplock bag inside it. They ordered *omakase,* chef's choice. After they had been eating for a few hours, her friend asked the waitress, in Japanese, for whale: *kujira*. According to Galbraith, it came to the table, sliced very thin, on a glass plate, with special soy sauce, accompanied by several pieces of dark reddish-brown sashimi that the waitress identified as horse, which has been illegal to serve to people in California for more than a decade. Galbraith's friend, who was seated facing the bar, had her leg pressed against Galbraith's; she moved it away whenever the chefs were watching. The women tasted both kinds of sashimi, while the chefs studied their reactions intently. As soon as the chefs turned away, Galbraith's friend touched her leg again, and Galbraith secreted two pieces of each kind of meat in a napkin, which she slipped into the ziplock. They left with a handwritten receipt, which included the words *whale* and *horse,* in English. The price for that course alone was $85.

Hambleton took the meat, froze it, and the following morning sent it by courier to Dr. Scott Baker, the associate director of the Marine Mammal Institute at Oregon State University, and an expert in cetacean molecular genetics. Baker, who recently established a database of whale, dolphin, and porpoise DNA, and has sampled cetacean meat sold in markets throughout Japan and Korea, identified the meat as sei, the fourth-largest of the baleen whales, behind blues, fins, and rights. Fast, sleek, and elusive, sei whales live far offshore and can travel at speeds up to thirty-five miles an hour. Baker called the National Oceanic and Atmospheric Association, which enforces the Marine Mammal Protection Act.

A few months later, federal investigators asked Galbraith to return to The Hump to collect more samples. Her Chinese friend had refused to go back, afraid that the *yakuza* were involved and might come after her, so Galbraith brought another friend, Heather Rally, a petite, part Asian woman in her early twenties. Hambleton tricked out the Guess purse with a better camera, from a top designer of surveillance equipment in New York, who helped with *The Cove* and, Hambleton told me, works with Israeli intelligence. "A lot of the cameras we get before the military does," he said.

Again the women ordered *omakase,* and when they asked specifically for whale they were allegedly served a plate of it. While they ate, Psyihoyos, who was in town getting ready for the Academy Awards, sat with Hambleton in an SUV in the parking lot, monitoring the audio feed. The filmmakers were as excited as they were appalled. "You could hear the live fish flapping at the table next to them!" Psihoyos told me. "The idea of taking apart a live animal for culinary enjoyment—now we're out of the food world and into the world of snuff films."

Meanwhile, a pair of agents from NOAA and the U.S. Fish and Wildlife Service had set up a base of operations at the Beverly Hills estate of an animal-loving former rock-and-roll manager. Leaving the restaurant with more samples, Galbraith and Rally headed to Beverly Hills. The house, vast and contemporary, with a waterfall, a room with a piano and eight guitars, and an extensive art collection, was also home to six rescue dogs. The agents turned a guest bathroom into a lab and tried to ignore the fact that the owner of the house, who had a serious medical condition, was walking around with a joint. "The look on their faces was great, like, 'Keep that away from us,'" Hambleton said.

In the bathroom, the agents worked late into the night debriefing Galbraith and Rally and preparing the samples. Hambleton secretly kept a little meat for himself; he didn't trust the feds to resist political pressure if someone decided it would be inconvenient for U.S.-Japan relations to find sei whale for sale in the United States. But he didn't have cause to use it: the NOAA lab the meat was sent to identified it as sei, too.

In early March 2010, the investigators asked Galbraith and Rally to make a final trip to The Hump. This time, the agents checked their purses before they went in and planted three of their own—from NOAA, Fish and Wildlife, and U.S. Customs and Border Protection—at the sushi bar. From the parking lot, Hambleton and Psihoyos listened to Galbraith and Rally and relayed information to them and to an agent stationed in the parking lot.

"They are ordering blowfish," Psihoyos texted one of the agents at the bar. The agents replied that there was only one chef in America licensed to prepare it, and he was based in New York. Then, "They were just served horse." Several minutes later, Psihoyos wrote again. "Just served the blowfish. What could possibly go wrong?"

After mackerel, toro, sea urchin, kobe beef, and sweet shrimp, Galbraith and Rally requested *kujira* by name. According to the affidavit, as the chef left to go outside, the Fish and Wildlife agent followed him and watched from a stairwell while he appeared to walk away from an old white Mercedes in the parking lot, carrying a hunk of meat wrapped in clear plastic.

"Nice," the agent in the parking lot texted Psihoyos.

"Bingo!" he responded.

Trailing the chef back inside, the agent who had been in the stairwell said he saw the chef slap it on the sushi bar in front of an underling, who cut it into small strips. Then, the agent said, he and his colleagues instigated speculation among the other patrons at the bar as to what kind of meat it was. Finally, the chef slicing it muttered "whale," at which point it was delivered to Galbraith and Rally.

Of all the things she ate in the name of saving animals, Galbraith found the alleged horse meat most disturbing. "Everything else was so good," she said. "I feel guilty saying it." Whale had the strange but not unpleasant flavor of "fishy beef," but horse she found altogether unpalatable. "It was pungent and gamey, really disgusting." she told me. To eat it, she had to fool herself back into a pre–*Skinny Bitch* mentality. Self-deception, as it happened, was not the only trickery at work on Galbraith's visits to The Hump. So committed was the restaurant to serving the outrageous and off-limits and hard-to-source that it resorted to a little subterfuge of its own. When Scott Baker's DNA tests came back, the horse that had assaulted her palate with its strangeness was revealed to have been beef.

A few days after *The Cove* won the Academy Award for Best Documentary Feature, The Hump's chef, Kiyoshiro Yamamoto, and Typhoon Restaurant, Inc., Vidor's company, were charged with violating the Marine Mammal Protection Act. People were shocked. "Short of putting human body parts on the menu, there isn't anything worse than serving whale to restaurant customers," Mark Gold wrote on his blog, *Spouting Off.* The invocation of cannibalism got my attention. It smelled of unexamined xenophobia: only a sub-human monster would eat another person. More important, it confused the nature of the issue, which is a problem of quantity not kind. Jonathan Gold, for his part, didn't take his brother's bait. He merely linked to his piece about eating whale in Korea.

An apology posted on The Hump's website doubled as a defense of culinary relativism. "The charge against the restaurant is true," it said. "The Hump served whale meat to customers looking to eat what in Japan is widely served as a delicacy." The message also said that The Hump would close, donate to conservation organizations, and pay whatever fine the court might deem appropriate (usually $100,000 for individuals and $200,000 for businesses). But then the charges against the restaurant and Yamamoto were abruptly dropped. Vidor, when I asked him about it in 2011, said he couldn't discuss the case. Prosecutors filed a separate charge—a misdemeanor—against the supplier, from whom, they claimed, Yamamoto had been getting whale for years. Using genetic information, Baker was able to trace the whale served at The Hump definitively to the Japanese scientific hunt.

At the end of 2012, a friend of mine told me that Yamamoto had opened Yamakase, a secret sushi bar with an unlisted phone number and address, accessible, according to its website, by invitation only. My friend had often entertained Japanese clients at The Hump. He told me stories of staying late, after all the other customers left, when the chefs locked the door and pulled out the strange stuff—tiny bright green turtles, rattlesnake moonshine—from coolers underneath the bar. He knew Yamamoto well enough to get us in. He also knew to bring enough sake to share with him. When we arrived, Yamamoto was standing outside, smoking a cigarette on an otherwise empty street. The restaurant, a onetime gelateria next to a place advertising itself as "Home of the Pregnant Burrito" had papered-over windows; behind them, a row of traditional narrow-necked bottles showed in silhouette, like a Morandi. The sign on the door said "Closed." It was the seafood equivalent of Totoraku, the invitation-only beef restaurant where I'd gone with the Hedonists, and in fact Yamamoto and the beef chef, Kaz Oyama, are great friends: the white Mercedes from which Yamamoto allegedly took the whale was registered to Oyama.

Inside: nine seats before a sushi bar, a glowing pink lump of Himalayan salt, and a gigantic, bristling Hokkaido crab with the face of an Irish brawler. Yamamoto had opened specially for us, and we were the only customers. He went behind the bar and sliced a piece of Japanese *wagyu* into sheets, grated a little salt on them, and seared them lightly. The ban on importing Japanese *wagyu* had just been lifted. "Only two weeks it's been available," he said when he looked up. "It's not on the open market yet." He offered to get us some to have at home.

We ate the beef, we ate the crab, we ate gumball-size baby peaches, olive-green and tasting like a 1940s perfume. There was slippery jellyfish in sesame-oil vinaigrette, and a raw oyster, poached quail egg, and crab guts, meant to be slurped together in one viscous spoonful. That dish—quiver on quiver on quiver—epitomized the convergence of the disgusting and the sublime typical of so much foodie food. It was almost impossible to swallow it, thinking ruined it, and submission to its alien texture rewarded you with a bracing, briny, primal rush.

"*Damn* good!" Yamamoto, a solid, gruff guy with bushy eyebrows, said, and took another swig of sake.

The restaurant was authentic and obscure, and demanded special willingness and stamina on the part of the eater. One influential blogger, who posted about eating twenty-six courses there with the French chef Ludo Lefebvre, wrote, "I think Yamakase's going to be the next big thing on the Japanese scene here in LA. I'm already thinking about my return trip—it's that good. Seriously though, if you care at all about Japanese dining, you owe it to yourself to give this place a try, *if* you can get in of course."

But in early 2013, Susumo Ueda and Yamamoto were indicted, along with Typhoon Restaurant, Inc., on charges that they conspired to smuggle and sell whale meat; Yamamoto was also charged with interfering with the investigation. This time the penalties were potentially severe: up to sixty-seven years in prison for Yamamoto and ten for Ueda, and a fine of $1.2 million for Typhoon Restaurant, Inc.

On the day of Ueda's arraignment, I went downtown to the Federal Building. In the hallway outside the courtroom, I noticed a young Japanese woman with a long black ponytail, shushing a baby. It was Ueda's wife, Yukiko; I went over to introduce myself. She said that her husband now had a job working at a sushi bar in Beverly Hills. "It's more conventional," she said. "Not so interesting as at The Hump. But you can call in advance. If he knows you're coming he will order something special for you."

Ueda, a kind-looking man with a graying buzz cut and a short goatee, used a Japanese interpreter to enter a plea of not guilty. Sei's status as an endangered animal was a legitimate source of outrage, but it wasn't the legal matter at issue; the law the chefs and the restaurant were charged with violating covers all cetaceans, endangered and not. In a sense, they were accused of not understanding that in America whales and their relatives are considered too smart—too human-like—to eat.

Brian Vidor built his businesses around the thrill of eating the forbidden: tiny insects downstairs, massive endangered species upstairs. One place represented rapacious, selfish, greedy devouring of all the world's creatures, the other broad-minded, virtuous, global humanism; one was theoretically sustainable, one likely not; both challenged notions of what is appropriate food. Vidor's lawyer entered a not-guilty plea for Typhoon Restaurant, Inc., too. After leaving the courtroom, he summed up his client's position and, as far as I could tell, the attitudes of the adventurous foodies who ate there and distanced themselves when the dark side of their thrill-seeking was exposed. "He owned the restaurant, but he's a Caucasian, he's a fun-loving guy—he wasn't involved day to day."

As a culinary prospect, horse presents a different problem to Anglo eaters. It is too familiar a creature for them to eat comfortably. But eat it they do. In early 2013, Tesco, the British supermarket chain, made a startling revelation: some of its frozen beef patties contained horse meat, one sample as much as 29 percent. Then Burger King, which used the same Irish supplier (who put the blame on *its* supplier, in Poland), admitted that its meat was potentially contaminated, too. A British food manufacturer disclosed that its beef lasagna was purely horse. Ikea pulled its meatballs—horse—from locations across Europe. For Americans who worried that something similar might happen here, it was hard to say what was more disconcerting, the idea that you wouldn't be able to taste the horse, or that you would. Foodies had the opposite reaction. Canada's CBC News reported that they were rushing to try it.

Horse meat is red, bloody, unmarbled, and is said to be

reminiscent of venison (venison, apparently, is the chicken of the alt-meat world). It takes a lot of grass to make a little bit of horse; given a choice, people have preferred to use horses as work animals, for transportation, and as instruments of war. In the first millennium, the Catholic Church, threatened by the stubborn pagan habit of ritual horse-eating—it was tied to Odin worship in Germany and Northern Europe—took the unusual step of banning it. Mostly, the ban was successful; only Iceland, which made exemption from the ban a condition of conversion, persisted.

Smart people have been making a logical argument in favor of horse meat for centuries. Parisians discovered it the hard way, as a food of last resort during the Revolution, but by the mid-nineteenth century—just in time for the Siege of Paris, when it came in handy again—intellectuals were promoting it as a cheap, nutritious, and tasty solution to the problem of hunger. The French zoologist Isidore Geoffroy Saint-Hilaire, who championed the cause, recommended horse by saying that "it has been sold in restaurants, even in the best, as venison, and without the customers ever suspecting the fraud or complaining of it." In *The Curiosities of Food,* published in 1859, Peter Lund Simmonds, a British journalist who fashioned himself as a Victorian-era Herodotus, reported, "Horse-flesh pie, too, eaten cold, is a dainty now at Berlin and Toulouse, and boiled horse, *rechauffé*, has usurped the place of ragouts and secondary dishes!" But trusty, tin-eared Anglo-Saxon—"horse-flesh pie"—was not the way to introduce the delicacy that, Simmonds said, was "at the present the rage" in Europe's dining clubs and salons. At home in England, members of the Society for the Propagation of Horse Flesh as an Article of Food hired French chefs to prepare banquets of *chevaline.* Previously, the English had known *chevaline* by the name "cat food."

Anxieties about sustainability also prompted another intellectual, Calvin W. Schwabe, the "father of veterinary epidemiology," to urge a reconsideration of the obvious, spurned protein. In 1979, he published *Unmentionable Cuisine,* which he described as "a practical guide to help us and our children prepare for the not too distant day when the world's growing food-population problem presses closer upon us and our overly restrictive eating habits become less tolerable." The taste for horse, he wrote, was "superficially latent" in many Americans. Case in point: a horse-meat shop in Westbrook, Connecticut, that opened during a period of high beef prices in the early seventies and was hugely successful. "I'll sell it as long as it moves," the proprietor told a reporter amid brisk sales on opening day, a cavalry of mounted protestors outside his door. Schwabe provided a recipe for meat loaf—three parts horse to one part pork—he and his wife made often during his years in vet school.

Horse advocacy groups have long pressed for a federal ban on horse slaughter, arguing that horses are companion animals and therefore should not end their lives as food. The "Americans don't eat pets" argument strikes me as a weak one, rooted in denial. Who's to say what is a pet, or under what circumstances? Besides, it's a standard that is unevenly applied. The rose-haired tarantula Daniella Martin made into sushi came from a pet store and was likely intended to be a friend for an introverted twelve-year-old, but inspired no extra sympathy as a result.

At the turn of the twenty-first century there were only three horse slaughterhouses operating in the United States, all foreign-owned, with all the meat going to Europe and Japan. In 2007, the last of them closed, and USDA inspections were struck from the federal budget, effectively banning domestic slaughter. Over the next five years, hundreds of thousands of live horses left America to be slaughtered in Canada and Mexico, under conditions advocates of domestic slaughter and animal-rights groups alike deplored. A report by ProPublica suggested that, in spite of laws against the practice, some of them might have been wild horses captured by the Bureau of Land Management in roundups and sold to "kill buyers"; others came from racetracks and were full of steroids, anti-inflammatories, and other medications prohibited in food animals.

In 2012, funding for USDA inspection was restored, and various companies have announced plans to open slaughterhouses. While the majority of the market will likely be foreign, boosters are making a direct appeal to adventurous American foodies, on the basis of the other exotic foods they have accepted. "The Promise of Cheval," a document recently produced by the International Equine Business Association, asks, "In a country where common gastronomic choices include everything from baby lambs and suckling pigs to grasshopper tacos and alligator tails, why can you not find the horse steak that was available on the menu of the Harvard dining room in the 1990s?" (The Faculty Club served it, with mushroom sauce and vegetables.) It goes on to describe a cheap, sweet, red meat, just out of reach. "When our Canadian neighbors are dining on delightful meals of Cheval au Porto, where is the same lean, tender dish to tempt our palates?" When I talked to Sue Wallis, a state legislator in

Wyoming who is trying to open a slaughterhouse in Missouri, she said, "There's great action going on with artisanal meats and butchery, and I think *cheval* would be interesting to those folks." Wallis is also a raw-milk advocate. Her favorite, of course, is raw horse milk, which she has tried courtesy of an Amish farmer who sells it to the cosmetics industry but holds some back to drink with his family.

The history of accidental horse-eating is long. Simmonds, in *The Curiosities of Food,* remarked that no one in the English knackers' yards could account for the hearts and tongues, and suggested that the "ox-tongues" sold as Russian imports might be equine instead. Upton Sinclair put it on par with the other horrors depicted in *The Jungle,* revealing that, until public outrage temporarily put a stop to it, the packers, in addition to all their other crimes against purse and palate, were slaughtering and tinning horses. At the turn of the last century, *The New York Times* reported frequently on a German butcher named Henry Bosse, "of horse-bologna-sausage fame," who operated a slaughterhouse beside the racetrack in Maspeth, Long Island. His business was "transforming decrepit quadrupeds into odiferous bologna sausages" for shipment to Belgium and Germany. Sometimes, the paper alleged, "after the horse meat was shipped to Europe and manufactured into sausage it was resent to this country and sold as some of the famous brands."

Hugue Dufour came by his "horse-bologna-sausage fame" differently—by openly appealing to the outré tastes of foodies. Dufour, who is Canadian, grew up on a working farm; sometimes the family slaughtered and ate their horses. Before coming to New York, he worked for Martin Picard at Au Pied du Cochon, in Montreal. The restaurant is known for its hedonistic foie gras and whole-animal frenzies: Animal plus Incanto. In an idiosyncratic homemade cookbook, *Au Pied de Cochon Sugar Shack,* Picard chronicles a sugaring season at a maple orchard forty-five minutes outside of town, where he has a second restaurant. Among photographs of syrup-immersed bacchantes and detailed instructions on how to make squirrel sushi, he writes, "I LOVE carcasses! I like tearing them apart and picking them clean with my fingers and I don't feel the slightest bit shy about doing it in public."

Au Pied du Cochon avoided serving beef, which it saw as the product of a wasteful, unwholesome industry. Under Picard, Dufour learned to cook red deer, venison, bison. Although the restaurant did not serve horse, he began to wonder about it. The stuff he'd eaten as a kid had not been good; he wanted to see if as a chef he could make it delicious. "It has long ribs so you can do a very Flintstoneish rack that's kind of cool," he said. He played around with tartare, a classic presentation—and the Tatars ate their horses, too. Ultimately, he decided that the leanness of the meat made it ideal for charcuterie.

In the spring of 2012, Dufour, by this time living in New York, was invited to participate in the Great Googa-Mooga, a food festival in Prospect Park, and was given a booth in Tony's Corner, an area overseen by Anthony Bourdain. "It's supposed to be the big foodie happening, so let's see how far foodies can go," Dufour recalled thinking. He sourced some horse from a friend with a slaughterhouse in Canada, and imported it legally, with the knowledge of the health department. His offering was a grilled horse-bologna, cheddar, and foie gras sandwich. At his booth, there was a horse cutout—you could stick your head through and get a picture taken. How's that for identification with your meal?

It was a moment of truth for the self-selected contingent that ventured over to Tony's Corner. "The foodies got torn," Dufour said. "Should I go for horse meat or should I not be a foodie?" Five thousand of them went for it. When the VIP section ran out of food, the organizers came to him to beg for horse.

For Dufour, the bologna was exploratory; he wanted to see what the public could tolerate. He was happily surprised. "They loved us so much," he said. "I was, like, 'New Yorkers are great. They have no problem with horse meat. Let's do it.'" Soon afterward, he announced that he would serve horse tartare at M. Wells Dinette, the new restaurant he was opening at MoMA PS1 in Queens. The response was so virulent—angry callers told him he didn't deserve to live in America and should leave—that he wrote a statement saying that he would drop the tartare from the menu. His motive, he wrote, had merely been to "offer customers new things," beyond the trinity of beef-chicken-pork. He went on, "It was certainly not our intent to insult American culture. However, it must be said, part of living in a city like New York means learning to tolerate different customs." Then he invited his critics to come in for a drink "and a bite of whatever animal they do consume (if any)"—which included, at the time, foie gras bread pudding, escargot and bone marrow, and blood pudding.

"Maybe the whole foodie counterculture is a reaction to the oppression of just a few things to eat and big supermarkets where you find everywhere the same thing," Dufour said. "For me, eating other animals, including horses, is a responsible thing to do. If you like meat, it's trying to find other sources, meat that is already around that would otherwise go to waste." Because it's not raised for human consumption, the meat sometimes poses a health risk—but, he says, so do conventionally raised beef and poultry. He finds the sentimental argument weak and insupportable. "It's more like recycling a dead animal," he said. "We can't start burying horses with tombstones every time."

For his next restaurant, M. Wells Steakhouse, Dufour envisions a "meat temple," where he will serve a zoo's worth of birds and beasts, and forgotten cuts of familiar animals. "When I call my butcher I ask for whatever people don't want, what's cheap, and make it nice," he said. His plans call for a wood-fired grill, next to a concrete trough filled with lobsters, trout, sea urchins. "Everything crawling and live," he said. "I grab and butcher them real quick and grill them really quickly." From time to time, he hopes to have exotic meats like rattlesnake and lion, which he imagines serving in a black peppercorn sauce. "I would have loved to do horse," he said ruefully.

Most people hold back some species or another from consideration as food, and the reasons can seem arbitrary. Usually it seems to come down to relatability. But to be upset only about the animals we identify with leads us, helpless, toward hypocrisy. Diana Reiss, the dolphin researcher, isn't vegetarian, and she has her doubts. "Different cultures have different accepted animals to eat," she says. "How do we grapple with that?" One former Hump regular I spoke with said he refuses to eat anything too smart, but, when it comes to pigs, he just avoids thinking about it, because he loves eating them so much. "In a perfect world, I'd be a vegetarian," he said. When I told Vidor, a snake-blood-drinker and scorpion-eater who closed one of his restaurants after admitting to serving an endangered mammal, that I had eaten dog in Vietnam, he was aghast. "See, I wouldn't eat dog," he said, withdrawing self-protectively, as if I might bite his hand.

For myself, I began to feel that the principle I had eaten by—I'll try anything once—was inadequate to the times. Foodie-ism is pushing things too far and too fast for that. I felt a new line etching itself on my conscience. The Tailless Whip Scorpion Rule was: Don't be the first to try something. After thinking about The Hump, I arrived at a new criterion for consumption: Don't be the last.

Nine

THE HUNT

At Starry Kitchen on the night of the *escamoles,* I struck up a conversation with a young chef named Craig Thornton, who was at the table next to me. He had on a camouflage hat and black T-shirt and was eating dinner with Eva Card, a dark-haired actress who models for women's magazines and was his girlfriend at the time. Habitual extreme eating had led her to conclude that ignorance was to be preferred. "I probably wouldn't have eaten it if I'd known what it was," she said about the ant pupae. "I don't ask anymore." Thornton said he'd had *escamoles* a bunch of times, and had even served them. "It's hard to find a clean source, though, and I'm very, very particular," he said. In order to find goat that meets his standards, for example, he drives to a farm forty miles east of L.A. and kills it himself. "When you're killing something, you have a whole new outlook," he said. Scarcity was on his mind, and the developing world's demand for meat. "I get more and more paranoid about food. It's affecting the way I'm cooking. I'm cooking thinking about the future of food rather than thinking about right now," he said. He was planning to start a hydroponic garden so he'd have more control over his produce. I asked him where his restaurant was. "My apartment," he said.

Jonathan Gold's ideal restaurant is one where people cook personal, home-style food in an intimate setting with the weird music they like and their strange art on the wall. For him, this means the "traditional" restaurants of Los Angeles: unassimilated ethnic cooking intended for a narrow audience. Thornton also cooks what he likes, on his own terms, for a tiny, very specific group; it's his music on the stereo, his bedroom just beyond that makeshift door. Here, I thought, was a chance to look unobstructed at the new American cooking that is taking shape. With no health department to worry about and no investors to please, and an audience made up of adoring foodies who have sometimes waited years for a spot, the features of the movement would be laid out plain.

Several nights a week, a group of sixteen strangers gathers around Thornton's dining-room table to eat delicacies he has handpicked and prepared for them, from a meticulously considered menu over which they have no say. It is the toughest reservation in the city: when he announces a dinner, hundreds of people typically respond. The group is selected with an eye toward occupational balance—all lawyers, a party foul that was recently avoided thanks to Google, would have been too monochrome—and, when possible, democracy. Your dinner companion might be a former UFC heavyweight champion,

Ludo Lefebvre, a foodie with a Lumix, or a kid who saved his money and drove four hours from Fresno to be there. At the end, you place a "donation"—whatever you think the meal was worth—in a desiccated crocodile head that sits in the middle of the table. Most people pay around $90; after buying the ingredients and paying a small crew, Thornton usually breaks even. The experiment is called Wolvesmouth, the loft Wolvesden; Thornton is the Wolf. "I grew up in a survival atmosphere," he says. "I like that aggressiveness. And I like that it's a shy animal that avoids confrontation."

Thornton is known never to prepare a dish the same way twice, an ideal conceit for the age of social media that also speaks to his nimbleness and resourcefulness, his hunter's sense of opportunity. From above, the food—smeared, brushed, and spattered with sauces in safety orange, violet, yolk yellow, acid green—is as vivid as a Kandinsky; from the table's edge, it forms eerie landscapes of hand-torn meat, loamy crumbles, and strewn blossoms. Being presented with a plate of Thornton's food often feels like stumbling upon a crime scene while running through the woods. A recipe for Wolves in the Snow, a dish of venison with cauliflower purée, hen-of-the-woods mushrooms, beet-blackberry gastrique, and Douglas-fir gelée, which Thornton published in the *LA Weekly,* instructs, "Rip venison apart with two forks, which will act as sharp teeth. . . . Attack the plate with your blackberry beet 'blood.'"

He introduces his courses with minimal fanfare, rattling off the main components almost dismissively. "This is rabbit, with poblano pepper, Monterey jack, sopapillas, apple, and zucchini," he announced at a recent dinner. Later, he told me, "We say 'apple.' But we took butter, vanilla, lemon juice, and cooked it at one twenty-eight—at that temperature, you're just opening up the pores to give it a little punch—then we took it out, cooled it, resealed it, compressed it. When you put it on the plate, it's just an apple. And then you're, like, 'Holy crap, this is intense.'"

For someone who makes beautiful-looking food—at a recent dinner, I heard an architecture student say that she'd based models for her thesis on dishes from Wolvesmouth—Thornton treats appearances as beside the point. For a time, when he felt that too much emphasis was being placed on the visuals, he instituted a brownout. "I started making ugly plates on purpose," he says. "Potato purée with a nicely cooked scallop." Of all the dishes I've eaten at Wolvesmouth, the one that lingers for me is among the unloveliest, a puce-colored pile of rabbit meatballs and mushrooms, leaning sloppily against a folded crêpe, in a puddle of yellow sauce: a briny, cool, and sour-sweet concoction made from lobster shell, shallot, vermouth, and tarragon, with a rich zap of lemon-lime curd. The rabbit still had the whiff of trembly, nervous game.

Thornton is thirty and skinny, five feet nine, with a lean, carved face and the playful, semiwild bearing of a stray animal that half remembers life at the hearth. People of an older generation adopt him. Three women consider themselves to be his mother; two men—neither one his father—call him son. Lost boys flock to him; at any given time, there are a couple of them camping on his floor, in tents and on bedrolls. He doesn't drink, smoke, or often sleep, and he once lost fifteen pounds driving across the country because he couldn't bring himself to eat road food. (At the end of the trip, he weighed 118.) It is hard for him to eat while working—which sometimes means fasting for days—and in any case he always leaves food on the plate. "I like the idea of discipline and restraint," he says. "You have to have that edge." He dresses in moody blacks and grays, with the occasional Iron Maiden T-shirt, and likes his jeans girl-tight. His hair hangs to his waist, but he keeps it tucked up in a newsboy cap with cutouts over the ears. I once saw him take it down and shake it for a second, to the delight of a couple of female diners, then, sheepish, return it to hiding. One of his great fears is to be known as the Axl Rose of cooking.

Dining at Wolvesmouth is a dramatic event: nine to twelve elaborately composed courses prepared in an open kitchen a few feet from the table. Thornton stands over a saucepan with his head bowed intently, his hands quick and careful, a sapper with a live one. Between maneuvers, he darts over to the refrigerator, where he posts the night's menu and, next to each course, the time it was served. Every so often, he steals a glance at the diners and makes a small adjustment on his iPhone, turning up the volume on the music to make people lean in if they seem hesitant to talk and turning it down once the social mood has been established. The first time I went, a few weeks after meeting him, there was half a roasted pig's head, teeth in, glistering fiendishly on the counter as a conversation starter for the guests.

The pressure involved in long-form, dinner-party-style cooking is extreme. "That food has to go out," Miles Thompson, a twenty-four-year-old alumnus of Nobu, who did a stage at

Wolvesmouth while figuring out his own underground concept, said. "You promised twelve courses, and you only have that one striped bass. There's no server error, no cook error, no 'Here, I'll buy you a cocktail.'" Thornton's menus are three-dimensional puzzles that remain in pieces until the final hours before the guests arrive. "Cooking is creating a big fucking problem and learning how to solve it," he says.

Because Thornton has no apparatus around him—no wall, even, separating the kitchen from the table—his diners can imagine he belongs to them. Without them, they sense, he would not exist. He is particularly beloved among a circle of Asian eaters who call themselves the Panda Clan and Team Fatass, referring to their panda-related Twitter handles and their appetite for food marathons. When he learned that one of them was about to turn forty, he proposed cooking him a forty-course meal to celebrate. It was a typical Wolvesmouth dinner, miniaturized and quadrupled, and served in four hours. Course No. 24: "chicken liver mousse, pickled pear, watermelon radish, brioche, fleur de sel." No. 31: "lobster, celery root remoulade, black sesame, cherry-white soy vinaigrette." Thornton didn't sleep for three days before the event. "I could've designed the menu differently, but I was, like, I gotta prep everything at the very last minute," he told me. The hardest part was trying not to repeat ingredients, given that each course had four or five components and each component had four or five elements. "All of a sudden, you're going through four hundred things," he said. One of the diners, Kevin Hsu, noted on his blog, *KevinEats,* that he ate more courses at the "40 at 40" than at Alinea, Grant Achatz's three-star restaurant in Chicago, where the tasting menu, which usually runs to twenty courses and costs around $200, is one of the most elaborate and extensive in America.

Wolvesmouth is part of a larger dismantling of fine dining. Nowadays, it's not just menus but restaurants themselves that are seasonal, popping up like chanterelles after a heavy rain. Established chefs, between gigs, squat in vacant commercial kitchens. Young, undercapitalized cooks with catchy ideas go in search of drunken undergraduates: gourmet food trucks. Cooks, both trained and not, host sporadic, legally questionable supper clubs and dinner parties wherever they want. You can pay for a meal in a West Hollywood apartment that belongs to a cook who is by day an assembler of mystery boxes on *MasterChef* and whose only oven is of the toaster variety. In New York, there are dinner parties on subway trains. In Austin, they hunt and field-dress wild boar. Often, you prepay for your "ticket" on PayPal. In most cases, these restaurants are underground in name only. Many of them have websites. A few have "underground restaurant" in the URL.

For chefs, being underground means sidestepping regulations they may find onerous. The ban on foie gras was meaningless to Quenioux, who before it took effect said, "We are known to be a little bit rebellious. They can fine me every day." After the ban, he sent me a picture of his fridge, loaded with glass jars full of gorgeous-looking product. "We have been serving foie at most pop up . . . I won't stop," he wrote. "It is my cultural heritage. It is like taking kimchi away from a Korean." Quenioux's itinerant cheese cart, which rivals Robuchon's, occasionally contains crottin, Rove des Garrigues, or Norman Camembert, all of which are made with unpasteurized milk and not aged the sixty days that the FDA insists upon. "We go *around,*" he told me. "I cannot say how. I know it's illegal to do so but I don't mind. Some of my cheeses cannot age that much because the taste changes." At CR8, an expensive dinner that attracts a wine-collecting clientele, the chef recently designed an Alexander McQueen–themed meal. The fifth course featured tonka beans, which he had smuggled from Berlin in his backpack. Tonka beans contain a fragrant compound called coumarin—it accounts for their vanilla-like aroma, and their popularity in European ice creams and desserts—which is also found in strawberries, sweet clover, and mown hay. Fermented, it converts to an anticoagulant and causes hemorrhaging, known as "sweet clover disease," in cattle. In 1954, the FDA deemed coumarin dangerous, and banned it as an additive; tonka beans are still on the FDA's list of "Substances Generally Prohibited from Direct Addition or Use as Human Food."

Chefs continued to cook with tonka beans anyway. "We had them until they went on a door-to-door jihad shutting people down who had them," Wylie Dufresne, the chef at WD-50, a highly regarded experimental restaurant in Manhattan, told me. "There was a moment when you were better off having a firearm than a tonka bean." In 2006, the FDA inspected Alinea's spice cabinet and ordered Achatz, who says he had no idea that it was illegal, to remove the offensive bean. The chef at CR8, whose kitchen doesn't exist, didn't have to worry about the feds. His dish involved a length of mushroom-filled puff pastry rolled to resemble a cinnamon stick, and a sabayon made with tonka bean and cinnamon oil. He said the inspiration came to him after looking at a bowl of potpourri in his bathroom.

"Whenever something is forbidden, it automatically gets cloaked in preciousness," he said. "My guests feel special because they get to experience something most people can't or won't."

Thornton uses the freedom that lack of scrutiny confers to offer ingredients that are impractical for most regular restaurants: too expensive (watershield, a kind of Northwestern lily pad), too weird (oak leaves, which he salted and served with pine broth and matsutake mushrooms), too fleeting (fiddlehead ferns, ramps), or too labor-intensive (cured bonito loin, which he shaves by hand). In the hundreds of meals he has prepared, he has only once served chicken meat, and that was for a private dinner, by request. Hanger steak, of which there are only two per cow, is an unthinkable waste; he serves rib-eye cap if he feels like cooking beef. Ideally, diners at Wolvesmouth will try three or four things they've never had before. Sourcing takes days, and Thornton does almost all of it himself.

In order to serve certain wild ingredients, chefs in regular restaurants must evade forest rangers, health inspectors, and, sometimes, the truth. "I'm very specific about sourcing," one prominent West Coast chef, who gathers by hand in places he's not necessarily permitted to but runs an otherwise very proper dining room, said. "But I don't tell our waitstaff where anything comes from. I just say 'nearby.'" In New York, a well-known chef told me that he has offered birds shot by friends upstate to diners who may or may not realize that what they're eating is illegal: because of the USDA's premortem inspection rule, you can't serve wild birds unless they are imported from the UK—which for some reason is allowed—or your hunting buddy happens to be an inspector. The chef said, "We've served whatever we can get our hands on as long as it's something we could use up quickly enough. It's a 'don't ask, don't tell' kind of thing. It's really not that we're trying to get away with something. It's just that we get excited about it and we know that our customer's expecting the greatest level of quality with all of our ingredients." Because of his unofficial status, Thornton can cook game without fear of losing his business. When the actor Jason Biggs shot a passel of pheasants, Thornton aged them for five days, plucked them, and served them to Biggs and his friends with handmade tagliatelle.

Wild products, the foraging West Coast chef told me, have "that frisson of death," which makes them extra delicious. Black trumpets—wizened, ash-gray eaters of the dead—are among Thornton's favorite ingredients. Their color speaks to his macabre side; he prefers to call them by their less common name, "death trumpets." Their smell is faintly sweet; they like the damp and dark and do not gather at the base of trees, as other mushrooms do. To find them, you have to look straight down. Some mushroom-hunters say that searching for them is like trying to find black holes. Others report the best luck finding them when peeing. Thornton sautés and lightly braises them so they keep their bite.

Recently, he got his hands on a few fiddlehead ferns from Oregon. "They're poisonous when they open up," he said, cleaning them carefully in the kitchen sink. "The toxin gets released. They can wreck you. They're, like, hospital poisonous." He served them, one per plate, on a just less intense green backdrop of puréed asparagus: a tight, poised coil. I had known him for a year at this point, and had seen him fastidiously source and prepare many meals. Eating is an act of trust, and I knew him to be a careful person with a great deal of integrity—a stress case, actually. I studied the coil: exactly how open is "open"? I ate around it for a while. I don't remember the moment of deciding to take a bite. I can imagine the concentrated earthy green flavor, slightly bitter, and feel the ropy, muscular texture of something from the forest floor that strains toward light. But the mind plays tricks.

Although investors have approached Thornton with plans for making Wolvesmouth into a household name, he has been reluctant to leave the safety of the den, where he exerts complete control. "I don't want a business partner who's, like, 'You know, my mom used to make a great meat loaf—I think we should do something with that,'" he told me. "I don't necessarily need seventeen restaurants serving the kind of food I do. When someone gets a seat at Wolvesmouth, they know I'm going to be behind the stove cooking." His stubbornness is attractive, particularly to an audience defined by its pursuit of singular food experiences. "He is obsessed with obscurity, which is why I love him," James Skotchdopole, one of Quentin Tarantino's producers and a frequent guest, says. Still, there is the problem of the neighbors, who let Thornton hold Wolvesmouth dinners only on weekends, when they are out of town. (He hosts smaller, private events, which pay the rent, throughout the week.)

But it is clear to Thornton that he has to bring Wolvesmouth into the light. His kitchen has three functioning burners and one small oven. Once, when the gas went off in the building, he prepped an entire Wolvesmouth dinner in a pair of pressure cookers. He has a dehydrator, an ice-cream maker, good knives, and, aside from a new, $3,000 Cryovac machine, nothing beyond what a moderately ambitious hobbyist might own. His version of the Smoking Gun is a gravity bong rigged from a plastic Voss bottle, a rubber stopper, and a head-shop pipe. One night he packed the bowl full of peachwood and lit it—only to discover, as his guests looked around in surprise, that Wolvesmouth's occasional dishwasher had used it for his own herb of choice and forgotten to clean it.

The Wolvesmouth crew is made up mostly of nonprofessionals; Thornton would like to be able to provide them with full-time work, and health insurance. Matthew Bone, a sweet, lugubrious man of six feet four, with tattoos up to his chin, is a painter; he and Thornton like to talk color theory while their girlfriends go out dancing. Andy Kireitov is an out-of-work heavy-metal guitarist from Siberia. Thornton went to high school with the dishwasher. Caleb Chen and Julian Fang came to Wolvesmouth as diners; so did Garrett Snyder, a husky, sweet-faced food writer in his early twenties who tweets as @searchanddevour. Thornton has taught them all to cook, after his painstaking example, slicing padrón peppers open with a razor blade and tweezing out the seeds. Lacking restaurant lingo, his crew members have evolved their own patois: "ramp" for a gentle-sided bowl that looks good for skating, "lifesaver" for one with a broad outer ring.

Only Greg Paz, a quiet, cat-like Filipino–Puerto Rican former skateboarder who serves as sous-chef, has professional experience. He went to cooking school and then worked at "turn and burn" joints before apprenticing himself to Thornton. Snyder likened Wolvesmouth's stature in the underground-dining scene to that of Kogi, the Korean-barbecue food truck. "There was nothing like it before and there's been nothing like it since," he said. "So many people want to be part of it."

One rainy spring day, a few hours before a Wolvesmouth dinner, Thornton stood over a tile fish, a dour, square-headed creature with a mosaic of silvery and mustard-yellow scales along its back. He wasn't yet sure what to do with it. The fish had come from a sushi wholesaler that supplies Nobu and ships choice specimens to Las Vegas and Aspen. "This morning, they called and said, 'Hey, we just got in some tile fish that's insane,'" Thornton told me. "They know with me I don't care what something costs."

The apartment was quiet and dimly lit. Small pelts were draped here and there; a preserved rat bobbed in a jar—a gift from Eva. Over a long dining table hung a mobile that Thornton fashioned from deer ribs and a jawbone he found in Oregon, and some lichen-covered pieces of applewood he once used to make ice cream. (He burned it, cut it, and soaked it in milk for a couple of days to make the base; finished, he said, it tasted like a campfire.) Paz, who, like Thornton, was dressed in dark, slim-fitting clothes and a black apron, cleaned vegetables. "People have this distaste for vegetables," Thornton said. "They're a lot more work. That's why I like cooking them."

After Thornton finished breaking down the fish, I went with him and Paz on a produce run, a fifty-mile round trip to a two-acre farm near the Long Beach airport. Thornton and a chef friend, Gary Menes, had persuaded the farmer to grow fava beans for them. By the time we arrived, it was pouring. Thornton jumped out of the car and spent the next hour ignoring lightning while picking the beans and a few handfuls of kale—only the smallest, purplest leaves closest to the heart. "Rather than getting it at the farmers' market, this is still alive," he said. "It will have that sweetness. This is what the diners want to hear about." He paused. "You couldn't do it in a restaurant." A patch of bronze fennel shivered in the wind. Thornton picked some and, a few hours later, served it with the final savory course: a tender piece of lamb half buried under snippets of cat grass, periwinkle-blue borage blossoms, yellow-foot mushrooms, and cocoa soil. One side of the plate was devoted to a splat of beet-rhubarb *verjus,* darkly clotting. He called it Spring Slaughter.

Thornton rarely has a chance to test dishes, and much of what he makes he has never eaten before. The education of his palate happened paradoxically: exposure to poor food made him hypersensitive to quality. Growing up, in Bullhead City, Arizona, he shopped for government-supplied groceries in the back room at the St. Vincent de Paul thrift shop. "The peanut butter came in a white jar and had the stamp of a peanut on it; we had powdered milk, powdered eggs, canned meat," he says. "I had a lot of bad, so I can detect bad quickly. I can taste it. I know when a piece of meat has been sitting and reheated, because it has the same flavor as that canned meat." The first meal he remembers making, in his grandmother's kitchen, was a turkey-pickle quesadilla, which he sold back to her for seventy-five cents. On Sunday nights, she made chicken-fried steak, fried okra, and collard greens, or white beans with ham hock and yeasty biscuits. In her honor, he sometimes pickles green strawberries or intentionally adds too much yeast when he bakes.

At Thornton's own house, a boarded-up travel trailer in a part of town that his cousin described to me as "the slum of Bullhead," there often wasn't any food at all. His mother, Elesa, and his stepfather, Emmett, would sell their food stamps to buy drugs. When they cooked, it was meth in the back room. In addition to being an addict, Thornton says, Elesa was mentally ill and susceptible to drug-induced paranoia. He remembers that one time when a social worker made her regular visit to the trailer, Elesa was naked on the couch repeating the sentence "I cut up and chop the hamburger meat"—the only thing she said for several weeks—while he watched *Dennis the Menace* on a TV set with the back torn off to expose the wires, in case they housed surveillance equipment. After thirty minutes, the social worker said, "OK, see you next month!" and left. "Why I have such a hard time with 'authority figures' who want to come in and tell me what to do is that they don't *do* anything," Thornton told me.

Emmett, who was covered in neo-Nazi tattoos and boasted to Thornton about having served time in the penitentiary, was violent and cruel. For fun, he would fill a Super Soaker water gun with gasoline and douse Thornton, threatening to light him on fire. He also hit, dragged, and pepper-sprayed him, and zipped him into a sleeping bag, which he filled with cigarette smoke. (Elesa denies that Emmett was abusive, and that she and Emmett used illegal drugs—though he has an arrest record for drug-related infractions.) At fourteen, Thornton, four feet eight and nicknamed Pudge, started lifting weights for baseball. One summer, he grew a foot. He thought about killing his torturer; instead, he planned his getaway.

Waiting till his mother was coming down from a binge and in need of cash, he paid her fifty dollars saved from his lunch money to sign a form, which he told her was a baseball permission slip. In fact, her signature transferred power of attorney over Thornton to his cousins, evangelical Christians in Riverside County, California, who had offered to take him in. He left the house with his bike and the clothes on his back, pretending that he was going to stay at a friend's. "See you Sunday," he told his mother, and never saw her again.

In 2003, Emmett died, from blunt-force head trauma and a possible overdose of methamphetamine, after he and Elesa had been fighting. She was not charged with a crime, but, according to the death investigation, she was "wishy-washy" about what had happened, and asked the firemen who responded to the scene if she had killed him.

Thornton's California cousins lived in a tract home in Menifee, which locals call Dirttown. To Thornton, it was a deliverance to middle-class normalcy. He rode his BMX, bleached his tips, and had a crush on a neighbor girl. When he went over to friends' houses, he spent his time talking to their parents and grandparents. After high school, he took classes at a local community college and worked at a skate-and-snowboarding shop, where he met Paz. He snowboarded at Mammoth and worked the night shift at Costco; because he didn't have a car, he ran to work four miles on the shoulder of the freeway.

Painting was his primary interest, and he considered going to art school, but he changed his mind and applied to Western

Culinary Institute, a branch of the Cordon Bleu, in Portland, Oregon. Wendy Bennett, a chef who taught him there, remembers him as being instinctive and original. "There are very few students that come through culinary school that get it on that level, that don't just rotely re-create what the chef made," she told me. "It's like going to a museum and you see a piece of art and it inspires you to make your own art piece. He wasn't afraid of anything." When class let out, in the late afternoon, he jogged forty blocks to Serrato, a Mediterranean restaurant where he'd landed a position after offering to work for free, and learned to prep in one hour what took the other cooks three.

After graduating, Thornton got a job in Las Vegas on the line at Bouchon, the French bistro owned by Thomas Keller, of The French Laundry and Per Se. Thornton worked eighty hours a week for minimum wage. A few months later, his student-loan debt became overwhelming and he left. Eventually, he moved to Los Angeles, and in 2007, through an agency, got a job working for Nicolas Cage and his family as a private chef. While with the Cages, he began to assemble the pieces to build Wolvesmouth: the table, the chairs, china, glasses, and flatware. "I didn't want to do it janky," he told me. He held his first dinners in an apartment near Larchmont Village, where he lived at the time, and then at a house in the Hollywood Hills belonging to the Olympic gold medalist Shaun White, a friend from his snowboarding days. (He cooked White's meal the night before he won gold in the half-pipe in Vancouver, in 2010.) In 2010, he left the Cages, moved to the loft downtown, and started working on Wolvesmouth full-time.

A hundred years ago, before Progressivism introduced

food-service regulations to cities, all restaurants were essentially underground. (As soon as there were regulations, people skirted them: Jacob Riis wrote about a sandwich, "two pieces of bread with a brick between," that sat on the bar at a drinking establishment to prove that it was a restaurant and therefore exempt from blue laws.) At the low end, there were taverns, frequently run out of people's houses, where strangers drank and dined communally on whatever the proprietor was making that night. The rich, on the other hand, entertained in formal hotel restaurants, working with the steward to devise intricate meals with musical and literary interludes. The underground restaurant in the twenty-first century reclaims features of both: the raucous dinner with random tablemates, and the self-conscious staging of an elevated social interaction. Michael Hebb and Naomi Pomeroy were originators of the movement, starting a restaurant in their house in Portland, in 2001. Hebb said that he saw an opportunity to "reinvigorate the convivial in this country." Thornton often finds himself still playing host at two in the morning, hours after the last dish has been served and the burners cleaned in full view of the guests.

Pomeroy and Hebb were inspired by an article that Michael had read about *paladares* in Cuba, and Family Supper, their event, had something of that subversive air. "It was challenging the notion of the restaurant and the limited number of responses to this basic idea of cooking for people and taking their money," Hebb told me. "It wasn't a middle finger to the health department so much as an indie-rock, anybody-can-do-it, DIY call to arms." He designed collapsible tables out of hollow-core doors, and later, when he and Pomeroy moved their catering business to a commercial kitchen and started holding dinners there, built Murphy tables that could disappear into the walls during the inspector's visits. "We'd get sloshy with our guests and do dishes in the morning," Pomeroy said. "It became a thing, like, 'Ooh, I got invited to Michael and Naomi's for dinner.'"

Eventually, they had ten thousand names on their e-mail list and were open for business five nights a week. With the success of Family Supper, Pomeroy and Hebb founded two restaurants in Portland; in spite of their popularity, food costs got out of control and they were forced to sell, losing hundreds of thousands of dollars of their investors' money. Pomeroy recovered by starting another underground, which she ran out of her backyard. There, Pomeroy, who has become a cooking-world star—a *Food & Wine* Best New Chef, a contestant on *Top Chef Masters*—perfected the ideas for her next restaurant, Beast, a twenty-six-seat place where, five nights a week, she cooks whatever she wants. "When major chefs hear about the way I run Beast, they say, 'You've created a chef's dream restaurant, because you don't have to compromise,'" she told me. "What happens when you do a million-dollar build-out is that you have to be open seven days a week, be really high end, and have a million choices, and that may not work in today's economy."

The lessons of the underground are spreading. "Suddenly, diners are along for the ride. You're paying for insight into one very specific idea of what food should be," Kaitlyn Goalen, an editor at the food newsletter *Tasting Table,* says. "Now it's 'If you don't want what we're offering, you can leave.'" Little Serow, in Washington, D.C., was named one of the country's ten best new restaurants by *Bon Appétit* in 2012; there are no choices and no substitutions, and the menu changes every week. Everybody who goes there knows that the food will be super spicy and the music very loud, and it'll cost $45 a head. Payment, the moment in the restaurant ritual that embodies the emotional drama at its core—you please me, I pay—is also being upended. At Next, which Grant Achatz opened after his success with Alinea, you reserve your seat and buy your meal in advance. As at the theater, you can get season tickets. You pay me, I cook.

The goal of this kind of dining is not seduction so much as it is experience. In the name of gathering some more, I went to pHeast, an itinerant underground restaurant that bills itself as "live art." Isaiah Frizzell, the chef at pHeast, is an amateur molecular gastronomist and a grandson of the honky-tonk singer Lefty Frizzell. "A lot of people claim to be the sons, daughters, and grandchildren of Lefty, but I have his ring in my pocket," he told me. We were standing at a tiny counter in the tiny kitchen of an architect's apartment in Santa Monica. On the floor was a sweating canister of liquid nitrogen. On the counter were deli cups filled with Seussian blobs of green-pea purée that had been spherified with sodium alginate and calcium lactate. "The skin on it creates a gusher inside," he said, depositing the blobs into bowls. They kept bursting. "It's OK, it's OK, if it's gone it's OK," he said nervously. "You still get the effect 'cause you get the gel for the skin."

Frizzell went out to the patio, where the guests were assembled at a long table. "This is nose-to-tail eating, in a vegetable fashion," he said, presenting the peas. Several courses followed, meager and mainly protein-free. At a certain point, even the hostess's enthusiasm seemed to be growing forced. "It is totally amazing what you can do with my tiny kitchen!" she chirped, over a plate of red-cabbage juice that had been turned into what Frizzell described as a "fluid gel" thickened with a tapioca starch. When a tray of bacon-infused whiskey cotton-candy pops, made by the bartender, came around, the diners snatched at them desperately. Then it was time for "nitrogen play." Luckily, one of the other diners was an emergency-room surgeon.

Frizzell decanted the liquid nitrogen into a small bottle with red-bell-pepper coulis and whippits inside, and shook it wildly before shooting the contents into a bowl. Cold smoke tumbled out and rolled down the long table. "Red-bell-pepper Dippin' Dots!" Frizzell announced triumphantly, spooning a pile onto every plate. They melted on my tongue—the ghost of nourishment. I thought of something the founder of a reservation site for underground dining had said about the industry. "We liken it to going to a doctor," she told me. "You don't say, 'This is the medicine I need.' They tell you what you need. The chef tells you what you should be eating." In this case, I was able to self-diagnose: what I needed was some food. I saw a gourmet truck on the way home and stopped for a hot dog.

The traditional restaurant business, with its expensive leases and fickle clientele, can be unforgiving. In the spring of 2007, Gonpachi, an izakaya-style place popular in Tokyo—scenes from *Kill Bill* were filmed there—came to Beverly Hills. It had three buildings and a large garden with a koi pond, and occupied thirteen thousand square feet on a stretch of La Cienega Boulevard. The build took three and a half years and cost more than $18 million. The beams in the main space, a two-story room meant to evoke a traditional village during a festival, were from a nineteenth-century house in Japan. Gonpachi offered sushi, yakitori, and sumiyaki, and had a glass-walled room where patrons could watch a soba master making noodles by hand. In the winter of 2011, it closed.

It was still sitting vacant the following June when Thornton and his crew found themselves with 2,500 servings of food and nowhere to serve it. An event that Dos Equis had planned to throw in an old Bank of America building downtown, with Thornton cooking (and belly dancers, Chinese acrobats, and Brazilian Carnival dancers performing), had been canceled that morning because of a problem with a permit. With half a day's notice, Thornton decided to pop up at Gonpachi.

When I arrived at Thornton's apartment in the late afternoon, I found him in an inside-out green army shirt and his camouflage cap, counting and quartering grilled peaches for a pork-belly dish. "This is a good opportunity to make some people happy who have never eaten the food," he said. The menu—eight courses, designed for a broader spectrum of the beer-drinking public and meant to be consumed in just twenty minutes—was the diffusion version of Wolvesmouth. "I'm trying to appeal to foodies with the technique and consistency but also to have a hook to bring in a mass audience," he had told me earlier. He went over to the fridge, where a menu was posted, and crossed out items that were completed. "Peach done," he muttered. "Tuna done. Tomato relish done. The rib eye we might be able to cook whole. Strawberry. *Tres leches* done. Done done done done done. Finishing fritter. Relish done."

At the dining table, Julian Fang, a heavyset Chinese-American man who is the slightly forbidding keeper of the Wolvesmouth e-mail list, leaned over an Apple computer. Beside him was another computer, a Dell, for his day job as a strategic-account manager at AT&T. He was trying to multitask, and his forehead was covered in sweat. He had written an e-mail to alert the list to the change of plans: the first two hundred to respond would be let into Gonpachi, starting at seven o'clock. The food would be free.

"Is that e-mail sent out?" Thornton asked.

"I can't get anything out of my outbox," Fang said. "It's three fifty-eight p.m. For the love of God, get this thing out!"

The e-mail finally sent, and ten minutes later Thornton peered over Fang's shoulder and said, "We're already half full. Crap." He laughed.

By six o'clock, Thornton and his crew had convened at Gonpachi, and were exploring the kitchen, with its array of burners, ovens, fridges, sinks. Amid the bounteous wreckage, they set up a survivalist kitchen: a fryer to make cheddar fritters, a circulator to *sous-vide* the pork belly. Thornton ran his hand along the *omakase* bar, disturbing a thick layer of dust. "If I had just this, like, permanently, I would be the happiest guy on the planet," he said.

Thornton showed Caleb Chen how to assemble his dish: corn soup with mole, lime gelée, and cotija cheese, designed to change from sweet to salty to sour to spicy in your mouth. To

Fang, he said, "Tuna, lingonberry, lime, black sesame, bok choy." He taught Garrett Snyder how to fan a stack of paper cocktail napkins with the back of his wrist.

The sky darkened and the smell of searing meat filled the garden. Lights came on in stone lanterns and the koi gulped at bubbles on the pond's surface. When the diners started to arrive, Thornton was still putting plastic forks out on the tables. He hurried back to the *omakase* bar and started slicing pork belly. "That gelatinous texture you sometimes get with pork belly doesn't necessarily translate, so I wanted to do a more porky texture that people are used to," he said. A crowd of foodies gathered around. One of them, a recent college graduate, told me that he worked at his aunt's software company, a job he despised, to finance his hobby. In the previous six months he had made two trips to New York, strictly to eat. On the first, he spent five nights in the city and went to eight restaurants, including Daniel and Le Bernardin, each of which has three stars from Michelin; on his second trip, a weekender, he had the extended menu at Per Se. During the same six months, miraculously, he had lost eighty pounds, due to a running regime and abstemiousness between sprees.

Matthew Selman, the *Simpsons* writer who cast Marge, Lisa, and Bart as food bloggers, leaned toward the bar. "I almost offered you our backyard," he told Thornton, as his wife, a willowy redhead, looked at him querulously. "Renee's given me permission to leave the marriage to eat," he said. "She eats gluten-free bread." The first trays of food went out and disappeared three seconds later. "Are these the guys that cook at Wolvesmouth?" a woman asked her date. "No," her date replied scornfully. "Wolvesmouth is not a *restaurant.*"

A hundred and fifty people showed up. At the end of the night, Chen said, "That felt like *Top Chef.* You're thrown into a space and it's, like, 'Now find some stuff to use.' We're so used to a home kitchen that we're, like, 'Oh, my God, what do you do with all this equipment?'" Thornton emerged from behind the bar. He looked a little stunned. "All I had was part of a sandwich today," he said. "I'm wiped." But he was happy. He'd talked to someone who'd been trying to get into Wolvesmouth for two years.

One late-summer evening, Thornton held a Wolvesmouth dinner at his apartment. Fang had his hands in a bowl of bitter steamed black-sesame cake, as porous as volcanic rock. He ripped it into pieces, which he placed on lifesavers lined up along the counter. "Smaller," Thornton said, looking over his shoulder. "We want one big one and one small, so it looks like two mountains." Thornton added chunks of compressed melon; they glowed like moonstones. He walked the length of the counter flicking lime curd from a metal bowl so that it pooled at the base of each mountain. "Saucing takes a confident stroke," he said. "It's messy without being messy. There's a feel you have to have, like being able to paint."

Matthew Bone stood nearby, moping. He was on day ten of a two-week raw vegan cleanse. He watched a plate sail past. "It kills me that he's making something and I don't know how it tastes," he said. He wrapped two cherry tomatoes in a piece of lettuce and took a big bite. "He never makes the same fucking flavors twice," he said. "They're rainbows. You can't catch them."

* * *

When I was twenty-four, my father died in a blind, hunting snow geese on an island in the Rio Grande. At home in suburban Maryland, in the basement where he kept guns locked in a huge steel safe the size of an upright man, we unpacked the duffel from that last trip: dark green, trimmed with tobacco-colored leather, sturdy, simple, well made. Inside, like outlines, were his waders and his crushed boots. There was a small silver flask, half filled with whiskey. My older brother, one of my sisters, and I each took a swig, and said good-bye. The elk that remained in the freezer fed us for years.

The first time I killed an animal, and there haven't been that many, my father dipped his finger in the blood and wiped it on my forehead. It's a rite that properly takes place between fathers and sons. One Thanksgiving, he made his three daughters necklaces from ivory elk canines—the teeth of six animals he had shot, over six seasons—strung with turquoise-colored beads he'd carefully picked out at Beadazzled in Dupont Circle, an image I treasure almost as much as the necklace. He left all of us with more, and more whimsical, taxidermy than you might care to envision. My friends used to take mushrooms just to watch the animals "talk." One of my favorite installations, a small, fierce honey badger—Pepé Le Pew, with fangs, mounted next to a fake fern—commanded particular respect from the handyman of my New York apartment building. I told him how a honey badger can take down a Cape buffalo by attacking its balls; after that, the grouchy, scarce super always got back to me right away. Tufts of fur, brass bullet shells, and pheasant feathers; pieces of skull, skin, and bone: that's what I call interior décor.

At Grant Achatz's Next, the menu is thematic, often historical, and changes four times a year: Paris 1906, traditional Japanese *kaiseki*. This past winter, the menu was "The Hunt." I couldn't resist it, and flew to Chicago to eat. I invited my mother, who lives in St. Louis. During ten years of marriage to my father, she had been handed her share of pheasants to hang.

Next is a windowless space in the West Loop, a meatpacking district that is being overtaken by culinary experiments. Its neighbors are Moto and iNG, restaurants belonging to Homaro Cantu, an inventor, cook, and consultant to industrial food companies. In a lab at Moto, he worked on making a vegan egg, and, in a closet-like "farm" off the kitchen, he grows his own microgreens, square watermelons, and heirloom tomatoes. iNG is devoted to taste-tripping with miracle berry, a West African fruit containing a protein that temporarily tricks the tongue into perceiving sour as sweet, which Cantu believes can alleviate world hunger and reduce carbon emissions by encouraging people to eat otherwise unpalatable plants. iNG's menus are double-designed, to taste like one thing before you eat the berry, and another altogether when the berry is in effect.

At Next, you are not a diner eating in a restaurant, you are an actor in a play about food. We took our seats. Over the white tablecloth the spotted pelt of a fawn was draped; before me was an eighteenth-century sterling walnut pick. "This is a rare opportunity to experience the flavors of the wild—foraged plants, hunted meats, offal—the more primal sensations that we don't get to encounter in our supermarkets," the waiter said. The menu would explore the hunt as an evolutionary necessity and a cultural artifact, from the prehistoric thrill of searing meat on a hot stone to the aristocratic indulgence of eating game from gilded plates.

A glass jewel box with brass hardware was placed on the pelt, steamy and green, a Kew Gardens in miniature. The waiter gave us each a wooden bowl and filled it, from a teapot, with maitake mushroom consommé. "Flip the lid," he said. I was preoccupied with the consommé, a salty, beefy, deep liquor I had to stop myself from drinking in one shot, and didn't hear him. "If you would, *flip the lid*." The box held two roasted maitake mushrooms, surrounded by snippets of herbs and a roasted onion. "Eat only the mushrooms out of the terrarium," the waiter said. As soon as he was gone, we stabbed the onion with our walnut picks and devoured it, too.

A tall, skinny server with a bushy red beard and a winking aspect slipped my mother a flask curved to fit a hip. "A wee bit of brandy to keep a hunter warm," he said. She waited a second, adjusting to the weird order of events—armagnac with the second course—and asked for something to pour it in.

"Oh! Did you want a glass?" He appeared genuinely confused. "The intention is to taste it out of the flask." She blushed and did what he said. The charcuterie—rabbit pâté, elk jerky, wild boar salami, blood sausage, venison-heart tartare—was served on disks of deer antler, set into a sap-oozing log. There were tiny deep purple hibiscus leaves grown in Ohio by Farmer Lee—he of the trademarked overalls—and caviar from sturgeon "wild-caught in the Caspian, then farm-raised in Florida."

A silver candelabra appeared, and was lit: time to play

nobility. Here came a cold course of woodcock, served with cocoa powder, black truffles, and a tangle of gold leaf. On one side of the plate was a dab of sauce made from hazelnuts and huckleberries, a culinary diorama that was the equivalent of a fake fern for a stuffed badger.

The next course was squab—baby pigeon—with all its parts, and offal en croute. The head, bisected, lay beside a fan of breast. At the edge of the plate was a talon. "Let's see if they eat it," the woman at the table next to us said. She and her husband hadn't; their grown kids, sitting across from them, had. I picked up the bird by the convenient tweezer of its beak and licked out the garlic-and-parsley-soaked brain. This time I was untroubled by the brain; maybe I have a mammalian prejudice. Or maybe I was seduced by surface: this plate was supremely beautiful, its challenging elements aestheticized. A stagehand, dressed in black, sweeping, stopped and whispered to us, "When Chef Morimoto"—the Iron Chef—"was here, there were no bones left on the plate."

It was an art-historical exegesis of a meal, with fifteen color plates. I have no idea what it might have meant to anyone else. For me, it was like feasting on my past. The smoky old flavors overwhelmed me, like a dream about a ghost that leaves you sad in the morning. I gnawed the meat from the talon, leaving the grip at the end of a spindly bone, the shrunken remains of a vanquished witch. My father would have made something fabulous from it. I almost put it in my purse. But in fairy tales purloined things have a way of turning into dust.

CODA

It was Easter week. My baby had just said her first word, "duck." Jonathan Gold was busy, doesn't much like Filipino food, and, besides, is afraid of eggs. Abby Abanes—who *is* Filipina—thinks *balut* is gross. I decided to face this beast on my own. It wasn't that I had a "list"; it was a personal test. I was curious, both about what it would taste like, and about whether I could stomach it. I thought of all the challenging things I had eaten over the past few years. How bad could it be? Maybe I would even like it.

I looked on Yelp and started calling. Nobody had it. Finally, I tried a place called Bahay Kubo, near downtown, run by someone with the perfectly discomfiting name Mommy Lucing. *"Balut?"* The woman who answered the phone said. "Come tomorrow at eleven."

The next morning, as the hour approached, I dawdled

around the house. I hadn't meant to go there hungry, but, stalling, let the morning slip by, and now it was lunchtime. I got in the car, and eventually I found myself driving in a part of the city I had first come to with Gold. There was Langer's, the pastrami place, and Mama's, where we went for tamales. I had my bearings. Passing MacArthur Park, I drove up a steep hill, around a corner, and into an unfamiliar Filipino pocket. Next to an apartment complex called Manila Terrace was a low building with a green awning and a Philippine National Bank Rapid Remit center. There was an "A" in the window.

Everyone inside was Filipino. A bamboo shanty on the patio housed a large TV; the TV inside was larger, and tuned to a Filipino talent show. The service was cafeteria-style, which meant I could talk to the lady behind me in line. "Don't eat that," she said, scrunching up her nose, when I told her I wanted to try *balut*. "What, you like feathers?" She cut me in line and left me on my own.

When it was my turn to order, I asked the man behind the counter for taro leaves in coconut milk. He was middle-aged and wore a tight red shirt, a white belt, and a diamond stud in his ear. "I don't think you're going to like it," he said, and made me taste it before he would put it on my plate. He was wrong, though. It was an island version of creamed spinach—bitter, rich, and sweet—and I liked it fine.

On top of the glass partition separating customers from the food was a small foam box secured with red, green, and yellow tape. A sign attached to it said "*Balut*, $1.85." "One of those," I said. Red Shirt raised his eyebrows, opened the box, and handed me a bluish-green duck egg, still warm, that fit in the palm of my hand. “Crack it, drink the juice, and then close your eyes,” he said. At the checkout, I asked for a 7-Up. If they’d sold ginger ale, I would have ordered that, remedy of childhood.

I carried my tray to a green faux-marbled table and sat down. Taking a bite of rice, I noticed that I was actually shaking. I cracked the bottom of the egg and peeled a little. Red Shirt had come out from behind the counter and was hovering around. “Wrong end,” he said. I kept going, chipping off pieces of shell. They were espaliered with dark red blood vessels. I had never seen this before. An unfertilized egg has no need of circuitry. I put my lips up to the hole I’d made and drank the liquid, a nice light chicken broth, then peeled some more, until I saw yolk.

I picked up a white chunk. In my mouth, I felt it give way into dark reddish brown meat. I didn’t need to take it out to examine it, I could see it with my tongue: my first and worst possible experience of synesthesia. I felt like a sharp-toothed animal, burrowing for meat. From my mouth, I pulled what was apparently a fingernail trimming. Meanwhile, I had to do something about the rest of the bite. Staring at nothing, keeping a bead on the talent show from the corner of my eye, like a seasick person trying to get steady, I swallowed.

I looked down at my tray. There, in the half shell, was a small creature, nestled into itself, a glazed eye, a billow of nourishing yolk. That is, *part* of a small creature.

“You should eat it all at once, if you can do it,” Red Shirt said, and handed me a shaker of salt.

Eating a creature and its food: aren’t whole lifestyles built on avoiding that? And isn’t foodie culture obsessed with artificially creating it? I thought of Cosentino’s pig and watercress, Achatz’s huckleberry and woodcock. I was a third of the way there. Why turn back now. I stole a sip of 7-Up and I took another bite. The familiar, not unpleasant taste of organ meat.

"It makes you strong," Red Shirt said. "It's the Filipino Viagra. It's like eating an oyster." I couldn't believe it—this darkest, most poignant maternal food, this was for men, too? I pulled the last piece of meat from the shell, determined to finish. This was a big bite, but I was almost there. Chewing, I hit an inexplicable texture, like a soft tooth. Single-minded, I mashed it to a paste and braced myself to swallow. Just as I was congratulating myself, thinking it was a mental game and I had won, something terrifying happened. From a deeper place than my taste buds—they could be tricked by a lick of chicken soup—rebellion. I felt a shift in my upper stomach, a violent bubbling, and the beginnings of a catastrophe.

Acknowledgments

I owe an incalculable debt of gratitude to *The New Yorker*, in particular to David Remnick, who has encouraged me at every turn; Dorothy Wickenden, a champion and a friend; and Nick Trautwein, a singularly gifted reader and collaborator. I want to thank Sarah McGrath for providing the spark and the fuel, and all the other thoughtful, smart people at Riverhead. Eric Simonoff for gracious stewardship. Stacey Kalish and Lila Byock for many meaningful contributions. Eliza Griswold, Claire Hoffman, Meghan O'Rourke, and Kevin West for reading and re-reading. Lila again, Eric Mercado, and Nate Stein for double-checking me.

I want to thank my mother for her curiosity, perceptivity, and steel trap. You inspired this.

To the people who let me into their kitchens, met me for

dinner, talked to me when they had other things that needed to be done: thank you. Your stories make the book.

My deepest thanks go to my husband, Billy, for supporting and sustaining me, and to our children for bringing me endless happiness.

About the Author

Dana Goodyear is a staff writer for *The New Yorker.* She teaches at the University of Southern California.

SEXUAL ASSAULT:
The Dilemma of Disclosure, The Question of Conviction

SEXUAL ASSAULT:

THE DILEMMA OF DISCLOSURE, THE QUESTION OF CONVICTION

Rita Gunn
Candice Minch

UNIVERSITY OF MANITOBA PRESS

Winnipeg, Manitoba R3T 2N2

Design: Norman Schmidt
Printed in Canada

Dedicated to all those who have suffered the degradation and violence of sexual assault. Your courage is an inspiration that change is possible.

The Outreach Fund of the University of Manitoba has assisted us in the distribution of this book.

Canadian Cataloguing in Publication Data

Gunn, Rita F.

Sexual assault

Includes bibliographical references and index.
ISBN 0-88755-144-0 (bound) - 0-88755-618-3 (pbk.)

1. Sex crimes - Canada. 2. Rape - Canada.
I. Minch, Candice P. II. Title.

KE8928.G86 1988 364.1'53'0971 C88-098096-6

CONTENTS

INTRODUCTION

Sexual assault enforces a restricted lifestyle on *all* women. The ever-conscious threat of an attack limits the behaviour and activities of females throughout their lives. Moreover, the actual occurrence of a sexual assault begins a process that does not end with the attack itself. The victim must face more than her own personal trauma in response to the event. She must decide whether and to whom she will disclose the incident. If she chooses to inform the police, she may be victimized again by the legal system.

Sexual assault is a criminal offence and, as for all criminal offences, an alleged offender is innocent until proven guilty. The legislation on sexual assault, however, is unique in its emphasis on consent and the character of the victim. Unlike most other offences, then, the victim of a sexual assault may feel that she is guilty until proven innocent. Consequently, in deciding whether to officially report an assault, the victim is caught in a dilemma. If she chooses not to report the assault, the offender goes unchallenged. If she chooses to report, she may be subjected to a legal process that has traditionally displayed skepticism toward females who report sexual assaults.

This book examines the anticipated and actual experiences of the sexual assault victim on both a personal and official level. We focus on the reactions of significant others (family, friends) and the criminal justice system (police, prosecution, courts) to the offence. The response by others is crucial, as it defines the event to the victim and ultimately to society.

The book is based on research undertaken in two separate studies, both of which confront systemic prejudices against women who have been sexually assaulted. The first study delves into the victim's perspective and exposes the internalized guilt that women endure when they have been victimized. The second scrutinizes the legal process and the inequities inherent in the system.

In research with victims we assess what led them to report a sexual assault to the police or to refrain from doing so. Other researchers (for example, Amir 1971) have identified possible contributing factors with the use of statistical data, but victim surveys have not systematically studied specific criteria. We isolated and tested several variables by gaining access to a crisis centre, an agency that provides victims with an alternative method of "unofficially" reporting sexual offences. Although crisis centres offer services to women who do report their victimization officially to the police, many of their clients choose not to become involved with the criminal justice system. Interviewing victims at such a facility provides first-hand information about women's perceptions of their assaults. With the results of these interviews, specific variables are correlated with individual decisions regarding disclosure of the incidents.

Our research at the criminal justice level reveals how the legal system deals with sexual assault. While the majority of research on sexual assault has concentrated on police-level processing (for example, Clark and Lewis 1977), we study the filtering system of the reports at the police, crown attorney, and court levels in order to examine the entire system. We also focus on the role of the prosecutor in sexual assault proceedings as the crucial link between the police and court levels. While crown attorneys have an obvious direct influence over charges in the court system, they also have an influence on police proceedings, albeit in a less direct manner. The police must make decisions on charges based on their expectations of the crown's willingness to accept and proceed with the charges in the court system.

At this level we deal with the legal offences of rape and attempted rape which were in effect at the time of the research. These data were collected prior to the enactment of the new sexual assault legislation which came into effect in January 1983. The new legislation replaces the former offences of rape, attempted rape and indecent assault with a three-tiered classification of sexual assault based on the degree of violence. Under the old law, if there was no vaginal penetration by a penis, a rape charge could not be laid.

Our intent was to examine the filtering system of sexual offences which were classified and handled as such by the criminal justice system. Obviously, the only way to achieve this was to obtain access to official police records. However, other offences, although sexual in nature, might not have been dealt with as sexual offences under the old legislation because of the extreme discretionary powers of the police and the limiting definitions under the old legislation. Consequently, to gather a sufficient number of cases with which to obtain detailed information for the following through of charges from the police level to final disposition, it became necessary to use the data that were available from an official source. We have utilized the broader term of sexual assault in the text of the monograph. Any reference to rape will relate to other studies cited prior to 1983 or where the former definition was associated with charges proceeding through the criminal justice system.

At the level of the victim, restricting ourselves to a legal definition of rape would have put severe limitations on the data that were available to us. The nature of the agency where the research was conducted allowed us access to victims of every type of sexual assault. Thus, it was possible to acquire a broad representation of all forms of sexual offences, irrespective of any legal definition. For this portion of the research, sexual assault has been defined as any sexual act perpetrated on a female against her will by means of physical force, intimidation, blackmail or authority.

The remainder of our discussion will be organized as follows: Chapter 1 describes the social context in which sexual assault occurs. Here it will be suggested that the occurrence of sexual assault can best be understood by viewing it in the context of a patriarchal society, where male aggression is fostered. Chapter 2 addresses the extent of under-reporting by sexual assault victims and the resulting myths and stereotypes that are perpetuated by the press and the legal system. Chapter 3 discusses the effects of socialization, including double standards of sexual behaviour, violence toward females and the resulting personal and legal responses. Chapters 4, 5 and 6 contain our research. Chapter 4 deals with the victim's response to sexual assault while chapters 5 and 6 address the response of the legal system and the role of the prosecutor, respectively. In chapter 7, we discuss the major features of the new sexual assault legislation and provide a preliminary analysis of the handling of sexual assault charges. Chapter 8 provides a synthesis of our research findings and ideas on the direction needed in further addressing the problem of sexual assault.

We undertook the writing this book with the intention of reaching a wide and diverse audience. It was important to us that the experience and knowledge we acquired as a result of our research would not sit on a shelf covered with a film of dust, retrieved occasionally, and purely for academic purposes. As such, we hope it will be read by students studying in the social sciences, sexual assault victims, those who counsel and provide support to victims, and the general public. To those who shared their experiences with us, this is a recognition of their courage and we hope they approve of our understanding and articulation of the dilemmas encountered by sexual assault victims.

SEXUAL ASSAULT:
The Dilemma of Disclosure, The Question of Conviction

CHAPTER I

The Social Context of Sexual Assault

THE widespread belief that women have made great strides toward equality with men is epitomized by the commercial cliché, "You've come a long way, baby!" It is a popular misconception that women have attained full freedom of choice and that authentic equality, based on ability and ambition, exists. Men are still at the helm of our economic, political, legal and religious institutions, making decisions that affect the lives of women.

The success of the women's movement in effecting social change through political pressure has been limited. Although advances have been made in the social, political and economic spheres, these changes have had little effect on the day-to-day lives of most women. The theoretical perspective that has guided and informed our inquiry on sexual assault focuses on the concept of "patriarchy" and its implications. Patriarchy refers to a gender-based differentiation of roles which becomes defined as a "natural" right of males to make decisions and monopolize positions of authority in society and its dominant institutions. This is not so much a deliberate, conscious effort on the part of males to control as it is a historically bound phenomenon in which women have been viewed as the property of men. Implicit in the concept of patriarchy is the notion of the power of males over females. If there is consensus in the assumption that sexual assault is a violent act involving power and dominance, then we must look at the differences in power between men and women in society.

The notion that women have achieved equal status in relation to men is contradicted by their continued subordination in virtually all spheres of social life. Men are still making the decisions that control the lives and the consciousness of women.

An important part of this reality and, hence, a real limitation is that women continue to occupy the traditional, low-paying, female-dominated occupations; that is, women's jobs are concentrated in the areas of sales, teaching, service, health and clerical work. In fact, their participation rate in these occupations rose from 71 percent in 1971 to 74 percent in 1981 (Statistics Canada 1984). The federal minister responsible for the status of women reported in 1986 that the wage gap between men and women for full-time work has persisted.

According to a 1987 Statistics Canada report, women currently earn 66 cents for every dollar earned by men, only a slight improvement over the 58 cents for every dollar figure they earned in 1967. This translates into average full-time salaries of $19,000 for women and $30,131 for men. Education is found to reduce the differential in wages, with a university degree resulting in women earning 19 percent less than their male counterparts. Although education may reduce the disparity somewhat, women in general continue to earn less than men.

Most part-time workers are women. Among the 1,477,000 part-time workers (13.5 percent of all workers) in the Canadian labour force in 1985, 71 percent were women. In general, part-time workers receive fewer benefits in terms of pensions, unionization, and job security and are paid less than full-time employees, even where there is no disparity in educational levels. While one-fifth of all part-time workers would prefer full-time employment, 70 percent of these dissatisfied workers are female (CACSW 1985a). Yet attitudes persist that women are taking jobs away from men and that this is a crucial factor in the Canadian unemployment situation. In fact, unemployment rates are consistently higher for women than men (NCW 1985).

These circumstances persist, in large part, because of the belief that women are secondary earners who are working, not out of economic necessity, but because of a so-called "boredom" with their domestic role. This idea, reinforced by the belief that the foremost obligation of women is within the domestic sphere, causes working women an enormous amount of self-doubt and guilt. If they have children, they bear the additional burden of being accused of maternal neglect. Delinquency is seldom attributed to working fathers. A Senate Committee report, "Child at Risk," claims that "maternal deprivation has a detrimental effect on character development" (1980, 33). It is a wretched double bind for women when nearly 61 percent of Canadian families would be living below the poverty line if wives and mothers were not contributing to the household income (CACSW 1985b). At the same time, although more men are claiming to be involved in household tasks, their participation remains relatively small. In a Gallup Poll taken in 1981, there was no significant change in the distribution of housework from an earlier poll taken in 1958 (Boyd 1984). Thus, while more women are required to work outside the home to supplement the family income, societal expectations still dictate that they retain the major responsibilities within the home.

These adversities are accompanied by the fact that most of the people who live at or below the poverty level are women. In 1984, according to a survey of Canadians by the National Council on Welfare, 43 percent of single women were found to be poor in contrast to 32 percent of single men. The gap widens with families headed by a female or male parent. Here, poverty levels for women are at 43 percent compared to those for men at 11 percent. The report describes Canada's elderly women as the most poverty stricken: 80 percent of women over the age of 65 are poor, compared to 29 percent of men (NCW 1985).

In political life, women are still found in the "housekeeping" tasks. With few exceptions, they participate in party organization and support functions at the citizen level, as opposed to acquiring true political authority. In 1983, for example, out of 1,018 members in federal and provincial politics, there were only 67 women, a representation of 6.6 percent. Federally, in the spring of 1988, they occupied 29 out of 282 seats in the House of Commons, with no representation from Manitoba, Saskatchewan, the Northwest Territories or the Atlantic provinces. This is clearly inadequate, as women constitute slightly over one-half of Canada's population. As a result, women retain minority status and have minimal input into the passing of laws, while men make the decisions that control the lives of women as well as their own.

Those women who do penetrate the male domain of politics and are elected members of government are often fielded into the area with the least power and status – the back-benches of government. Here women have little power, and primarily serve to raise regional or local concerns and to support the positions and decisions taken by the party's hierarchy. Positions of power in government are rarely accorded to women, whose portfolios usually include those that are less desirable and therefore less sought after by men.

A few women who have achieved some measure of political status have complained that voicing concern for women's issues causes them to be labelled "radical feminists" and results in the tendency for male colleagues to dismiss their opinions on that basis. This is the sort of disparagement that women find defeating and frustrating when they rise to a position of some power. The quandary they face is how to maintain political effectiveness in establishing rights for women and still retain the respect of male colleagues who are less concerned with human issues when they relate to women. Until female representation in politics is increased and there is a corresponding sensitivity to the rights and needs of women, there will continue to be little concern for realizing real equality and enshrining it in the law.

While parliament legislates, the laws are interpreted and applied by the legal profession. This has traditionally meant that laws made by men have been interpreted and applied by men. It appears that women are advancing in this institution, as shown by law school enrollments and bar admissions which indicate that more women are pursuing law degrees. But these gains are not found among practising lawyers. Statistics obtained from the provincial law societies list 7,049 women out of a total of 46,036 practising lawyers in Canada, as of July 1985 (Manitoba Bar Assn. 1986). This translates into female representation of only 15 percent in the legal profession.

The low status of women lawyers is reflected in an analysis of their placement within the legal hierarchy. At the top of the pyramid are judges, the large majority of whom are male. In 1979 there were 18 federally appointed female superior court judges out of a total of 630 in Canadian courtrooms (CACSW 1979). In 1985, female federal appointees rose from 18 to 28, a 36 percent increase in six years, but still only an insignificant proportion overall (Egan 1985). A 1982 survey of provincial judges in Canada (except Quebec which did not provide data) shows 22 women out of a total of 572 in the six provinces with at least minimal female representation (Zwarun 1985). As of 1988 there have been three women appointed to the Manitoba Court of Queen's Bench, with two assigned to the Family Division. A woman's place, even in the courtroom, is found to be in the realm of the family. Women's nature is assumed to be intrinsically bound up with domestic life and the courtroom is no exception. Of a total of 77 Manitoba judges in spring 1988, there were 6 women.

It is evident from the above data that women are still largely excluded from the major roles outside the home, relegated to domestic life and the responsibilities associated with the family. There is no denying that these duties are honourable and essential, but little status is bestowed upon those who perform them. Patriarchy does not provide choices. A society that places a high value on economic reward and achievement does not allow freedom to decide one's role. Free choice is illusionary when social expectations and social structure designate roles. Competition for high status and lucrative positions is limited to persons (mainly male) who can afford the time and dedication that is demanded of them. We are aware of the rising number of "superwomen" who manage, albeit with guilt, stress and exhaustion, both family and career. But major advances in the economic and political spheres cannot be achieved with a half-time commitment. It is apparent that men have had the freedom to pursue power and claim access to most of the resources that perpetuate their power, because of a notable biological difference: they cannot give birth to children! While the dictionary defines the term parent as a mother or father, parenting is mainly performed by the child-bearer – the mother.

Although child-bearing is a biological fact associated with women, the assignment of child-rearing has been socially designated to females. One of the major ways in which patriarchy is perpetuated is through the existence of the traditional nuclear family, consisting of a father, mother and children. The role of the female as wife and mother within this framework involves the provision of domestic labour and sexual services, as well as the reproduction and care of children. These services are provided for men and are controlled by men. This work differs substantially from paid male labour in the public sphere, as women provide these services for social, not financial, rewards. Male control of women's labour (production/reproduction) enhances their dominant position and maintains women in a dependent role.

The preparation of the sexes for their respective roles in a society dominated by a male power structure is accomplished through gender-based socialization. The most reliable predictor of future behaviour is likely the assignment of gender at birth. It is the categorization of expectations that accompany being "male" or "female" that will define the path of the socialized person. In general, females are encouraged to be nurturing, deferring and dependent, while males are taught to be aggressive, strong and independent. Such pre-defined behavioural traits become a blueprint for what is considered "normal" behaviour. Males and females are treated differently, are subject to differing expectations, and get rewarded for responding appropriately. That is the way the world unfolds for each human as they learn the norms of society. In this way, our reality and our world are socially constructed and we learn to interpret our experiences according to a prescribed frame of reference.

One of the obvious vehicles for perpetuating the prevalent image of males and females is the media. Given the pervasiveness of its influence, the media plays a crucial role in socialization. Sex-role stereotyping is actually a technique which is purposely used by advertisers in the media to create an idealized image of reality (Supply and Services Canada 1982). Not only are adults having their harmful and inaccurate beliefs validated, but children are being indoctrinated and absorbed into patriarchal society. Relatively few attempts have been made to reverse roles and balance the portrayal of males and females and these have been insufficient to ward off the cumulative effects of yet another male-dominated institution.

The roles we enact, then, are socially created and reflect accepted patterns of behaviour in society. For example, in Canadian society, as in others, it is appropriate for females to defer to males. This "norm" is supported by the social structure through, for example, the family and the legal system, so that learning through interaction in society is supported and perpetuated by its institutions.

Organized religion, another major social institution, offers a system of beliefs and values irreconcilable with the principle of women's equality. Therefore changes to improve the status of women are inhibited by religious beliefs which are culturally bound and only applicable to the historical context of their origin. Portrayal of the deity as male and the ideology of male supremacy in the nuclear family perpetuates restrictive gender roles. This is not surprising, since religious laws, like secular laws, have been written, interpreted and primarily enforced by men. This can be seen in the way that churches still retain control over women's bodies with women often having little or no voice in matters pertaining to birth control and abortion.

We have provided an examination of institutions and the power base in society in an attempt to understand the social context in which sexual assault occurs. Institutional inequality and rigid roles based on gender maintain and perpetuate the inferior status of females. The traditional definition of female behaviour as subordinate has been strengthened by the training we give our female children to be passive and nurturant. Male superiority, on the other hand, has been enhanced by the way we train male children to be aggressive and to succeed in the economic and political spheres. This extends to their interpersonal relationships with females. Male sexuality is linked to the role of aggressor and some degree of force or coercion is acceptable; importance is placed on the end result, reaching an objective. There is sufficient evidence now that assures us that sexual assault is not motivated by uncontrollable sexual desire. Sexual assault has been exposed as a violent offence involving power and domination (Brownmiller 1975; Clark and Lewis 1977). Whether females are accosted on the street, harassed in the workplace, or fondled at home by their fathers, there is one common theme – an imbalance of power in which violence is implicit. Sexual exploitation, in any form, exemplifies the vulnerability of females because it involves acts that are primarily directed at females in a male dominated society. As such, it is a method by which males can exert control over females in an extreme form along a continuum of male aggressiveness.

CHAPTER II

Understanding Sexual Assault

THE EXTENT OF THE PROBLEM

ONE of the primary obstacles in viewing sexual assault as a significant social problem has been the absence of accurate information on its occurrence. It is a crime that is grossly under-reported. Since it is clear that statistics do not reflect the actual incidence of the crime, it has been impossible to view the severity and extent of the problem in a realistic light. Our work, which examines incidents reported to a crisis centre as well as to the legal system, supplements official statistics by providing information on assaults that have not necessarily been reported to the police. An examination of the criteria differentiating women who make official reports from those who attempt to deal with the assaults in other ways shows that unreported cases are not necessarily comparable to those reported. As stated by Clark and Lewis, "We cannot hope to have anything like a complete picture of rape until all victims are willing to report the crime" (1977, 41).

A victimization survey of 551 women in Winnipeg revealed that one out of every four females had been sexually victimized at some point in her life (Brickman et al. 1980). If this proportion holds for the rest of the country as well, then just over 3 million Canadian women are, or will be victims of sexual assaults. The victimization survey, while more representative than official statistics, nonetheless is not comprehensive and reflects rates based on the sample used. Moreover, it should not be assumed that all the respondents would admit having been sexually assaulted. For the victim who has never disclosed the incident, it might be easier to deny it happened than to allow the stigma and emotional pain associated with the offence to surface. The result is that the least conservative estimates of sexual assault are probably the most representative in gauging its incidence.

PERPETUATION OF MYTHS BY THE PRESS AND THE LEGAL SYSTEM

There is a double standard of sexual behaviour for males and females which is maintained by popular myths. Females are expected to behave in a "virtuous" manner and are condemned for having sexual desires. Males, on the other hand are perceived as "naturally sexual" and are assumed to be unable to control themselves once they have become aroused. It is a common belief that a woman who has been assaulted may have been the cause of her own victimization by behaving in a "promiscuous" manner – a classic example of "blaming the victim" (see Ryan 1974).

The idea that the sexual revolution of the 1960s and 1970s brought about a change in these attitudes is perhaps the most pervasive myth of all. With the onset of the so-called "new morality" it was believed that women were finally entitled to their sexual freedom. Women were being encouraged to be sexually expressive and free from guilt. These ideas were popularized by the media, but society in general still held fast to the old stereotypes. So while women were trying to become less inhibited, they were still feeling guilty. To this day, there are double standards of sexual freedom for women and men.

The persistence of myths and stereotypes is well illustrated by statements made by the media, police, attorneys and judges. The following account describes a case which commanded considerable attention from the media and mobilized a city-wide program to apprehend a "legitimate" assailant. The view that the victim could in no way be blameworthy is obvious in the description of her activity at the time of the assault: "At three in the afternoon, a 22-year-old woman was walking home. She was pushing her 20-month-old daughter in a stroller and was on a path...crossing a field.... There was a male walking behind her. He grabbed her and forced her into some nearby bushes. He began choking her and forcibly removing her clothing. The baby began to cry. The mother was struggling...." (*Winnipeg Free Press* Oct. 1984). In addition, the writer inserts his own opinion as he begins the article with the comment: "It was mid-afternoon on a weekday, an unlikely time for an attempted rape." He also suggests that, "Police found the circumstances of the daylight attack on a young mother were good reasons for making it...crime of the week."

This case is a conspicuous contrast to the next report. Consider the obvious value judgments being made despite the fact that in both cases a woman has been assaulted. "At about 2 a.m. Sunday a 20-year-old woman was about to enter her apartment block when two men approached her and invited her to a party. She agreed to accompany them but when they arrived at an apartment she found there was no party. She attempted to leave twice but accepted a drink from the men...." (*Winnipeg Free Press* Dec. 1984). This story was contained in a single article describing several different sexual assaults, including attacks on a "deaf woman" and a "61-year-old woman". Of the four assaults reported, the attack on the 20-year-old woman was deemed the one worthy of embellishment. Emphasizing the fact that the woman accepted an invitation from two strangers at 2:00 a.m. and focussing on her acceptance of a drink suggests to the reader that the victim was deserving of her fate. By blaming the victim, the perpetrators have been relieved of responsibility for their conduct. The previous account of a woman fulfilling the most traditional of roles, along with the imagery of her crying baby conjures up a portrait of a woman deserving of protection. The facts about both cases could have been presented more objectively, without comments on the victims' characteristics and activities.

The use of headlines by the media to attract attention can also serve to reinforce inaccurate views on sexual assault. The relationship between hitchhiking and sexual assault is distorted by a police official's comment that appeared as a newspaper heading: "Three young women learn painful hitchhiking lesson" (*Winnipeg Free Press* July 1982). The suggestion evident in the headline is that the victims suffered the due consequences of their own behaviour.

The attitude of the police to victims of sexual assault has been under attack by feminists and other concerned groups. Victims themselves most often report fear of police (and the courts) as a major reason not to report an assault (Solicitor General 1984, 10). This concern is justified when one considers that the police represent the initial contact with the criminal justice system. The police also have a great deal of discretionary power in deciding to proceed with an investigation; they are the first "judges" of whether or not, in their minds, a real assault took place. A statement made by a senior police officer that "spring fever" was to blame for a recent increase of sexual assaults (*Winnipeg Sun* April 1984) is indicative of the kind of attitude that reinforces harmful stereotypes and discourages women from reporting attacks. The suggestion that because women wear less clothing in spring, they inevitably excite normal unsuspecting males, perpetuates the idea that women provoke men into assaulting them.

Responsibility can be attributed to the police for intimidating victims of sexual assault with inaccurate statements like the following: "police walk a tightrope whenever someone cries rape" and "one in four reports are false" (*Winnipeg Sun* Nov. 1981). The expression "cries rape" has become a familiar cliché, alluding to deceit. The designation of a rape charge as "false" when it does not proceed through to the court and result in conviction is misleading. As our research demonstrates, there are many reasons why a complaint may not be pursued (such as an uncooperative victim or insufficient evidence), although an assault took place. The impression given by such statements is that women tend to lie and are untrustworthy.

Defence lawyers have routinely tried to benefit by drawing upon misconceptions and harmful stereotypes of female sexuality in defending rapists. At a Winnipeg rape trial in 1987 the defence lawyer attempted to undermine the victim's credibility with the following statements: "Your honor has seen many black eyes in the courtroom and does not consider those to be bodily harm. I submit it (the laceration) is even less than that. It's not as if he beat her up." The lawyer further stated that his client had no idea that the woman was a virgin. In another case, defence counsel for a 22-year-old man who assaulted a 13-year-old-girl in the basement of a high school suggested that his client "thought the complainant was someone he knew and would not object to his conduct." The judge, responding with humour at the expense of the victim said, "It is an odd way to say hello" (*Winnipeg Free Press* May 1982). In another story, a defence lawyer rationalizes the attack by a 26-year-old on a child of 6 by suggesting that his client was "sexually immature" (*Winnipeg Free Press* May 1983). Lawyers are notorious for using questionable tactics in courtrooms. Yet, the distrust is always directed at the victims.

Nor do crown attorneys resist negative stereotyping when presenting their cases to juries. The following attack on a woman who aided a motorist stuck in a ditch outside her home is described with poetic fervor by the crown attorney. The assault, he said was not "the case of some healthy, young lass walking brazenly...braless, clad in tight fitting shorts on a sunny Manitoba morn raising the passions of some hot-blooded youths. Rather, it involved a housewife playing a Good Samaritan role" (*Winnipeg Free Press* Sept. 1980). Evidently, the jury and judge were in agreement and the offender was sentenced to three years imprisonment after a half-day trial for attempted rape. Many perpetrators have been given shorter sentences for more violent attacks. Should we then assume that young women must walk around in heavy clothing during the summer in order to avoid sexual assault?

In the next case, note the qualifying adjectives used by a crown attorney in describing the attempted rape and beating of a woman: "To assault and attempt to rape an 82-year-old woman who was walking down the street with a bag of groceries in broad daylight...is a crime of utmost cowardice" (*Winnipeg Free Press* April 1979). The point to be made here is that the assault was a crime, but the impact of the statement is due to the age of the victim, the time of day and the victim's activities at the time of the assault.

Judges, who represent the height of legal knowledge and experience, have unfortunately not been exempt from relying on myths and misconceptions in exercising their legal powers in the system. Several comments offered by judges presiding over sexual assault cases are worthy of mention. The *Edmonton Journal* (Feb. 1982) contains two such quotes. The first case involves a 5-year-old female assaulted by her mother's live-in boyfriend. In sentencing the 24-year-old offender to a 90-day work release program, the judge explained: "I am satisfied we have an unusually sexually promiscuous young lady. And he (the defendant) did not know enough to refuse. No way do I believe (the man) initiated sexual contact." Perhaps the judge in question was a proponent of Dr. Spock's world-renowned child care book which warns against seductive females in the 3-to-5-year age range! (See Rush 1980.)

The second case concerns three boys aged 15 to 16 years who received no punishment for a sexual assault other than one of the boys being banned from his school for one year. The judge, in attempting to rationalize his decision on their attack of a 16-year-old female, stated in court: "This community is well-known to be sexually permissive. Too many women go around in provocative clothing. Should we punish a 15- or 16-year-old boy who reacts to it normally?"

Another court case reported in the *Winnipeg Free Press* (Jan. 1984) quotes a judge who sentenced a 20-year-old man to four years in prison for the rape of a 33-year-old woman: "One a scale of one to 10, I'd rate this about a two." The victim happened to be an exotic dancer on her way home from work. The crown attorney in objecting to the judge's assessment of the offence retorted in similar vein, using a rating scale: "It should be a seven or eight."

More recently a judge sentenced a 22-year-old offender to a 90-day jail term for the beating and sexual assault of a 27-year-old victim. The offender was allowed to serve his time on weekends. The judge rationalized the sentence by saying that the offender was from a good family and had learned his lesson. He further suggested that there was "no evidence of lasting emotional or psychological harm" even though it took two weeks for the victim to recover from bruises and cuts to her face (*Winnipeg Free Press* Jan. 1988). The judge clearly failed to understand the longer lasting emotional trauma.

THE VICTIM'S INTERNALIZATION OF GUILT

The under-representation of particular kinds of sexual assault in official statistics has also brought about a misunderstanding of the problem for the victim herself. Because of the prevalence of stereotypes, even victims may be unable to define an offence. The belief that only young, attractive, and perhaps careless females are assaulted causes them to define themselves within this context (because nice girls don't get raped). This contradicts the real facts about the offence. Small babies and elderly women are also victims of sexual assaults. Married women are attacked by their husbands and young girls are sexually abused by their fathers. The socialization of women is so powerful that regardless of circumstances, self-blame is inevitable. It should be mentioned here that no value judgment is being made regarding the comparative seriousness of assaults. Socializing at bars and hitching rides are activities engaged in by both men and women for purposes of recreation and transportation, respectively. Women who are sexually assaulted in those situations should not be accused of "asking for it."

LACK OF IMPETUS BY THE LEGAL SYSTEM

Clearly, the most harmful aspect of the under-reporting of sexual assault has been that we know little about those assaults which are not reported. This has two consequences: the perpetuation of assaults which are perceived to be "legitimate" and are the ones usually reported; and a lack of impetus by the criminal justice system to view sexual assault as a significant social problem meriting legal action. Conventional notions regarding male and female sexuality are extended to sexual assault offences. This results in a harrowing experience for all victims, even those females who are perceived as faultless, when attempting to gain redress through the legal system.

The low number of reported assaults conceals the actual nature of the offence on both a personal and institutional level. A vicious circle emerges whereby the stereotypes of "legitimate" victims and assaults are upheld by society and the legal system. The victim responds in kind by experiencing shame, guilt and fear, and this response limits use of the legal system as a means of justice for the offence committed.

CHAPTER III

The Effects of Socialization

WOMEN AS OBJECTS OF SEXUAL ENTERTAINMENT

IN a society where women can be bought on the street or viewed in pornographic magazines and films (bound, beaten and mutilated) for the enjoyment of men, a belief system has developed which says that this is how females should be treated. The image of the unwilling woman who is overpowered by a passionate man is a popular movie theme and one which provides implicit cultural approval for this type of sexual interaction. The impression derived from this aggressive–passive form of behaviour is that women want (or need) to be dominated.

The most destructive manifestation of the differing sexual roles for males and females is evident in the violence against women found in "sexual entertainment". Pornography and prostitution exist primarily because there is a male demand for them. There is an unrealistic connotation of glamour attached to the life of prostitutes and women in pornographic films. Yet, the sobering reality is that the great majority of these women work out of economic necessity, and many have suffered sexual abuse as children.

Several recent studies have examined the economics of prostitution. Researchers in Winnipeg discovered that, of 54 prostitutes interviewed, virtually all the respondents cited a need for money as the primary reason for entering prostitution (Elizabeth Fry Society 1985). Most were supporting another adult from their income (77 percent), and over half were supporting dependent children (54 percent). Of equal importance was the fact that a substantial proportion (88 percent) of the prostitutes interviewed reported instances of physical, sexual and verbal/emotional abuse as children. Of this group, nearly 70 percent had specifically experienced physical or sexual abuse. Without exception, those who suffered from sexual abuse recalled the abuser as someone they were close to as opposed to a stranger, with 95 percent of the sexual abusers identified as a blood or legal relative. Only 12 percent reported no abuse as a child.

The Fraser Commission on Pornography and Prostitution also provided some facts on prostitution in Canada. For example, the Vancouver study of prostitution (Lowman 1984) reported that one-third of the prostitutes interviewed had experienced family sexual abuse and more than two-thirds were victims of non-family sexual abuse. Among those who were still active, 84 percent stated that they would leave the profession if an alternative well-paying job were available to them. The Prairie Region component of the study (Lautt 1984) revealed that all the prostitutes cited money as the reason for entering prostitution.

In the Winnipeg study, the prostitutes were asked to identify what they disliked about working on the streets. The most common responses given were not liking the "johns" and the sexual act itself, along with the violence and harassment encountered on the job. Seventy-eight percent had experienced either physical or sexual assaults while one-half had been subjected to both forms of violence since they began prostituting. Almost all the women (94 percent) responded that they drank and used drugs. Their reasons for alcohol and drug use focused primarily on making their lives tolerable. Responses included: "Makes this job a little easier"; "Reality can be dulled"; and, "I can't work unless I'm drunk or high." One woman expressed her feelings in the following way: "It's hard to keep smiling and pretend you're interested in the men you're dealing with. Alcohol and drugs make it easier."

The experiences of women in pornography are similar to those of prostitutes. Personal accounts from women involved in pornography suggest that economic necessity is a definite factor leading to involvement in pornography. Physical and sexual violence are also present in the course of their work (see Lederer 1980; Lovelace 1980). This violence is very often intimated if not actually carried out in the course of producing pornographic material. The progression to pornography can be gradual, beginning with sexually suggestive photos to sexually explicit photos and finally pornographic pictures and films. In fact, the similarities between pornography and prostitution may well be more real than is apparent. One ex-pornographic model summed up the two occupations in the following manner: "A prostitute is just being more honest about what she's doing. A pornography model can fool herself and we did. We called what we were doing 'modeling' or 'acting'. Pornography models have the illusion that they're not hooking. It's called acting instead of sex. Or it's labeled 'simulated sex' – even sometimes when it's not simulated, it's called simulated. But it's all a form of rape because women who are involved in it don't know how to get out" (Lederer 1980, 64).

The condemnation of prostitution and women in such films is not intended to be moralistic or critical of erotica, which portrays consensual sexual relations between adults. Rather, the distinction occurs when these activities become degrading to women. Helen Lagino, in Lederer's book, *Take Back the Night*, provides a concise definition of degrading behaviour: "Behavior that is degrading or abusive includes physical harm or abuse, and physical or psychological coercion. In addition, behavior which ignores or devalues the real interests, desires and experiences of one or more participants in any way is degrading. Finally, that a person has chosen or consented to be harmed, abused or subjected to coercion does not alter the degrading character of such behavior" (1980, 29-30). In other words, prostitution and the depiction of women in films and magazines become destructive when women are degraded and abused for the purpose of entertainment.

On a societal level, violence directed toward women under the guise of enjoyment produces injurious consequences. First, it impedes healthy and equitable relationships between the sexes. It takes from women the human qualities, turning them into objects of sex, devoid of dignity and respect. Second, exposure to violence has been found to facilitate and encourage aggressive behaviour among those who view it.[1] The need to address the abuse of women in prostitution and pornography cannot be ignored. A society which allows this form of degradation cannot be left blameless for the violence directed toward all females in the threat of sexual assault.

1 In the United States the National Institute of Mental Health (1982) reviewed empirical research on the relationship between viewing violence on television and later aggressive behaviour. Donnerstein and Linz (1984) reviewed research on the connection between reading pornography and subsequent aggressive behaviour toward women.

THE INDIVIDUAL'S RESPONSE

As part of the pattern of sex role socialization, women internalize the ideology of sexual assault, which causes them to look for fault within themselves. A woman may question her own behaviour and appearance to assess what she has done to deserve an attack. In many cases, if there is little violence, or if she knows her assailant, a woman may not identify herself as a victim of sexual assault (Clark and Lewis 1977). Since aggression and brutality are commonplace to many women in their relationships, a sexual assault may be just a step further along a continuum of violence.

In contrast, it is not unusual for some men to believe they have been unfairly accused when they overpower women sexually because sexual conquest is part of the patriarchal ideology. Within this context, power and dominance are the key elements. Several researchers studying offenders found no evidence to suggest that men assault because of sexual arousal (Wilson and Nias 1976; Wilson 1978; Groth 1979). As long as women continue to accept responsibility for being assaulted, offenders will continue to rationalize or excuse their own behaviour. Nicholas Groth clearly stated the truth about sexual assault: "...all nonconsenting sexual encounters are assaults" (1979, 2). Only when this statement is fully understood and accepted by those in positions of responsibility in our legal system will assailants be forced to accept responsibility for their acts of aggression.

Since the majority of sexual assaults take place between persons who are, at the very least, acquainted and more often are intimately known to each other, it is misleading to consider that it is the behaviour of females being out alone at night, dressing provocatively, or hitchhiking that causes sexual assaults to occur. Assaults between strangers are comparatively rare and disguise the more subtle and private forms of abuse that are kept hidden. Sexual assault victims are extremely isolated and, rather than seeing themselves in the larger social context, they feel as though they are the only victims in their circumstances. In reality, sexual assault is much more common than official statistics indicate. It must be recognized that the issue to consider is not women's behaviour, but the more pervasive combination of male domination and female submissiveness rooted in the patriarchal structure of society that leads to the violence.

THE LEGAL RESPONSE

The repercussions of differing expectations for male and female behaviour are illustrated in the legal response to sexual assault. In conjunction with societal attitudes, both the law and the criminal justice system emerge as being biased against the victim. There are three legal issues which determine the point at which a sexual assault report may be filtered out of the legal system: consent, corroboration and the character of the victim.

Consent

The notion of consent, in legal terms, refers to resistance. Resistance must be sufficient to prove lack of consent. The determination of nonconsent is essentially a subjective one, resulting in arbitrary decisions being made by members of the criminal justice system. They determine whether or not the resistance offered by the victim is sufficient to cause the attack to be labelled as a sexual assault. Circumstances of attacks differ and each victim will react individually to the incident. Her behaviour cannot be prescribed by anyone other than herself. In a crisis situation, this may be particularly significant since the ability of an individual to think clearly, make rational decisions or recall details may be impaired.

A comparison of the behaviour of victims in other violent crimes underlines the exceptional nature of the consent standard for sexual assault cases. Not only are robbery victims encouraged to comply with their assailants, but research indicates that they usually do not offer any resistance. A study of robbery victims by Conklin (1972) revealed that only one in ten offered resistance either by refusal or force. In sexual assault cases as well, police warn victims not to resist. Yet at the same time, the onus is on the victim to prevent the offence from occurring.

Clark and Lewis contest the appropriateness of the issue of consent: "Only in the case of sexual transactions do we refuse to acknowledge that the relevant issue is the offender's behaviour rather than the victim's state of mind" (1977, 164). The victim is placed in the precarious position of having to prove that her reaction was sufficient to establish nonconsent. The telltale signs of nonconsent then become the physical injuries, even though cases of forced consent in the presence of threats (either verbal or by use of a weapon) are no less intimidating to the victim.

Corroboration

The corroboration requirement, in general, relates to testimony or evidence that is provided by anyone other than the victim of a crime. Such evidence is significant in the successful prosecution of sexual assault cases and refers to evidentiary factors independent of the victim's account of the crime. Corroboration is supplied by the testimony of witnesses or through circumstantial evidence. The general components of corroborative evidence include the following: the victim's injuries, medical evidence and testimony, the promptness of the complaint to the police (or other witness), the emotional condition of the victim, lack of motive to falsify and the presence of semen or blood on the clothing of the victim and accused. It is noteworthy that more than half of the components mentioned are related to the victim's behaviour and condition. Although questions may be directed at the victim on the corroborative evidence, the basis of the evidence will be given by others: namely, police officers and medical personnel.

The importance of corroborative evidence was underlined by a requirement prior to 1976 that instructed judges to warn juries of the danger in convicting a defendant without any corroborative evidence apart from the victim's testimony. The warning to the jury was required for no other criminal charges. A 1976 Criminal Code amendment abolished the requirement, but until the legislation on sexual assault was revised in 1983, judges continued to have discretion in presenting the cautionary instruction to juries. Although this practice has been discontinued, the credibility of the complainant is still bolstered by corroborative evidence. An illustration of this point is found in a case cited in *Criminal Reports*: "The trial judge accepted the evidence of the girl, which although corroboration was not necessary, was corroborated by the medical evidence of bruises to the right breast" (1984, 40, 284).

Implicit in this notion is the fear that women will make false accusations against innocent men. The motives attributed to fabricated reports include guilt, protection of an innocent party, hatred, revenge, blackmail and notoriety. These assumptions, however, disregard both the victim's apprehension about reporting and the legal rules and methods of investigation which effectively minimize the possibility of deceit.

Character and Status of the Victim

The character and status of the victim is another issue that influences the extent to which a sexual assault is prosecuted. According to Clark and Lewis, "Because rape is a crime against property, its key legal element is the status and character of the victim; that is, the judgment of wrongdoing depends upon the nature of the property in question". They continue: "It is hardly surprising, therefore, that virgins and chaste wives are the most highly protected forms of sexual property within the system, and that these are the women which the law perceived as credible...victims" (1977, 117).

An illustration of such values is expressed by a Winnipeg judge in sentencing a defendant to a lengthier than usual sentence of seven years: "What we have here is a brutal rape with violence on an innocent girl, a 15-year-old virgin. He has probably affected her life for her lifetime" (*Winnipeg Sun* July 1982). The offender was further described as "without merit as a human being". The judge's obvious show of contempt is for the attack on a virgin who is deserving of the court's protection, and he has thereby deemed the offence worthy of extreme punishment. The description of the victim as "innocent" implicitly suggests that if she were not a virgin, she would be less than innocent (perhaps guilty) of her fate. If this were so, what protection would she deserve?

Even with restrictions on the questioning of a victim as to her character and past sexual experiences with other men, certain questions may still be raised. An amendment to the Canadian Criminal Code, effective in 1976, required advance notice in writing for any questions regarding the past sexual conduct of the victim with someone other than the accused. The judge then decided during an *in-camera*[2] hearing whether the evidence was "necessary for a just determination of the case". The major drawback was that the decision on such questioning was left to the discretion of the presiding judge. Consequently, the reform leaves open the possibility of allowing the questioning of each victim. This procedure, while further restricted, continues under the 1983 legislation (see chapter 6).

The double standard in the law which concentrates solely on the character of the victim, as opposed to the actions of the defendant who is being tried, may be further aided by a subconscious adherence of the public at large to a double standard of sexual behaviour for men and women. Gager and Schurr elaborate: "Defense attorneys have routinely benefited from this fact, deliberately introducing questions which they know are not permitted merely to plant suspicion against the victim in the minds of judge and jury. Even if the prosecutor is on his toes and quickly voices objection, sustained by the judge, the damage is done, the victim is made suspect; her 'morality' rather than the accused's behavior becomes a central issue" (1976, 156-57). The unreasonable relationship is drawn between the victim's prior sexual activities, whether factual or intimated by defence counsel, and the likelihood that she would have consented to the offence

2 An in-camera hearing is a private consultation between the judge and legal counsel, which excludes the jury and general public from the courtroom.

in question. Within this context, the perceived character and status of the victim exert considerable influence on the outcome of the charges.

The legal issues that have been examined here indicate that the victim, rather than the defendant, may be put on trial. Carrow states further: "In fact, there is evidence to suggest that rather than allowing false complaints to go to trial, this (trial) process tends to discourage many legitimate complaints" (1980, 175).

The foregoing discussion emphasizes the strength of socialization in contributing to the objectification and secondary status of females. As illustrated, some of the more extreme manifestations of violence against women are seen in pornography, prostitution and sexual assault. The personal and legal responses to sexual assault serve to support the status quo and perpetuate the effects of socialization.

CHAPTER IV

The Response of the Victim

EVERY victim of a sexual assault is faced with the dilemma of disclosure. Should she report the assault? Whom can she trust? Who will believe her? Her decision is based on social factors in which the circumstances and effects of the incident, along with other facets of the her life experience, must be examined. Not all victims react the same way in seemingly similar circumstances. Consequently, how this dilemma is resolved must be determined by factors other than the assault itself.

METHODOLOGY

Access to this sort of information can come only from victims. By using the victim's perception of her victimization as well as her manifest act of disclosure, we believed that we could objectively define the relevant factors that would lead a victim to report the assault to the police. In other words, the victim's description of the assault and her actual response of reporting it to the police or dealing with it in some other way would provide us with subjective data (socialization) and hard data (reporting).

With this intention, we approached Klinic, a Community Health Centre based in Winnipeg. Klinic is the only agency of its kind in the province, serving an urban community of 600,000. The agency's sexual assault program offers 24-hour service, providing information, advocacy, support and counselling to victims, via telephone or personal contact with counsellors.

Initially, our request for access to victims and files was regarded with some concern by the clinical director and other agency personnel. Eventually, after considerable negotiation, Klinic granted access with two stipulations. The first was that the researcher collecting the data undergo a training program by the agency as a sexual assault counsellor. The agency wanted the interviewer to be informed about and sensitive to the issue of sexual assault and to be equipped to deal with potential traumatic effects resulting from an interview. The second requirement was that absolute confidentiality of names and identifying information was to be respected. Once these issues were resolved, the study was approved.

Interviewing did not begin immediately after the training was concluded. Before formulating the questionnaire the researcher needed some experience in the "field" in order to be aware of the types of questions that should be asked. This process, however, took much longer than anticipated. The exposure to women who had undergone every sort of violence imaginable opened up a new world for the naive researcher. Some of the women were recent victims, and of those several turned to the agency immediately after an assault. They called from phone booths and hospitals, or just appeared at Klinic, still in shock following an attack. A large number of victims were "survivors," women who were dealing with assaults from the past, possibly never revealed to anyone before. No longer academic theory and discourse, this was reality – the horrifying details of torture, mutilation and psychological terror suffered by women at the hands of other human beings.

DESCRIPTION OF THE SAMPLE

Most of the 75 victims selected for the study came to Klinic for sexual assault counselling, but some initially contacted the agency for other problems such as depression or suicidal tendencies. These clients were often recognized by crisis workers to be victims of sexual assault and were thus referred to the sexual assault program.

The occupational status of the victims or victims' families ranged from unskilled labour (29 percent) to management and professionals (27 percent), with 35 percent falling between the extremes of the occupational scale. The remaining 9 percent were unemployed or could not be classified by the scale we used (Blishen 1967). This evidence contradicts the popular belief that sexual assault is predominantly associated with low social status. It was found that women with high occupational status were more likely to report an assault than were those with lower status. This was consistent with Bart's findings (1975), which indicated that women with professional occupations tended to report assault more often than did other women. This may be because professional women are more likely to be believed by the police (Clark and Lewis 1977) or because they are likely to be better informed of their rights.

Well over half of the victims (59 percent) were under 19 at the time of the offence. Thirty percent were in their twenties and only 11 percent were over 30. Age distribution was similar in Schram's and Meyer's research (1978; 1979). Brickman et al. (1980) in the Winnipeg Rape Incidence Survey found that more than half of the respondents reported being under 17 at the time of their assaults. The results of this study showed that reporting increased with age. These findings were also consistent with those of Bart (1975).

More than three-quarters of the victims in the study were single when they were assaulted, while 12 percent were divorced or widowed and 9 percent were married or living as married. Meyer's findings were identical to these. Clark and Lewis (1977) indicated that 54 percent of their sample were single, 17 percent were separated or divorced and 20 percent were married or living as married. Some of the differences between the findings of Clark and Lewis and those of the present study are likely due to the fact that girls under 14 were not included in their study.

The majority of the sample in this study were Caucasian women; thirteen percent were Asian, Native Indian or Métis. This distribution may not, however, reflect actual victimization patterns. Kilpatrick, Veronen and Resick (1979) conducted a study at a rape crisis centre in South Carolina and found that despite the large Black population, 61 percent of the respondents were Caucasian, while only 37 percent were Black. Crisis centres have typically been staffed by white middle class women, and poor women or women of other races may be less likely to seek help from these agencies.

RESULTS

In assessing the social stimuli that would ostensibly influence a victim's decision to report a sexual assault to the police, several factors were considered: the victim's attribution of blame; the nature of the response of the first person informed; the background experience of the victim (violence, incest); the relationship between the victim and the offender; the extent of injury to the victim; the-amount of resistance by the victim; the victim's attitude to the police. Each of these factors was used to formulate propositions which could be tested with the data and each will be discussed individually.

Victim's Attribution of Blame

Unlike other crimes, there is a stigma attached to being a victim of a "sexual crime". A victim is often considered responsible for causing the assault by placing herself in a vulnerable situation or by behaving irresponsibly and "asking for it". Historically, women have been delegated the responsibility of controlling men's sexual behaviour as well as their own (Brownmiller 1975). Consequently, women who have been assaulted believe they must be accountable. Child and incest victims are also guilt-ridden. In these cases, an adult in authority uses power to gain compliance. Self-condemnation builds up because these victims can do nothing to stop the activity. Since most victims hold themselves to some extent responsible for being sexually assaulted and since society is known to condemn victims, it is not unlikely that they will refrain from reporting the assault. This leads to the first proposition: *The more blame a victim attributes to herself, the less likely she is to report a sexual assault to the police.*

Our results in Table I (factor 1) show that, of the victims who reported, those who blamed themselves for the assault (31 percent) were less likely to report the incident than were those who felt they shared blame with the offender (48 percent). Victims were most likely to report when they believed the assailant was totally responsible (90 percent). It is instructive to note that almost all respondents (87 percent) believed they were entirely or partly to blame for the offence.

TABLE I
Factors Influencing Victim's Decision to Report Sexual Assault to Police

	Reported to Police		
Factor	Yes (%)	No (%)	(N)
1. Victim's attribution of blame			
self	31	69	(42)
shared	48	52	(23)
assailant	90	10	(10)
2. Nature of response of first person told			
supportive	47	53	(51)
non-supportive	21	79	(19)
3. Violence in victim's background			
yes	41	59	(46)
no	48	52	(29)
4. Previous sexual assault			
yes	36	64	(33)
no	48	52	(40)
5. Victim-offender relationship			
stranger	75	25	(16)
casually known	47	53	(17)
familiarly known	43	57	(14)
family	25	75	(28)
6. Injury to victim			
yes	68	32	(25)
no	32	68	(50)
7. Resistance by victim			
yes	47	53	(34)
no	42	58	(40)
8. Victim's opinion of police			
negative	39	61	(28)
neutral	30	70	(20)
positive	59	41	(27)

As Wilson (1978) indicated in his research, the predominant effects experienced by sexual assault victims were feelings of "degradation, humiliation, and self-incrimination". This was blatantly evident during the interviewing, and the results demonstrate that these feelings did influence reporting behaviour.

One of the victims who did not report being assaulted explained that her boyfriend had been "taking advantage" of her, spending her money and "cheating". She had decided to end the relationship and refused to see him. One night he knocked on the door, pleading for a chance to speak to her. When she unlocked the door, he grabbed her and began tearing at her clothes. As she cried and pleaded, he dragged her into the bedroom, sexually assaulted her and walked out, leaving her on the bed shaken. During the interview, she said, "After he left me, I laid there for a long time, not believing what had happened. I wondered if my blouse had been too revealing or if I had just hurt him so much that he had to hurt me back. Maybe I made him remember being rejected by his mother". At no time did it occur to this woman that the responsibility for the attack should have been solely attributed to the offender.

Another striking example of self-blame was disclosed during an interview with a woman who had responded to a request for directions while walking home from the library one afternoon. A male stopped his car and called out to her, indicating that he was looking for a street that she recognized as being only two blocks away. She walked over to the car to assist him and he pointed a gun at her, ordering her to get into the car. She was blindfolded and taken to a place where she was sexually assaulted and tortured for the next fifteen hours. This assault, obviously an extreme of the media stereotype, was reported directly to the police. The victim, however, maintained that the fault was hers because she "should have known better than to speak to a stranger."

Nature of Response from First Person Informed

Notman and Nadelson (1980) point out that the reaction of significant others is an important aspect of how a victim reacts to an assault. Accordingly, it follows that this is a vital issue when a victim must decide whether or not to make a report. The sexual assault victim has been socialized to feel guilty, regardless of the circumstances of the offence. Vulnerability to these emotions is reinforced by negative attitudes and judgments of those with whom she has an emotional attachment. For instance, husbands may view the assault as a form of adultery, while parents may respond with anger because they feel guilty and helpless for having been unable to protect the victim. Children and incest victims often get no support from their families and are subject to disbelief or accusations. Although a supportive response does not eradicate the humiliation, it can ease the burden of guilt for the victim. If a response reinforces the guilt and shame already felt by most sexual assault victims, it is not likely that an attempt will be made to seek justice from the legal system. This leads to the second proposition: *A victim will more likely report a sexual assault to the police if a supportive response has been given by the first person informed of the attack.*

As shown in Table I (factor 2), of the victims who reported, those who received a supportive response from the first person they told (47 percent) were more likely to report the offence than those who received a nonsupportive response (21 percent). Thus, the support a victim receives initially after an assault is a factor which does influence victim reporting.

One young victim talked about being awakened and assaulted by a stranger while on summer vacation. She had been sleeping with her dog in a tent near her parents' trailer because the trailer was too small to accommodate the family and the dog. Her mother angrily declared that it was her own fault because she had insisted on taking her dog. She was told, "Next time you'll know better!" No report was made in this case by parents or victim.

In another case, a woman decided to seek counselling after several attempts to commit suicide. She recalled her mother walking into her bedroom while her father was in the process of molesting her. The memory she retained was, "My mother started screaming and became hysterical. I always thought I had done something wrong." Subsequent assaults reinforced her guilt.

Many victims who had experienced support and sympathy from the first person they told of an assault said that it helped to diminish some of the guilt they were feeling. One victim described a series of clandestine visits from her stepfather that progressed from sexual touching to intercourse. He had always warned that she would be blamed if anyone found out. She finally decided to run away from home, but before leaving, told her sister about the assaults. To her surprise, she discovered that her sister had also been enduring these violations. They held each other and cried, feeling somewhat relieved that they were not alone. Together they informed their mother and subsequently the police were notified. She said, "It was so important to be believed. I always thought it happened because of something I was doing. I felt dirty and ashamed.

When my sister told me it happened to her, I started to understand."

Background Experience of Victim

Groth has said that "many women have such a low sense of self-worth that they don't feel they can expect to be treated as equal, worthy people" (1979, 81). To the extent that females are socialized in their feminine role as the property of males, they are limited in their view of personal freedom. Some women have been trained to perceive violence as normal and may learn at an early age to submit to being sexually used: "Children who have been sexually abused and children and women who have been raped have their concepts of themselves as sex objects strengthened" (Hirsch 1981, 62). Kinnon reported that previous assaults led to further victimization, predisposing women to feel like they were "damaged goods," making them believe they were "unworthy of respect" (1981, 7). An important part of the socialization of women is interpreting violence and control as normal interaction between males and females. If a woman has always been subjected to physical or sexual abuse, she will be more likely to define an aggressive situation as normal. The expectations and definitions that women have internalized serve to maintain the secrecy surrounding sexual assault. Therefore, it is our expectation that reporting a sexual assault is contingent on factors relating to the individual's experience, which affects her perception of how she defines the assault. The third proposition thus states: *A victim will be less likely to report a sexual assault to the police if she has a history of being subjected to violence.*

We found that victims who had been subjected to past violence were somewhat less likely to report an assault

(Table I, factor 3). Of the women who reported, 41 percent said they had experienced violence in the past, while 48 percent had not. Of those who had suffered previous sexual assaults (Table I, factor 4), 36 percent reported the current offence to the police, compared to 48 percent who had not been sexually assaulted before. The fact that some women have learned to expect aggression or forced sex during their lifetime was evident from the interviews. For these women, a sexual assault was merely another incident along a continuum of violence.

One respondent who had never officially reported an assault told of a series of abusive relationships and sexual assaults throughout her life. When asked about violence in her background, she replied, "Not really. My parents punished me, but they weren't what I would call violent. They used to make me keep hot pepper sauce in my mouth for an hour and they'd hit me with a metal belt. My counsellor said that was violence, but I never had anything to compare it with."

Another woman who dismissed the option of reporting an assault, described a father who was inclined to "blow up" without any warning. "He often beat me with a belt until I was black and blue and several times he cut me with a knife. I never thought that treatment was extraordinary. I thought that was what happened to bad people."

Yet another nonreporting victim described the punishment she and her sisters received for being "bad". "My father used to make us kneel down without shirts and then he hit us across our backs with his razor-strop" (a leather band used by barbers for sharpening razors).

Forty-six victims told of varying degrees of cruelty that they had suffered at the hands of parents, step-parents, etc. The least dramatic were comments such as, "Oh, my parents knocked me around a little" or "My father beat my mother and they both beat me and my brothers."

Among the women who said they were victims of incest, many had never thought about reporting as an option. "I didn't know I had any rights, I was only a kid" or "I never thought of it" were replies often heard.

One of the respondents recalled her experience: "My father used to come into our bedroom at night and point to one of us. That meant it was our turn and we knew what was expected of us. We each tried to sleep farthest from the door because the one closest seemed to get picked most often."

Another woman described being kept a prisoner by her father for twenty years. "My stepmother knew what was happening, but she didn't do anything, so I never told anyone." Still another case involved a second generation, "My grandfather would always come to my bed when I slept there. He used to touch me and masturbate on me. I always felt so badly, but I didn't know what to do."

Research points to the possibility that one in four female children could be subject to some sort of encounter before the age of 14 (Russell 1984) and that about 80 percent of these assaults are committed by a male relative or close family friend (Rush 1980). This early socialization teaches children to accept sexual assault as normal. The results of this study offer some evidence that the acquired self-concept continues long after the incest has ceased.

Relationship Between Victim and Offender

Many sources have indicated that the victim who knows the offender experiences more self-blame than if the attack was perpetrated by a stranger (Brodyaga et al., 1975).

If self-blame is a factor that inhibits women from reporting an assault (proposition 1), then the relationship between the offender and the victim is significant. An attack by a stranger fits the public image of a "real" assault. As the relationship between victim and offender becomes closer, defining the assault as a criminal offence becomes more difficult. Furthermore, interpreting sexual assault as an act of passion, rather than what it is – an expression of power and hostility – shifts the responsibility for the act from the offender to the victim. Depending on whether he is a former lover, friend, acquaintance, stranger, or a family member, the victim of a sexual assault will usually experience varying degrees of reluctance to report. The fourth proposition states: *Police reporting will differ according to the degree of familiarity between a victim and offender, with strangers being reported most often.*

We found that strangers were the most likely to be reported (75 percent), while family members were the least reported (25 percent). See Table I (factor 5) for distribution. Although the smallest percentage of offences reported to the police were committed by family members, they constituted the greatest number of offenders of any of the four relationship categories in the study.

Previous researchers have suggested that sexual assaults by strangers are more likely to be reported because these assaults reflect cultural assumptions and are more readily perceived as authentic by others as well as by the victim herself. One item on the questionnaire asked women why they had decided not to report an assault. Most respondents who knew the offenders did not consider reporting to be a legitimate alternative because the relationships often disguised the culpability of the offenders. As self-blame has been found to inhibit reporting, it follows than an offence is less likely to be reported if it does not fit the stereotypical notion of what women themselves have been socialized to believe. Replies such as, "The police wouldn't care," "I didn't think it was a police matter," "I didn't think I would be believed," were typical of the 60 percent who did not report and whose assailants were categorized as closely related (i.e. familiar and family). Although research suggests that the most prevalent type of assaults are those which occur between people who know each other, they are the most underreported (Lott et al. 1982).

Extent of Injury to Victim

Skelton and Burkhart (1980) found that the degree of force used was an important factor in the decision to report a rape. A victim who is injured finds it easier to define the attack according to the "social stereotype" of an authentic assault, thus acting to diminish guilt. The assumption that a crime of violence must be accompanied by injuries, communicates the message that if sexual assault is a violent crime and there are no injuries sustained, there must not have been a sexual assault. Therefore, a victim without injury may fear that it will be hopeless to attempt to prove that a crime took place, and this is likely to deter her from reporting. The fifth proposition states: *Police reporting will differ according to the degree of injury sustained by the victim, with greater injury being positively related to reporting.*

Table I (factor 6) demonstrates that respondents were twice as likely to report an assault to the police if they sustained visible injury (68 percent) than if they suffered less perceptible harm (32 percent). Notably, of all victims who were injured (33 percent of the total sample), 68 percent reported the offence.

An assault that results in visible injury conforms to the acceptable social criterion of a violent crime. Therefore, injury may permit a victim to more easily define a sexual assault as an illegal act. As one victim stated, "I didn't think there was any sense in reporting it. I had no injuries...who would believe me?" Another woman said, "I knew it would be my word against his. I wasn't even sure it was a crime."

Amount of Resistance by Victim

Although police generally advise women not to resist an attack in order to avoid serious injury or death, Curtis (1974) has suggested that physical resistance results in less emotional trauma for the victim. Weis and Borges (1973) have proposed an inverse relationship between greater trauma and the likelihood of reporting a sexual assault to the police. This leads to the sixth proposition which states: *Police reporting will differ according to the degree of resistance exhibited by the victim, with greater resistance being positively related to reporting.*

Resistance showed a slight positive correlation to reporting (see Table I, factor 7). Of those victims who did resist, 47 percent reported the offence as compared to 42 percent who did not resist.

Women are expected to protect themselves from sexual assault, but their resistance is often seen as teasing or an expression of a desire to be overcome. In order for resistance to be taken seriously, even by the victims, it might require severe injury and that would seem to encourage reporting.

Additionally, individual definitions of the circumstance must be considered when assessing these findings. For example, one respondent who had taken eight years of instruction in tai kwan do recalled the warning of her instructor: "He told us if we didn't think we could overpower the enemy, we shouldn't try. This guy told me he was trained to kill and I wasn't about to test his ability. So I didn't use what I'd learned and at least I didn't get beaten up or killed." This woman did not report the assault, but justified her compliance by reiterating what the instructor had told her. Assaults by strangers were often accompanied by a threat to kill, and although most of the women did not resist when confronted in this manner, their interpretation of the situation in some cases warranted a report to the police.

Attitude of Victim To Police

According to the literature, the victim's opinion of the police appeared to be a generally accepted factor influencing reporting (Ennis 1967; Robin 1977; Schram 1978; Williams and Holmes 1981; Dean and de Bruyn-Kops 1982). Only one study found little support for concern about police hostility as a factor of nonreporting (Wilson 1978).

During the interviewing for this study, however, it seemed apparent that views toward police did not affect reporting. Rather, other factors seemed far more relevant. In general, when offences conformed to the classic or stereotypical version of a sexual assault, victims were more likely to report regardless of their opinion of police. This was the rationale leading up to the seventh proposition: *Police reporting will not differ according to victims' attitudes to the police.*

In Table I (factor 8) we see that although victims who

had a positive opinion of police reported most often (59 percent), those who did not have a positive opinion reported more often (39 percent) than those who were neutral (30 percent). Our results suggest that even if a victim articulates a negative opinion of police, this does not necessarily preclude a report. Many of the nonreporting victims made positive statements about the police, while others were neutral and still did not report. Conversely, some victims who expressed negative feelings about the police did report.

The research also revealed that the manner in which a victim was treated by the police when she did report a sexual assault had some bearing on her impression of them. If she was treated badly, that was reflected in her attitude to them. Kindness on the part of police almost always resulted in a positive opinion of them. These findings suggest that some of the attitudes toward police may be a consequence of reporting rather than a cause.

SUMMARY

To summarize the findings from this study, we found that victims were more likely to report assaults to the police when: (1) they blamed the assailant; (2) they received a supportive response from the first person they told about the assault; (3) they had not experienced physical or sexual violence in their backgrounds; (4) the attack was perpetrated by a stranger; (5) there were visible injuries; (6) and they resisted vigorously, thus increasing the likelihood of injury.

CHAPTER V

The Response of the Criminal Justice System

UNTIL recently, much of the research concerning sexual assault has focussed either on the characteristics surrounding the offence or on the police handling of the reports (Clark and Lewis 1977; Amir 1971; Gager and Schurr 1976). Our research attempts to expand the focus by examining the response of the criminal justice system from the time a victim has contact with the police to the final disposition of the charges. Consequently, the police, prosecution and court levels were included in the analysis. Specifically, an examination was made of the filtering system whereby reported offences are diverted out of the legal system. Filtering refers to the termination or reduction of sexual assault charges as they proceed through the criminal justice system.

METHODOLOGY

We used police file data to obtain information on reports of rape and attempted rape made to the Winnipeg Police Department for the years 1976 and 1977. The file information was supplemented by interviews with the prosecutors assigned to each of the cases that proceeded beyond the police level. These interviews with crown attornies were used to obtain information on the course of the charges once they reached the crown and court levels. Access to file data at the crown level could not be secured because the files are confidential.

The total number of cases that emerged from the study was 154. For each case there was one victim, and one to five offenders. The victims in all cases were female and in all but one case the offenders were male. The total number of offenders, with the inclusion of multiple offender cases, was 211.

The use of data collected in a single jurisdiction proved to be beneficial in several respects. First, official statistics from national data sources used in research have been criticized for the fact that comparability was often lacking for data from different levels of the criminal justice system (Connidis 1979). However, in the present study the same reports were followed through the system, by charge, from the initial contact of the victim with the police to the final disposition. This allowed us to examine the reasons for case attrition where charges are filtered out of the criminal justice system. By using this procedure, the loss of cases in the analysis was avoided. In addition, the data provided information on any reduction of charges so that information was not lost as a result of the re-classification.

As our previous discussion indicates, data utilized in the present study are not representative of sexual assaults in Winnipeg for the two-year study period. Rather, they are representative of the victims who reported the offence to the police and subsequently had a police file prepared. The use of official statistics is reliable to the extent that it represents a select group of sexual assault victims whose victimization is made known to a police agency.

Nonetheless, the information from the police files, used in perspective, provided an excellent opportunity to examine the official response of the criminal justice system to the reports that began at the law enforcement level. There is a filtering system that operates from the police to the judicial level and determines the final outcome of the charges. Connidis (1979) cautions against research that focuses on only one subsystem such as the police and advocates increased research where the entire criminal justice system is examined.

RESULTS

The filtering system of the rape and attempted rape reports was analysed at three levels: the police, crown and court. Each of the three levels have termination points in filtering. The police level deals with charges until they are handed over to the crown prosecutor's office. The prosecutor level processes the cases up to the preliminary hearing. Finally, the court level begins with the preliminary hearing and ends with the final disposition.

The Police Level

The filtering system is evident from the time a report is made by the victim to the police. The level of the police is the first official stage where reports may be filtered out of the system. Here we classified reports as either proceeding to the office of the prosecution or terminating at the police level. Of the 154 incidents reported, 73 were sent to the prosecutor after the initial screening by the police. Of these, the police classified 68 as founded and left 5 reports unclassified (leaving the designation to the prosecutor's office).

Fifty-three percent of the total did not proceed beyond the police level, involving 58 percent of the reported offenders. A summary of the filtering system at the police level is presented in Table II.

TABLE II
Summary of the Filtering System of Rape and Attempted Rape Reports at the Police Level by Case and Number of Offenders, 1976 and 1977

Initial Reports Made to the Police		Number of Cases 154		Number of Offenders 211
Filtering System at the Police Level	**Number**	**Percent**	**Number**	**Percent**
Unfounded designation	42	27.3	61	28.9
No formal complaint made by the victim	10	6.5	22	10.4
Victim drops charges	7	4.5	16	7.6
No suspect apprehended	22	14.3	23	10.3
Total filtering out of charges at the police level	81	52.6	122	57.8
Number of charges remaining	73	47.4	89	42.2

Cases were terminated for three major reasons: first, the charged was designated unfounded; secondly, no formal complaint was made by the victim or charges were dropped at the police level; or, thirdly, no suspect was apprehended.

Unfounded Designation

The rationale for an unfounded designation on the part of the police can be either subjective or practical. Sometimes the police simply do not believe that a rape or attempted rape has occurred. Police bias was evident in some of the reports. The following comment by police reflects the skepticism directed toward victims' allegations of sexual assault: "She had been in the suite for a period of about four or five hours and it is doubtful that any victim would be attractive enough for an assailant to wait for that period of time."

In other cases, the police foresee that the prosecutor will have difficulty in proceeding with the charge. Regardless of the veracity of a particular charge, problems related to the victim or to the evidence can affect the chances of proving in court that a rape has occurred. The police classified one report as unfounded with the following justification: "I do not feel that we will be able to present a case against the accused that will result in a conviction. Consent will be the issue and I do not feel that the complainant will be able to convince a court that she said 'no' in a manner that the accused clearly understood."

We also found that the reaction of the victim to the sexual assault was being evaluated on the basis of stereotypical notions of how victims should react, irrespective of individual differences in dealing with the offence. In one case a police officer commented: "I found her to be extremely composed and rational. She did not show any of the usual emotional trauma one would associate with being a rape victim."

The police, however, should not carry the sole burden for an apparent thwarting of justice at this point. The police must be realistic to a certain extent in foreseeing the reactions and prejudices that may emerge from the prosecutors, judges and juries who will ultimately make the decisions regarding the charges. The police must also give some consideration to the efficiency of the police, crown attorney and court system in deciding whether to retain or to filter out a charge. "As a result, the police are forced to operate as an elaborate screening device, a highly selective filter, through which only the 'best' of even the founded cases proceed" (Clark and Lewis 1977, 59). Consequently, one would expect to find the greatest amount of filtering out of reports at the level of the police. In addition, there are cases where the victim's denial of the offence or apprehension about proceeding with a charge lead to an unfounded designation. The police classified 27 percent of the cases as unfounded. The specific reasons for classifying a case as unfounded was given in all but two instances.

In 5 percent of the cases the police referred specifically to problems with evidence as the basis for an unfounded report. The evidentiary problems concerned lack of evidence, lack of resistance and the drunk or drugged condition of the victim at the time of the offence. Intoxication of the victim, according to the police files, was a factor in six of the reports.

For 10 percent of the cases, a combination of police and victim apprehension about proceeding with a charge led to an unfounded report. The victim, in most cases, was generally uncooperative and apprehensive about proceeding with a report. In one case the victim was legally separated from the offender and in another two cases the offender was the ex-boyfriend of the victim. Three of the victims in this group were referred to as having serious drinking problems while two were referred to as "simple minded" and one as severely retarded.

In 5 percent of the cases the unfounded reports were labelled as false complaints. In five of the reports the victim told the police that the allegation of rape was false. Out of this group, police files contained descriptions of one of the victims as incorrigible, one as a neglected child and one as being involved in a lovers' quarrel. There were three cases where the police classified a false complaint without an actual denial of the offence from the victim. Two of these victims were described as being in need of psychiatric help. An unfounded designation was given by the police on the first interview with the victim in four of the reports, on the second interview for three of the reports and on the third interview for one of the reports.

Finally, in 5 percent of the cases the victim did not initially contact the police. Instead, a family relative or witness made the decision to report the offence to the police. The victims in this group, when contacted by the police, denied that a sexual assault had taken place or refused to speak to the police about the incident. One victim's assault was summed up as follows on a police report after the police attended a hospital and were told by the victim she refused to continue any further: "It appears that the complainant was taken in by a 'smooth' operator and is more ashamed of herself than anything. It appears doubtful that there was any offence of rape here as no threats, violence etc. were used." In all but one of the cases, the report was terminated after the initial interview between the police and the victim.

No Formal Complaint by the Victim/ Victim Drops Charges at the Police Level

The next two types of situation which resulted in the termination of a report at the level of the police were initiated by the victim. In some instances, the victim refuses to make a formal complaint after relating the offence to the police. In other cases, the victim decided to drop charges at the police level before it was handed over to the office of the prosecution. A victim might have changed her mind and decided that she did not want to participate in the lengthy process required for a criminal prosecution. The probability of reliving the sexual assault while testifying in the courtroom is an effective deterrent to many victims in the initial stages of police action. A victim who refused to attend court stated to police that her report was for police information only, as the offender might commit the offence against someone else again. Fear of testifying and refusal to participate in the judicial system proceedings caused some victims to refuse to make a formal complaint or to drop a complaint. There are also many victims who decide not to report the offence to the police at all and consequently are not represented in the study. As seen in the previous chapter, many of the clients of the sexual assault centre chose not to report.

We found that other victims did not want any police involvement in response to the offence. One victim had not intended to call police but her friend had contacted them. After the victim related the offence to the police she stated she did not want involvement in any legal proceedings and only wanted the offender to leave her alone. She revealed that the offender, who was living with her sister, had also attempted to sexually assault her on a previous occasion. In the present study, 6 percent of the victims refused to make a formal complaint. Further, 4 percent had the charges dropped at the police level before crown involvement.

The reasons given by the victim to the police for refusing to press charges are as follows (with the number of times shown in parentheses): family pressures (2); refusal to testify in court (5); victim did not initially make the report (3); fear of reprisal from the offender (1); victim only wanted stolen items returned (1); and victim decided against any further police action (5). With reference to the final category, the police did not hesitate to make broad assumptions regarding the victim's intentions. One of the victims who decided against further police action and was said to be intoxicated was described in the following way: "It would appear she was upset about being dropped out of the car and using the rape accusation as an excuse to try and get back at the guy. It was quite likely he had attempted some sexual activity; however, upon her refusal she was dropped off. She refused any medical attention."

Non-supportive responses affect the victim's decision either to initiate or to continue with a report. These issues add to the notion of the victim's responsibility, whereby the victimization is minimized in seriousness by the stereotyping that plagues the offence. These factors were found to have considerable impact on the victim's decision to report the offence to the police as determined from the research with victims discussed previously.

No Suspect Apprehended

Finally, we found there are some reports made where the victim wishes to proceed on a sexual assault charge but a failure to apprehend the offender renders further police action impossible. At times, a victim does not get a good enough look at the offender to give the police an adequate description. In other instances, even a thorough description does not suffice; a name or a licence number might be needed in order for the police to apprehend the suspect. The absence of witnesses during the offence further complicates the problem of identifying and apprehending the suspect. In the study, 14 percent of the cases had no suspect(s) identified. Reports of this nature are generally kept on file should any new information concerning the identity of the suspect become available.

Summary

The filtering out of reports at the police level accounted for the termination of 53 percent, or 81, of the cases and 58 percent, or 122, of the offenders' charges in the criminal justice system. Apprehension on the part of the police or the victim about proceeding with a report, in addition to the failure to identify and locate a suspect, emerged as the salient factors in the termination of rape and attempted rape reports at the police level.

The Crown Level

The next official to deal with a report of rape or attempted rape is the crown attorney in the provincial Attorney General's Department. "After a case has been referred to the Crown counsel, it may be proceeded with, withdrawn or the charge originally laid may be altered.... The decisions of prosecutors will reflect the priorities of their office which may not be similar to those of the police" (Griffiths et al. 1980, 53).

As mentioned previously, 47 percent, or 73, of the cases were passed on to the level of the crown from the offences reported during the two year study period, involving 42 percent, or 89, of the offenders. For 2 percent of the reports police were unsure whether they should be classified as founded or unfounded. The reports were given to the crown attorney's office for an opinion as to the correct classification. In such cases, the decision was made by a senior prosecutor in the Attorney General's Department..

The crown classified three of these reports as founded and two as unfounded. The two unfounded reports resulted in the termination of charges for 2 percent of the offenders. Preliminary screening by the crown resulted in

46 percent of the cases being proceeded with, comprising 40 percent of the offenders.

Our results on the initial screening at the crown's office reveal consensus between the police and prosecutors, implying similar priorities at the two levels. In fact, the only cases terminated at the crown level were those left unclassified by the police. The data from this study indicate the adeptness with which the police bring forward cases in terms of "second guessing" their acceptance at the crown level.

For 3 percent, however, the victim was instrumental in a total dismissal of charges after the case had reached the prosecutor's office. In these cases, the victim decided that she did not want to proceed any further with the case. In all cases, this occurred before the preliminary hearing had begun. If the victim refuses to continue with the case, the prosecutor generally has no recourse but to drop the charges for want of prosecution.[1] It would be difficult to conduct a trial without the victim for she is the key witness for the crown's case.

Filtering out of charges at the crown level resulted in 6 percent of the charges being terminated. The percentage of offenders whose charges remained in effect now stands at 37. Although we found the actual filtering out of charges at the crown level was relatively minimal, there were modifications that took place respecting the remaining charges. Included were reclassification of original police charges, the use of concomitant and directly related

1 While the prosecutor does have a legal recourse provided for in the Criminal Code (Section 635) to send a victim (in her role as a witness) to jail until she agrees to testify, the use of this method is generally considered to be outweighed by the prospect of an uncooperative victim in the proceedings.

TABLE III
Summary of the Filtering System of Reports at the Crown Level by the Number of Offenders

Filtering System at the Crown Level	Number of Offenders Number	Percent
Charges terminated		
a) Crown unfounded	5	2.4
b) Victim withdraws participation before preliminary hearing	7	3.3
Charges plea bargained		
a) Plea bargain charge	7	3.3
b) Plea bargain sentence	3	1.4
TOTAL	22	10.4

additional charges, and the use of plea bargaining on charge and sentence. The crown, like the police, assess the chances of success in the court system.

Regardless of the subjective, extra-legal factors such as the victim's demeanour and the circumstances of the offence, the crown tries to predict whether a particular female will be seen as a 'genuine' victim by the judges and juries who will make the decision at the court level.

Reclassification of Police Charges

At this point the crown attorney is in charge of the reports and may classify charges according to his or her discretion. Charges may be re-classified to lesser ones, or to alternate charges that are deemed to be more appropriate for the particular offence involved. We found that initially the prosecutor's office did not dismiss any of the charges altogether, but rather decided to file charges less serious than the original police classification for 4 percent of the offenders. The study found that three charges of indecent assault on a female, three charges of contributing to juvenile delinquency, two charges of sexual intercourse with a female between fourteen and sixteen years and one charge of break and enter with intent to commit rape were laid as alternatives to the original police charges.

Additional Charges

The prosecutor may also decide to include additional charges apart from the major charge. The information that is contained in the crown report during the filing of charges will serve to accommodate the inclusion of additional charges. The additional charges that are laid can serve two major purposes. A case in which there are foreseeable problems with the evidence or the victim's testimony can often be remedied with the possibility of conviction on one of the lesser additional charges, should the case result in an acquittal for the accused on the major charge at trial. A charge of rape where proof of penetration is uncertain could contain a back-up charge of indecent assault on a female so that acquittal of the major charge leaves open the option of guilt on the latter charge.

The second purpose for the prosecutor is the use of additional charges as a plea bargaining tool (Buckle and Buckle 1977). The problematic case may best be served by a negotiated plea or sentence where conviction is almost certain. Plea bargaining eliminates the need for a trial and the uncertain outcome inherent in court proceedings. There are two types of additional charges that were utilized by the crown for the study period: concomitant offence charges and directly related additional charges.

Our information taken from the police reports indicates that the police listed separate additional offence charges for 6 percent of the offenders apart from the sexual assault charge. These charges comprised robbery or theft, attempted murder, assault, and theft and assault causing bodily harm. The crown acted on only one of the additional charges, that being assault (on a relative of the victim by the offender). For the remaining concomitant offences there were two instances where the crown did not file the robbery or theft charges with the major charges; the rest of the charges were contained in the categories of "no suspect apprehended" and "victim did not make a formal complaint."

Directly related additional charges are those involved in the commission of the sexual assault. Offences that are directly related include forcible confinement and gross indecency. The data reveal that of the 12 percent of offenders who went to trial on the original charge(s) laid by the crown, there were six percent who had directly related additional charges included with the major sexual assault charge. A frequency distribution of directly related additional charges for those offenders whose original crown charge was retained, is presented in Table IV. Further examination of the data from the study period indicate that there were no instances where the accused was acquitted on the major sexual assault trial charge and found guilty of the directly related additional charges. Our findings reveal that conviction resulted for one-half of the applicable 6 percent of the offenders who were found guilty of both the major charge and at least one of the additional charges; the remaining 3 percent of the offenders were either found guilty of the major charge only (2 percent) or

TABLE IV
Frequency Distribution of Directly-related Additional Charges Included with Original Crown Charges, 1976 and 1977*

Directly-Related Additional Charges	Number of Offenders
Assault causing bodily harm	4
Gross indecency	6
Indecent assault	4
Possession of a dangerous weapon	1
Kidnapping	1
Unlawful confinement	1
Forcible confinement	4

*For some of the offenders there were several additional charges laid. The number of offenders with at least one additional charge was 12.

acquitted on the major charge and the directly-related additional charges (1 percent).

Plea Bargaining

Plea bargaining as a method of disposing of cases can be facilitated by the use of additional charges. The crown is able to secure a conviction without a trial. The defence is able to achieve the dismissal of the major and more serious charge and offer the accused a lower penalty for a less serious charge (Klein 1976; Huemann 1978). The accused may also be offered a pre-determined sentence or sentence range in exchange for a guilty plea to the original charge. In plea bargaining arrangements, the prosecutor and defence counsel confer with each other, and they may reach a mutually satisfactory agreement approved by the defendant that will be subject to judicial approval.

In the present study, 3 percent of the offenders agreed

TABLE V
Plea Bargaining in Relation to Charge that Took Place Before the Commencement of the Preliminary Hearing, 1976 and 1977

Plea Bargain Charge	Original Crown Charge	Number of Offenders
Sexual intercourse with a female between 14-16 years	Rape	1
Contributing to juvenile delinquency	Rape	2
Indecent assault on a female	Rape	1
Indecent assault on a female	Attempted rape	3
TOTAL		7 (3.3%)

to plea bargain for a lesser charge before the preliminary hearing began.[2] The alternative charges that were accepted in exchange for a guilty plea are shown in Table V.

Another 1 percent of the offenders plea bargained for a lighter sentence prior to the preliminary hearing.[3] The charges that were plea bargained on sentence as submitted by the crown and defence counsel are presented in Table VI.

Summary

The filtering system in effect at the crown level resulted in 22, or 10 percent, of the offenders' charges being terminated or disposed of in the criminal justice system. Of

2 Information on the stage at which plea bargaining took place was obtained from personal interviews with the prosecutors who had handled the charges.

3 One of the offenders had two separate charges of rape plea bargained in relation to sentence. The offender is represented as two offenders, reflecting the two separate reports of rape involved.

TABLE VI
Plea Bargaining in Relation to Sentence that Took Place Before the Commencement of the Preliminary Hearing, 1976 and 1977

Pre-Determined Sentence	Crown Charge	Number of Offenders
5-10 year sentence range for charges of rape	Rape	2
1 year sentence	Attempted rape	1
TOTAL		3 (1.4%)

these 22 offenders, 12 had their charges terminated altogether, while 10 were involved in a plea bargain with respect to charge or sentence in exchange for a guilty plea. Sixty-seven offenders, or 32 percent of those charged, remained in the criminal justice system for disposition of their charges.

The Court Level

The next stage, the court, results in the final disposition of charges for those offenders still in the criminal justice system. The full spectrum of the court level can involve a preliminary hearing, a trial, sentencing and an appeal. Charges at the final level can be disposed of in a number of different ways: charges may be dismissed, plea bargained on charge, plea bargained on sentence, retained, or finally, may involve a guilty plea without concessions. The crown continues to be very influential at the court level and may attempt to alter the course of the proceedings at any point. The purpose of the preliminary hearing is to determine whether or not the crown has sufficient evidence to proceed with the charges laid. The judge who presides over the hearing is responsible for the determination of sufficient evidence. "At the hearing...the judge determines whether a *prima facie* case exists, and thus, whether a trial...is warranted" (McCahill, Meyer and Fischman 1979, 160). The crown prosecutor is responsible for presenting the evidence against the accused. Defence counsel attempts to undermine the validity of the evidence, presented by way of victim cross-examination, on behalf of their client. The preliminary hearing is the testing ground for the defence and, to a lesser extent, the crown in terms of attempting to expose any victim or evidentiary weaknesses.

The initial pre-trial hearing has been aptly referred to as a "fishing expedition" for the defence counsel. Intimidation of the victim by way of irrelevant and personal questioning is by no means ruled out, as it reflects on the victim's credibility. "If the defence can show that the victim is not the kind of person who can be believed, then her claim that she did not consent to this particular act of sexual intercourse will be thrown into question" (Clark and Lewis 1977, 47).

Defence counsel works toward a dismissal of the charges at most, and intimidation of the victim at least. It is crucial that the crown counsel intervene and put forth objections to the harassment of the victim by defence counsel. It is the responsibility of the presiding judge to determine which questions are pertinent; the degree of intimidation to the victim ultimately depends on the particular judge, prompted by crown objections at the preliminary hearing.

The preliminary hearing emerges as the crucial phase of the court level since it affects the charges and all that follows. First, the charges may be dismissed by the judge at the conclusion of the hearing if he or she does not think that the evidence warrants a trial. Second, the crown may assess their chances at trial as poor, based on the victim's performance and evidence presented, and opt for plea bargaining. Finally, the victim may terminate the charges by withdrawing her participation in the proceedings.

A trial will follow the preliminary hearing if the judge has decided that a case exists based on the original charges, or if the crown has laid subsequent charges after an initial judicial dismissal of the original crown charge. The mode of trial may be either by a judge sitting alone or by a judge and a jury. The disposition of charges at the court level is shown in Table VII.

Dismissal of Charges

The dismissal of crown charges at the court level can occur at any time after a preliminary hearing date has been set and can result from decisions made by the various persons involved at this level. Our data from the study period indicate that the victim, the crown psychiatrist, the accused and the judge at the preliminary hearing were instrumental in a dismissal of the crown charges.

The preliminary hearing can be a time of apprehension for the victim. Her fears about testifying at the hearing can lead her to withdraw from the process at this stage. McCahill, Meyer and Fischman attribute this phenomenon to a number of factors: "The lack of preparation or support, the prospect of speaking publicly (often for the first time) about a humiliating experience, and the necessity of confronting the offender may contribute to the high rate of victim absence at the preliminary hearing" (1979, 167).

TABLE VII
The Disposition of the Charges at the Court Level by the Number of Offenders, 1976 and 1977

Disposition of Charges	Number of Offenders Number	Percent
Termination of Charges	8	3.8
Subsequent Charges Laid by the Crown		
a) Plea bargain charge	3	1.4
b) Offender found guilty	6	2.8
c) Offender found not guilty	2	0.9
Original Crown Charges		
a) Plea bargained charge	16	7.6
b) Plea bargained sentence	2	0.9
Original Crown Charges Retained		
a) Offender pled guilty - no concessions	2	0.9
b) Consent committal	2	0.9
c) Offender found guilty - all trial charges	15	7.1
d) Offender found guilty - major charge only	4	1.9
e) Offender found guilty of attempted rape instead of the trial charge of rape	1	0.5
f) Offender acquitted of all charges	6	2.8
TOTAL	67	31.8

At the court level, 2 percent of the offenders had their charges terminated because the victim withdrew her participation in the proceedings. In one instance the victim withdrew once the preliminary hearing was in progress. The remaining offenders had their charges terminated after the victim refused to appear at the trial.

The crown psychiatrist was the major force behind a

dismissal of charges for 2 (or 1 percent) of the offenders. In these cases, the psychiatrist came to the conclusion that the accused was insane and therefore not fit to stand trial. The crown, in light of the psychiatrist's decision, dismissed the charges. The crown and defence counsel then agreed upon a consent committal. This resulted in the accused being kept in custody for mental rehabilitation for a indeterminate period of time. In both cases, the consent committal was agreed upon before the preliminary hearing began; these cases will not be considered as valid dismissals given that a period of detention is involved.

In addition, there was one accused (.5 percent) who had his charge dismissed at the request of his co-accused. The crown accepted the offer in exchange for a guilty plea from the co-accused, against whom more evidence was held. The dismissal of charge for one of the accused occurred before the trial. This case represents the single occasion where a plea bargain was achieved by way of a concession for the co-accused.

Finally we found the judge responsible for the termination of some of the charges at the conclusion of the preliminary hearing. The judge determines whether the charges will be brought to trial or dismissed. The data indicate that the charges for 4 percent of the offenders were determined to contain insufficient evidence and were subsequently dismissed by the judge.The total percentage of offenders whose charges were initially dismissed stands at 9 percent, or 19 offenders.[4]

4 Aside from the 13 recorded dismissals, there were 6 accused for whom there was no information available as to when the charges were initially dismissed and whether the victim, the prosecutor or the judge was instrumental in that decision.

The crown, in turn, laid subsequent charges for 6 percent of the accused males who had their original crown charges dismissed. The judge at the preliminary hearing was responsible for the initial dismissal of charges for 5 of the accused. In another case, the victim decided to discontinue with the charges before the preliminary hearing began, whereupon the crown laid a charge of assault causing bodily harm on behalf of the victim's sister against the accused.

For the remaining 3 percent of offenders, there was no information available as to the initial dismissal of charges. Data were available for the outcome of the subsequent charges: 3 percent of the accused were found guilty; 1 percent were found not guilty; 1 percent had their subsequent charges dismissed as the victim withdrew her support before the trial began; and a further 1 percent pled guilty before the trial. The conviction rate from the initial dismissals reveals that of 9 percent, or 19, of the accused who had their original crown charges dismissed, only 4 percent, or 9 of the accused were eventually found guilty by way of a trial or a negotiated plea on the lesser charges. In addition, 1 percent of the accused were dealt with by consent committals.

Retained Charges

Charges filed by the prosecutor were retained for 12 percent of the offenders and were subject to both a preliminary hearing and a trial. Among retained charges, the use of plea bargaining was discussed by legal counsel for just over one-half of the offenders. The prosecutor was instrumental in refusing a guilty plea for roughly 70 percent of those charges. The crown's refusal to accept a guilty plea was most often related to having a "strong case" against the accused. Charges of rape were applicable to 9 percent of the offenders, with attempted rape charges at 2 percent and contributing to juvenile delinquency at 1 percent. Additional charges at trial were included for 7 percent of the accused. The results at trial are as follows: 3 percent of the accused were acquitted on all charges; 7 percent of the accused were found guilty of the major charge only; and .5 percent of the accused was found guilty of attempted rape instead of the original trial charge of rape.

Our results from the study reveal that few crown charges are retained and result in a trial. Out of the 211 persons originally accused of rape or attempted rape, there were only 26 (12 percent)[5] whose original crown charge(s) reached a trial solution. Further, only 19 (9 percent) of the accused were found guilty of at least the major crown charge at trial.

Plea Bargained Charges

The pervasiveness of plea bargaining has been well documented. Counsel on both sides must assess the characteristics of the offence, the credibility of the victim and the amount of crown evidence and must develop strategies to further their respective goals. Realistically, however, success for either counsel is never assured. Plea bargaining provides a means whereby each can benefit; the crown can obtain an admission of guilt from the accused and the defence can obtain the probability of a less harsh outcome for the accused in terms of charge and/or sentence. The

5 Three of the accused went to trial on a reduced crown charge of contributing to juvenile delinquency. The remainder of the charges were either rape or attempted rape.

time and energies required by a trial are spared everyone involved in the court proceedings by a guilty plea, especially where there is reasonable doubt about the chances of success for either the crown or the defence.

The benefits of a negotiated guilty plea in a rape or attempted rape case may be obvious to everyone except the victim, who often may feel that the legal process is working to the offender's advantage. A plea of guilty to a reduced charge will be of a less serious nature in legal terms. The pre-determined sentence will specify a sentence or sentence range that will place length of sentence below the maximum penalty allowable to the offender. The plea bargain emerges as a viable alternative to the accused who may not be willing to face the uncertainty of a trial.

A reduction of charge in exchange for a guilty plea resulted for nearly 6 percent of the offenders at the court level. A reduced charge was accepted for 1 percent of the offenders during the preliminary hearing and for 4 percent of the offenders before the court trial. A frequency distribution of the reduced charges accepted by counsel at the court level is presented in Table VIII.

In addition, 2 percent of the offenders had their charges plea bargained but there was no information available as to when the negotiated plea was obtained.[6] Incorporating the above cases into the group of plea bargained cases at the court level results in nearly 8 percent of the offenders being involved in a guilty plea in exchange for a reduced charge.

6 No information was available on the prosecutors who had handled the cases.

TABLE VIII
Plea Bargaining in Relation to Charge that Took Place from the Time of the Preliminary Hearing to the Trial, 1976 and 1977

Plea Bargained Charge	Original Crown Charge	When Plea Bargained	Number of Offenders
Gross indecency	Rape	During preliminary hearing	3
Indecent assault	Rape	Before trial	3
Contributing to juvenile delinquency	Rape	Before trial	1
Gross indecency	Rape	Before trial	3
Common assault	Attempted rape	Before trial	1
Indecent assault	Attempted rape	Before trial	1
TOTAL			12 (5.7%)

Plea Bargained Sentence

A total of 1 percent of the offenders were involved in a plea bargain in relation to sentence. A pre-determined sentence or sentence range was agreed upon by the crown and defence counsel from the time of the preliminary hearing to the court trial. The sentences agreed upon at the court level are presented in Table IX.

Offender Pled Guilty – No Concessions

The final route that crown charges may take at the court level is a plea of guilty by the offender without any concessions in the form of plea bargaining. This applied to 1 percent of the offenders from the study period. Both of the

TABLE IX
Plea Bargaining in Relation to Sentence that Took Place from the Time of the Preliminary Hearing to the Trial, 1976 and 1977

Sentence Range	Crown Charges	When Plea Bargained	Number of Offenders
9-18 months	Break and enter with intent to commit rape	During preliminary hearing	1
3-5 years	Rape	Before trial	1
10-12 years	Rape	Before trial	1
TOTAL			3 (1.4%)

offenders agreed to a guilty plea on the rape charge after a preliminary hearing had taken place.

Summary

The filtering system at the court level resulted in nearly 8 percent, or 16, of the accused having their charges terminated either by a dismissal (4 percent) or by an acquittal (4 percent). Twenty-four percent, or 51 of the offenders, were found guilty. Of those persons found guilty, 10 percent were found guilty of reduced charges or had sentences reduced through plea bargaining, 3 percent were found guilty of subsequent charges after an initial dismissal of the original crown charges, 1 percent were involved in a guilty plea to the original crown charges without any plea bargaining concessions, 1 percent were involved in a consent committal, and .5 percent were found guilty of attempted rape instead of the trial charge of rape. Finally, 9 percent of the accused were found guilty of at least the major crown charges at trial.

Conclusion

The filtering system at the police, crown and court levels resulted in a loss of 150 (71 percent) of the original 211 accused persons. Most were filtered out by the police (58 percent, or 122 offenders), with the crown and court levels following at 6 percent (12 offenders) and 8 percent (16 offenders), respectively. The total percentage of offenders convicted for the two-year period was 29 (61 offenders) and comprised findings of guilt on the original crown charges, reduced charges and plea bargained charges.

Our findings confirm that among those sexual assault charges reported, only a select few proceed through the legal system and result in a finding of guilt. The disparity widens when convictions on the original sexual assault charges are examined. A summary regarding the filtering out of charges is presented in Table X.

DEMOGRAPHICS FROM THE STUDY

The Victim and the Offender

Of the 155 victims who reported offences to the police, the majority were under the age of 30 (86 percent). The largest age category was the 15-19 year range representing 38 percent of the victims, followed by the 20-24 year group at 23 percent. Two-thirds of the victims were single (62 percent), which is to be expected given the relative youth of the majority. The category of cohabitation followed at 14 percent. Occupational status revealed that nearly one-half (49 percent) were students or worked in occupations ranging from waitressing to unskilled labour where no special training beyond basic schooling was required (21 percent). The victims in the study did not emerge as a particularly criminal group with only 6 percent of them having a criminal record mentioned in their files.

The 211 offenders from the study were, for the most part, young in age. The largest age category was the 20-24 year group (36 percent), followed by the 15-19 and the 25-29 year categories at 24 percent each. Just over 58 percent of the offenders were classified as single, with married (21 percent) and cohabitation (11 percent) categories following in frequency. Unskilled labour was the most common occupation listed for the offender (47 percent) with only 2 percent classified as students. Twenty-four percent of the offenders had criminal records; 6 percent had records for previous sexual offences.

Just over half of the reports (56 percent) involved complete strangers. The next largest group involved offenders who could be identified but were not acquainted with the victim (18 percent). Acquaintances accounted for 10 percent. Nearly 10 percent of the cases involved family friends, boyfriends and relatives.

The Offence

The characteristics of the offence revealed that the reported assaults occurred primarily at night and on the weekend (57 and 56 percent, respectively), and during the spring and fall (41 percent). The majority of the reported offences took place in inner city Winnipeg where most of the hotels, drinking establishments and business offices are concentrated. Assaults in vehicles (29 percent) and at an indoor location (22 percent) were more frequent than those at outdoor locations (16 percent). The majority of the offences were reported by someone other than the vic-

TABLE X
Total Filtering Out of Offenders' Charges

Reduction of Charges	Original Crown Charges N=211	Termination of Charges
	Police level N=211	Police unfounded n=61 Charges dropped by victim n=38 No suspect apprehended n=23
Plea bargained charges n=10	**Crown level n=89**	Victim initiated n=7 Crown unfounded n=5
Plea bargained charges n=21 Guilty at trial on reduced charges n=7	**Court level n=67**	Charges terminated (by victim or judges at preliminary hearing) n=8 Acquittal at trial n=8 not guilty by reason of insanity n=2
	Guilty at trial n=21	
TOTAL n=38 18%	TOTAL n=21 10%	TOTAL n=152 72%

tim(58 percent). While the victim made the initial report in 42 percent of the offences, the next three largest categories were stranger/passerby (17 percent), parent/guardian (14 percent) and friend (8 percent).

Stereotypes Not Supported by Data

Several stereotypes and myths have been dispelled by our examination of the characteristics of the offence. The young, "sexually attractive" female was not the only type of victim, as evidenced by an age range that included the very young (1-9 years of age) and the older victim (40-59 years of age). Likewise, the unmarried offender, while constituting the majority, was not the sole type of perpetrator. Nearly one-third of the offenders were in a cohabiting relationship.

Sexual assault occurred primarily in the spring and fall months as opposed to the thermic notion of crime which asserts that most sexual assaults occur in the hot summer months. Further, a sudden outdoor attack was less frequent than attacks in a vehicle, at an indoor residence (other than that of the victim or the offender) and at the victim's residence. These results are not consistent with many of the inaccurate stereotypes held by the public. Importantly, they serve to provide a more realistic picture of the sexual assaults reported.

CHAPTER VI

The Role of the Prosecutor

THE role of the prosecutor was highlighted in our examination of the response of the criminal justice system to sexual assault. The considerable discretion of the prosecutor in legal proceedings has been addressed by numerous researchers (Grosman 1970; Chambliss and Seidman 1971; and LaFave 1970). In addition, the involvement of the prosecutor emerged in our research as being substantial, given that the crown has responsibility for the charges in the judicial system up to their final disposition. Consequently, the practices and procedures of the crown were integral in gaining insight into the handling of sexual assault charges.

METHODOLOGY

Prosecutors in the Manitoba Attorney-General's Department who had handled sexual assault cases during the two-year study period were interviewed with respect to their general practices and procedures in prosecuting such cases. In addition, the problematic aspects of legal and societal guidelines concerning sexual assault were investigated.

A profile of the prosecutors revealed that of the eighteen prosecutors interviewed, all but one were male. Their ages ranged from 28 years to 45 years with the average age being 33 years. Ten of the respondents had performed other types of legal work before becoming crown attorneys; seven of them had been in private practice, with the remaining lawyers having done defence work, labour relations and police work, respectively. Eight did not have work experience in other areas of legal work. An examination of years of experience in prosecuting sexual assault cases revealed that 56 percent had up to 5 years experience, with an overall range of 2 to 13 years among the prosecutors interviewed.

RESULTS OF STUDY

The Discretion of the Prosecutor

Background

It has been said that prosecutors have the greatest discretionary powers in the criminal justice system (Reiss 1974). In order to understand discretion in the context of the prosecutor's role, the following definition should be considered: "...a public officer has discretion whenever the effective limits on his power leave him free to make a choice among possible courses of action or inaction" (Davis 1969, 4). Discretion here, according to LaFave, may be "...exercised by doing nothing and may exist without express recognition in law" (1970, 532).

The impact of the prosecutor's discretion on the processing of charges of sexual assault is evident. Because the police must anticipate the decision the crown attorney will make on a charge, the prosecutor has an influence on whether the police decide to lay the charge. At the crown and court levels it is the prosecutor who is responsible for proceding with the charge.

Considerable criticism has arisen over the use of plea bargaining as a necessary component of prosecutorial discretion, rather than from the use of discretion *per se*. Plea bargaining is frequently considered illegitimate, stemming from the motivations involved when the prosecutor exercises this form of discretion. Various explanations for the use of plea bargaining have been put forward. The most frequent explanation is that plea bargaining may serve to reduce a backlog of cases. However, some prosecutors do not agree that case overload is the major determinant for the existence of plea bargaining (Heumann 1978). It may be more appropriate to consider a number of factors that, when combined, explain prosecutorial plea bargaining.

Plea bargaining tends to result from various pressures to which the prosecutor is subject. One of the most significant is the "winner take all" adversarial system where the crown and defence are on opposite sides in a trial, culminating in a finding of innocence or guilt for the defendant. Uncertainty about the outcome of a trial figures strongly in the prosecutor's use of discretion. The prosecutor displays his or her competence and efficiency by way of the conviction rate (Buckle and Buckle 1977; Klein 1976). In this sense, a conviction can be achieved by either a plea bargain or a trial conforming to the adversarial model. The prosecutor's record is commonly based on the gross number of convictions and, should he or she lose too many cases, serious questions of competence may arise. In simple terms, the more trials there are, the greater the potential for an acquittal or the loss of a conviction for the crown.

The unpredictability of juries is also a major incentive for a negotiated plea (Heumann 1978). Most prosecutors have had personal experience with the court veterans' adage that "no case is 100 percent certain one way or the other". The implication is not that the prosecutor will negotiate every case. Rather, knowledge and experience will enable the prosecutor to make realistic predictions of the outcome of a trial and to weigh carefully the advantages of a negotiated plea as opposed to a trial.

Problems with prosecuting a case may also prompt the prosecutor to accept a guilty plea to a lesser charge. The chances of success usually involve the strength of evidence and the credibility of witnesses. One prosecutor in a study by Grosman indicated: "...it may just be a matter of logistics and witnesses don't show up and all you can salvage is a plea to something less. It's the best you can do under the circumstances" (1969, 34).

In addition, the prosecutor may have more influence on the sentence with plea bargaining. If the case goes to trial, the judge may be more familiar with the facts and less inclined to concur with prosecutor's recommended sentence. On the other hand, the sentence given by the judge at a trial may correspond roughly to one which might have been achieved through plea bargaining. In this case, the trial may have a marginal effect on the final disposition and the prosecutor may wonder whether it merited so much time and energy.

The prosecutor must also respond to pressures from the various bodies of the criminal justice system: police, defence counsel, judges and social services personnel. Prosecutorial negotiations require mutual cooperation between the various agencies in the system. The concept of a "community game" is used by Cole in a study of a Washington prosecutor's office: "The participants in the legal system (game) share a common territorial field and collaborate for different and particular ends. They interact on a continuing basis as their responsibilities demand contact with other participants in the process. Thus, the need for cooperation of other participants can have a bearing on the decision to prosecute" (1976, 235).

Pressures may be placed on the prosecutor by other members of the criminal justice system for the use of plea bargaining. Plea bargaining can then serve to facilitate the administrative and professional demands placed upon the various agencies with whom the prosecutor interacts.

In Canada, estimates of guilty pleas from regional studies ranged from a low of 44 percent (Hann 1973) to a high of 69 percent (Friedland 1965). However, Hogarth maintains that a 90 percent plus figure for guilty pleas, similar to figures obtained from U.S. studies, is reflective of the Canadian situation (1974).

Initial Charging Phase

The range of prosecutorial discretion is realized in numerous ways. Initially, when the prosecutor receives a report, the decision is made as to whether prosecution is warranted and on what legal grounds. For a sexual assault charge this involves acceptance of that charge at the crown level and the determination of the charge designation; whether it is proceeded with under the original police classification or on an alternative charge. The next step involves the recording of specific information that will serve to accommodate the charging decision. Overcharging may occur at this point in anticipation of plea bargaining. In fact, the interviews with the prosecutors revealed that a sizeable number of them (44 percent) considered directly related additional charges appropriate for use as a plea bargaining tool in sexual assault cases. One of the respondents went so far as to say: "I initially charge 'heavy' in the hopes that the offender will plead guilty and then drop the lesser ones to spare the complainant testifying (in court)...if you can get a decent plea for the particular rape involved. "

A further 22 percent of the respondents referred to the use of such additional charges as back-ups should the main charge be dismissed or problematic in terms of proof of its occurrence. One prosecutor summed up the use of additional charges in the following way: "The only rationalization is that you have a sneaking feeling that the offender will be acquitted so you hope that the offender will at least be convicted on one of the additional charges."

Plea Bargaining

The crown may retain the original charge or may negotiate with defence counsel for a reduction of charge or a predetermined sentence in exchange for a guilty plea, instead of having the case go to trial. While, in theory, plea bargaining is subject to judicial approval, LaFave asserts that the judicial practice is to follow the prosecutor's recommendations (1970). The prosecutors interviewed for this study unanimously agreed that judges almost always accepted their plea bargaining recommendation.

When questioned as to their opinion of plea bargaining in their jurisdiction, all prosecutors replied they were in favour of it, with one-half of them advocating that certain changes should be made. The respondents who expressed satisfaction with the existing plea bargaining system most often reported that it allowed for a satisfactory agreement for everyone involved. However, data from the study of the filtering system indicated that a satisfactory agreement primarily involved the defence, offender and the crown. The victim was not consulted during the plea bargaining process for just over 70 percent of the guilty plea arrangements that involved a concession for the offender. Explanations given to victims regarding the acceptance of a guilty plea almost always concerned evidentiary problems with the case.

Among the prosecutors who felt that plea bargaining should be retained but changed, the most common objection voiced was the use of last-minute plea bargaining after the court phase had been arranged or was in progress. The study data revealed that such last-minute plea bargaining occurred for 44 percent of the offenders. One solution offered by several respondents was the institution of stricter guidelines governing the timing of plea bargaining. Another solution involved the use of penalties in the form of a fine or an increased jail sentence for the offender who pleads guilty just before the trial.

Several of the respondents were critical of the secrecy surrounding guilty-plea agreements between defence and crown counsel. Disclosure of the reasons for a plea bargain by both counsel in open court was advocated as a means of accountability of counsel to both the judge and the general public. The use of plea bargaining by junior crown attorneys without consulting senior crown attorneys was also a source of dissatisfaction. None of the respondents favoured the elimination of the existing plea bargaining system altogether. However, one of the prosecutors who favoured changes in the system remarked: "If a backlog of cases would not result from the elimination of plea bargaining, I personally would rather work without it."

Pre-Trial Disclosure

The pre-trial disclosure of the crown's information to

defence counsel, beyond the minimum required by law, is also left to the discretion of the prosecutor. The crown decides whether the disclosure will exceed the minimal requirements. The interview results indicated that 22 percent of the prosecutors allowed only minimal disclosure as their usual procedure, while only one of the respondents indicated that full access to information (including witness statements) was allowed. The majority of the respondents (72 percent) revealed that the disclosure of the particulars of the case, excluding witness statements, was the procedure followed. When asked for the circumstances where minimal disclosure was considered appropriate, the responses included: where harassment of the victim was likely; where the prosecutor had a poor relationship with defence counsel; and where there was a weak case or weak complainant. One prosecutor underlined the importance of the victim being a strong witness in court: "The trial is so dependent on the articulation and the confidence of the victim. So, an ethnic thing enters here. Native girls generally aren't as articulate or as confident."

Court Proceedings

The crown also exerts considerable influence on the amount of bail, if any, that is granted, on the selection of the judge who will hear or try the case and on the calendar dates for the case at any stage of the proceedings. The interview results confirmed that prosecutors believe they exert considerable influence over the areas of bail (78 percent) and calendar dates (89 percent). However, all prosecutors denied they had considerable influence over the selection of the judge who presides over a case. When asked to compare their influence with that of the defence counsel, the majority of the respondents (72 percent) estimated that they had the same influence or more than the defence counsel in those three areas.

This discussion of prosecutorial discretion has provided a realistic examination of the extent of its use. Professional and administrative demands have emerged as the guiding principles in the discharging of that discretion. It was anticipated that the majority of sexual assault charges from the study period would be dealt with as altered charges (plea bargained or reduced crown charges) as opposed to being retained as original crown charges of rape or attempted rape. The data revealed that the majority of charges accepted by the prosecution and disposed of in court were in fact altered by way of plea bargaining or trial on a reduced charge. The figures from the study indicated that 60 percent of the charges were dealt with as altered charges while 40 percent were dealt with on the original crown charge. The use of plea bargaining was considerable, representing almost one-half of the total charges disposed of in court. With reference to the utility of plea bargaining to prosecutors, one of the respondents made the following remark: "It allows you to have the discretion not to waste valuable court time when it's not appropriate – if the outcome is likely to be negative."

The use of altered charges in sexual assault cases was predominant in both the present study and comparable research. Guilty pleas in sexual assault cases have been documented by several researchers, for example, LaFree, 59 percent (1982), and Galvin and Polk, 71 percent (1983). Further, a study by Williams (1978) revealed that 66 percent of defendants in sexual assault cases were convicted on reduced charges, while the remaining 34 percent were convicted on the original sexual assault charge. Conversely, Williams reported that robbery cases resulted in conviction for 73 percent of those tried on a type of robbery-charge. The legal premise of acquittal should reasonable doubt exist[1] emerges as problematic in sexual assault cases where societal attitudes and legal practice place the onus on the victim. Her character, motives and behaviour, areas beyond the scope of the offence itself, are frequently questioned, something that does not happen for most other offences.

Prosecutorial Practices in Sexual Assault Cases

Interaction Between the Prosecutor and the Victim

The prosecutors were asked how many times the victim was usually interviewed prior to the trial. The majority of the prosecutors (72 percent) indicated that the victim was generally interviewed by them twice before the trial. The remainder replied that the victim was either interviewed once before the trial (22 percent) or more than twice before the trial (6 percent). In addition, the prosecutors revealed that the most intensive interviewing usually took place before the preliminary hearing (72 percent) as opposed to before trial (17 percent), with several of the respondents giving equal weight to the interviewing process before both the preliminary hearing and the trial.

Most of the respondents indicated that there was

1 Dean and deBruyn-Kops (1982, 84) indicate that a reasonable doubt on the part of the judge or jury may be based on an evidentiary weakness as opposed to a sincere belief that the accused is innocent of the crime.

usually no one present during the interview other than the prosecutor and the victim (61 percent). The remainder reported that the police officer involved in the case (22 percent) or a victim advocate from a crisis centre (17 percent) was present during the interviewing.

All prosecutors felt that counselling services should be provided for sexual assault victims. When questioned as to which agencies could best deliver the counselling, equal weight was given to professionals (psychologists, social workers) and specially trained volunteers at 50 percent each. Hospital-based programs and a combination of the above-mentioned agencies with law enforcement workers was supported by 11 percent and 6 percent of the respondents, respectively. None of the respondents chose the option of the law enforcement agency handling the counselling independently.

The prosecutors were also questioned about the frequency with which victims withdraw complaints after a suspect has been charged. Most of the respondents (61 percent) estimated that 10 percent or less of the victims withdrew charges. The rest (39 percent) indicated that withdrawal by the victim accounted for 20 to 33 percent, with one of the respondents stating that an estimate was difficult to make. One of the prosecutors noted a difference in charge withdrawal by a victim depending on whether she resides in a rural community in northern Manitoba (80 percent) or Winnipeg (10 percent).

The present study revealed that 13 percent of the victims withdrew their complaints after the police had laid charges, with the result that 27 offenders were filtered out of the criminal justice system after being charged with rape or attempted rape. However, a higher percentage of victims (18 percent) withdrew before charges were laid;

proceedings were terminated either at the instigation of the victim (in 22 cases), or because of apprehension about proceeding on the part of both the victim and the police (in 16 cases).

The prosecutors were asked to identify the major reasons for the victim's withdrawal of a complaint after a suspect has been charged. The majority of the respondents (83 percent) identified the fear of testifying in court as the major reason for the victim's withdrawal after a suspect had been charged, indicating an awareness of the trauma involved in the court phase for the victim. The victim's fear may be either perceived (withdrawing before the preliminary hearing) or real (withdrawing at some point after the preliminary hearing). Nonetheless, since the victim is the main (and usually the only) witness in sexual assault cases, the traumatic effect on the victim must be addressed and remedied in order to improve the prosecution of rape cases.

The reason mentioned next in frequency by the prosecutors was that, in their opinion, the victim did not make a sincere complaint (44 percent). The respondents felt that if the legal system does not filter out a false complaint, the victim might take the initiative and withdraw the complaint. One prosecutor commented: "If the victim is not telling the truth she'll probably withdraw at some point. Thorough investigation methods by police and judicial system ensure that a false complaint is discovered. This assures that innocent accused are not convicted." Perhaps this category is also used for reports by victims who withdraw or disappear without giving an explanation, with the prosecutor assuming that the victim had not told the truth about the assault. This, however, is only an assumption as there are cases where there are no explanations given for the victim's withdrawal from the proceedings.

The remaining factors noted by the prosecutors involved personal reasons, the most frequent of which was fear of reprisal from the offender (28 percent). Pressure on the victim from her family or friends to drop the complaint (22 percent) was considered a major factor in the victim's withdrawal. Acquaintance of the victim with the offender (17 percent) may also be related to the fear of reprisal and pressures from family and friends. Sympathy for the offender (akin to victim responsibility) was noted by 11 percent of the prosecutors. Finally, the fear of being known as a rape victim and wanting to forget the assault were given as single responses.

Apart from the above-mentioned reasons given by the prosecutors for the victim's withdrawal after a suspect has been charged, there is an additional factor that may act as a deterrent. A victim who refuses to testify can legally be charged with contempt of court under the Canadian Criminal Code (Section 635), although this rarely occurs.

Relationship Between the Crown and Police

The prosecutors were questioned about their relationship with the police in handling sexual assault cases. All but one of the respondents considered that the degree of cooperation between the two agencies was excellent. The remaining respondent replied that the degree of cooperation was acceptable. None of the prosecutors felt that the relationship needed improvement. The most common response concerning the favourable relationship was that it was necessary for them to work together to ensure the best results. One prosecutor commented: "We're both playing on the same team. We're both in law enforcement.

The only way that a case can be successfully prosecuted is for full disclosure of its strengths and weaknesses between both agencies."

Another prosecutor underlined the importance of working together in the following way: "The necessity of both [agencies] to determine a rapport with respect to the complainant – to screen out any weak complainants." The degree of cooperation between the two agencies was seen in our research, where the crown initially accepted all the reports designated by the police as founded.

Difficulties in Obtaining a Jury Conviction

The prosecutors were asked what they felt were the two major difficulties they found in getting juries to convict for forcible rape. It is interesting to note that all but one of the respondents interviewed felt that the credibility of the victim was one of the major difficulties. Included in this category, apart from the veracity of the victim's account of the offence, were the character and background of the victim. The importance of the victim's credibility in a jury situation is acknowledged by Chappell: "Because of the necessity to prove force or threat of force and lack of consent, and since the victim is usually the prosecutor's only witness, her credibility becomes extremely salient in influencing the decision of jury members"(1975, 85).

The category which followed in terms of frequency of response was that the corroboration requirements are too strict (39 percent). Since this study was completed, the corroboration requirements have been tempered by the new sexual assault legislation (see our discussion in chapter 8).

Other difficulties noted by prosecutors were: the

presentation of the case is limited (22 percent) and the penalties are too severe (6 percent). The additional response category provided specific examples of victim credibility: the notion that 'good girls' don't get raped and the behaviour and conduct of the victim just before the actual offence. The final response concerned the lapse of time in having the case concluded, which corresponds to the notion that "the heart may soften with the passage of time".

The prosecutors were also queried as to the importance of a number of legal and social factors both in terms of the filing of charges and in obtaining a conviction for rape. The five most important factors in the decision to file charges included three elements that are not necessary components of the offence: physical force, injury to the victim and the relationship between the victim and the suspect. The same three elements emerged among the top five factors for obtaining a conviction, with the addition to a further element that is not a necessary component of the offence – the use of a weapon.

Consequently, the data support the assertion that the greater the amount of force and injury, the greater are the chances that a rape charge will be fully prosecuted. There is evidently a shared social consensus by victims and the judicial system about when a case is likely to be taken seriously. The study of the victim's response clearly indicates that a decision to report an offence to the police is contingent on the same factors that are used to justify prosecution. Thus, not only are these elements likely to encourage entry to the system, they also legitimate the charges for legal proceedings. Aside from the injustice of predetermining the legitimacy of an assault, victims are subject to contradictory messages. While, under the "acceptable" circumstances of attacks by strangers, victims are expected to vigorously resist (with possible allowances for threats with a weapon), they are at the same time told not to resist in order to avoid severe injury or death.

Average Sentence for Rape

The respondents were asked to give an estimate of the average sentence actually imposed for forcible rape in Manitoba. The lowest estimate given was 1.5 years while the highest estimate given was 5 years. The average estimate was 3.5 years. The mean sentence imposed for forcible rape in our study was 3.2 years. The majority of the prosecutors interviewed felt that the average sentence imposed was inappropriate in terms of being too lenient for the offence involved (61 percent).

Criticisms of sentencing by prosecutors revealed the following information. Some respondents said that rape is one of the most serious criminal offences and is potentially punishable by life imprisonment (22 percent). Several of the respondents (17 percent) felt that rapes involving violence should have higher sentences than they do at present. It was also felt that the emotional damage to the victim should be reflected in higher sentences (17 percent). The opinion that low sentences are not an effective deterrent to potential offenders (17 percent) was also cited. A final concern regarding low sentences was that they are inadequate in terms of punishment of the offender (28 percent).

The remainder of the prosecutors interviewed (39 percent) were of the opinion that the average sentence imposed for rape in Manitoba was appropriate. Several of the prosecutors referred to sexual assaults without a lot of violence as either "poor salesmanship" or "over-zealous seductions". This group of respondents felt that the sentence involved generally corresponded to the type of rape involved.

Major Improvements Needed to Deal with Sexual Assault

The prosecutors were queried as to the most important improvements needed in dealing with the problem of sexual assault. Once again, they expressed their dissatisfaction with the sentencing in sexual assault cases. Most of the respondents (61 percent) indicated that sentencing improvements were the most important changes needed in dealing with sexual assault. Public education dealing with the realities of the offence as opposed to the stereotypes followed in terms of frequency (50 percent). Improvement in the area of services for better aiding the victim and ultimately leading to a higher rate of reporting, was voiced as a major concern (44 percent).

The next two improvements were concerned with controlling the incidence of sexual assault. These were the treatment and rehabilitation of offenders (39 percent) and the teaching of prevention techniques to potential victims (33 percent). It is curious that the prosecutors ranked victim avoidance techniques closely behind treatment for offenders, given that the latter group are the actual perpetrators of the crime.

Legal reform was ranked rather low at 22 percent. Police investigation techniques and prosecution policies were also considered relatively insignificant (11 and 6 percent, respectively). Finally, the under-reporting of the offence was noted by one of the prosecutors and can be linked to the improvement of victim services and public education.

It would appear that the prosecutors interviewed do not see the criminal justice system as a whole playing a significant role in dealing with the problem of sexual assault. The problems cited least often by the prosecutors concerned legal reform, prosecution policies, police training and police investigative techniques. Although sentencing and victim services were among the major problems listed, there was emphasis on the prevention of sexual assault by way of victim avoidance and offender treatment and rehabilitation. While public education about the realities of the offence was deemed significant, the responsibilities of the legal system in addressing sexual assault were not given comparable consideration. In this sense, the use of the legal system was overlooked in importance by the prosecutors as one of the potential educators of the public.

In the context of the theoretical orientation advocated by the authors, it is noteworthy that respondents have proposed a micro solution to a macro problem. Treating offenders (those few who are convicted) and trying to teach potential victims how not to be victimized suggest "band-aid" solutions to much deeper social/structural problems. The notion propagated by this theme is that the issue is one to be dealt with on an individual, rather than a societal, level. However, as long as males and females are operating from unequal positions, violence will continue to be perpetrated on those who have less power.

CHAPTER VII

The New Sexual Assault Legislation

FEATURES OF THE NEW LAW

IN January 1983, the existing rape law in Canada was replaced by sexual assault legislation. The first and most obvious change is that of the designation of the offence. The former offences of rape, attempted rape, and indecent assault on a female or male have been replaced by the offence of sexual assault. The designation is crucial as it correctly shifts the emphasis from sex to violence. As a result, the necessity of penetration has been replaced by the violence of the entire offence. However, the label of "rape" persists and with it the preoccupation with the connotation of sex as opposed to the violence. A media report from Vancouver (*Winnipeg Free Press*, May 1983), in referring to a man thought to be responsible for numerous sexual assaults and not yet apprehended, stated: "The man plans his ambush in advance...sexually assaults or rapes them after luring them into bush areas". Even four to five years later, media accounts continue to label sexual assaults as rape. A headline reading "Rapid Fire Sex Ruled Rape" actually referred to a case in which the accused was found guilty of sexual assault (*Winnipeg Sun*, Aug. 1987). Confusion as to the new sexual assault legislation is heightened by media accounts which continue to distinguish between sexual assault and rape.

Under the new legislation, either a male or female can be classified as a victim or an offender. This change removes the stigmatization of the "female victim" and replaces it with a more equitable definition that includes either of the sexes. The "degenderizing" of offences, however, applies only to those charges replaced by the new sexual assault law. Charges applying only to females, including sexual intercourse with a female under 14 years, with a female between 14 and 16 years and seduction of female passengers on vessels, still remain in the Criminal Code. In addition, the offences of buggery, gross indecency and incest are still accorded separate status and are dealt with outside of the sexual assault legislation.

Sexual assault contains a three-tiered structure of degrees of assault, and includes sexual assault, sexual assault with threats or bodily harm, and aggravated sexual assault. The categories are delineated by factors such as use of a weapon, threat to a third party, victim injury, the number of offenders and the endangerment of life. The maximum sentences vary from 6 months for simple sexual assault to life imprisonment for aggravated sexual assault, depending upon the severity of the offence. The Criminal Code provisions for sexual assault are given below.

SEXUAL ASSAULT - No Defence

246.1

1)Every one who commits a sexual assault is guilty of

a)an indictable offence and is liable to imprisonment for ten years; or

b)an offence punishable on summary conviction.

2)Where an accused is charged with an offence under subsection (1) or section 246.2 or 246.3 in respect of a person under the age of fourteen years, it is not a defence that the complainant consented to the activity that forms the subject-matter of the charge unless the accused is less than three years older than the complainant. 1980-81-82, c. 125, 19.

SEXUAL ASSAULT WITH A WEAPON, THREATS TO A THIRD PARTY OR CAUSING BODILY HARM

246.2

Everyone who, in committing a sexual assault,

a)carries, uses or threatens to use a weapon or on imitation thereof;

b)threatens to cause bodily harm to a person other than the complainant; or

c)causes bodily harm to the complainant; or

d)is a party to the offence with any other person,

is guilty of an indictable offence and is liable to imprisonment for fourteen years. 1980-81-82,c.125,s.19.

AGGRAVATED SEXUAL ASSAULT - Punishment

246.3

1)Every one commits an aggravated sexual assault who, in committing a sexual assault, wounds, maims, disfigures or endangers the life of the complainant.

2)Every one who commits an aggravated sexual assault is guilty of an indictable offence and is liable to imprisonment for life. 1980-81-82, c. 125, s. 19.

CORROBORATION NOT REQUIRED

246.4

Where an accused is charged with an offence under section 150 (incest), 157 (gross indecency), 246.1 (sexual assault), 246.2 (sexual assault with a weapon, threats to a third party or causing bodily harm) or 246.3 (aggravated sexual assault), no corroboration is required for a conviction and the judge shall not instruct the jury that it is unsafe to find the accused guilty in the absence of corroboration. 1980-81-82, c. 125, s. 19.

The new sexual assault law has now been in effect for over five years since its proclamation in January of 1983. We have examined cases tried under the new legislation and have prepared some recommendations aimed at enabling more effective prosecution of sexual offences. The major areas of the legislation analysed are: the meaning of sexual assault; corroboration and recent complaint; the sexual background of the victim; sexual assault of a spouse; prior relationship; the young victims of sexual assault; and the ban on publication of the victim's identity.

ANALYSIS OF KEY AREAS

The Meaning of Sexual Assault

One of the major problem areas identified in the sexual assault legislation is the lack of a definition that sets the offence apart from non-sexual assault. As it stands, the same necessary elements are applied to both assault and sexual assault. The result is the potential for differing interpretations of the actions that constitute a sexual assault. In other words, when does an assault become a sexual assault and what are the necessary elements that make up the offence? A review of cases prosecuted under the new legislation reveals some of the discrepancies in interpreting actions and applying the legislation.

A decision by the New Brunswick Court of Appeal in *R. v. Chase* held that sexual assault as related in the Criminal Code provisions was restricted to an assault on the sexual organs or genitalia and did not include the touching of a woman's breasts. One of the appeal judges stated: "The problem in this case is that the contact was not with the sexual organs of the victim but with the mammary gland, a secondary sexual characteristic" (1984, 286-87). Further, the grabbing of a woman's breasts was equated with other secondary sexual characteristics such as a man's beard. The appeal judge struck down the original conviction for sexual assault and substituted it with a verdict of guilty of common assault.

Several other appeals of sexual assault convictions were subsequently made which were based on the Chase decision. One such case involved an appeal to the Ontario Court of Appeal in *R. v. Gardynik* (1984) on a sexual assault conviction. The argument was made that the accused's actions of trying to kiss a woman, lying on top of her and biting her breast did not constitute a sexual assault as there was no involvement of the complainant's primary sexual organs. The Ontario Court dismissed the appeal, rejecting the Chase decision, and held that when the primary sexual organs were not involved, it was appropriate to determine all the facts in considering whether a sexual assault had occurred. They decided that the assault being appealed had in fact been appropriately defined at trial as a sexual assault. In October 1987 the Supreme Court of Canada clarified the legislation by stating that the touching of breasts was indeed sexual, and therefore constituted a sexual assault.

Another case, that of *R. v. Cook*, heard in the B.C. Court of Appeal, concerned the accused's appeal on conviction for sexual assault. It was questioned whether the touching of the thighs, stomach and breasts of the victim were applicable elements of the offence of sexual assault or nonsexual assault. The B.C. court also rejected the Chase decision and dismissed the appeal. According to one of the judges who heard the appeal: "I do not propose to offer a definition for sexual assault, where Parliament has declined to do so. But I do not think that the characteristic that turns a simple assault into a sexual assault is solely a matter of anatomy. I think that a real affront to sexual integrity and sexual dignity may be sufficient" (1985, 149).

The Cook case also addressed the inappropriateness of equating the old offences (rape, indecent assault) with the new sexual assault provisions. One of the judges remarked that a charge of sexual assault might not sustain a charge of indecent assault and vice versa, citing *R. v. Burden* (1982) from the B.C. Court of Appeal, in which an accused was acquitted of indecent assault for sitting next to the victim on a near-empty bus and putting his hand on her thigh for five to ten seconds. The accused in this case was subsequently convicted of common assault after a crown appeal. The judge from the current case further commented: "I think the assault in the Burden case might well be characterized as a sexual assault, though it was not characterized in the Burden case as indecent assault.... If a light but intentional touching may constitute an assault, then I think that a light but intentional sexual touching may constitute a sexual assault" (1985, 148).

A further example dealing with the meaning of sexual assault is the crown appeal of an accused's acquittal on assault, sexual assault and confinement charges in *R. v. Taylor* (1985). The charges related to the punishment of a 16-year-old female on several occasions by a male acting in a role of parental authority. The punishment included taping the victim's hands to a post and pulling her nightgown up to her neck where she would be forced to stand for a period of time. On one of these occasions, the accused used a wooden paddle on the bare buttocks of the victim while she was so confined. The charges resulted in an acquittal, as the judge decided the acts did not have a sexual connotation. It was also concluded that a conviction for assault was unwarranted according to Sec. 43 of the Criminal Code which states:

> 43. Every schoolteacher, parent or person standing the place of a parent is justified in using force by way of correction toward a pupil or child, as the case may be, who is under his care, if the force does not exceed what is reasonable under the circumstances.

It was apparently concluded that the punishment given to the victim fell within the parameters of the above Criminal Code provision. The Alberta Court of Appeal rejected the acquittal and ordered a new trial on all the original charges, defining a sexual assault as an act which was intended to degrade or demean another person for sexual gratification, and not restricted only to acts of force involving the sexual organs (1985, 269). The decision further stated that an objective test of whether the actions had sexual or carnal aspects in the opinion of a reasonable observer was sufficient evidence, regardless of the victim's perception of the presence of such sexual aspects.

Definitions for the offence are also needed for setting the parameters as to what reasonably constitutes a sexual assault so as not to unduly trivialize the offence. An illustrative example occurred in the case of *R. v. Thorne* (1985) where an 18-year-old accused was convicted of sexual assault for forcibly kissing the hand of a young female. An appeal by the accused from his conviction to the Ontario Court of Appeal resulted in a verdict of guilty with a conditional discharge. The offence was appropriately classified in appeal court as one without sufficient sexual connotation to be deemed a sexual assault.

The use of the term "rape" lingers on, despite the fact that it no longer applies (legally) to the offence. Since the word can be found in any English dictionary, citing forced sexual intercourse among its meanings, "rape" will undoubtedly persist as the term which is used to define that particular act. However, members of the judiciary and the media have a responsibility to change public perception of the offence by using terms that are consistent with the new law. Otherwise, the power and violence of the assaults will remain trivial in relation to the sexual aspect, thus defeating the motive for changing the law in the first place.

Another problem to consider pertaining to the new term is that it continues to be translated according to the older, more familiar one. This is analogous to the practice utilized by immigrants in attempting to translate a second language by tacitly decoding it through their mother-tongue before uttering their thoughts. Judges, however, are obligated to learn the new "language" and recognize any incongruity. At the trial of *R. v. Daychief* (1985), the judge referred to the term "rape" in sentencing the offender and the decision was appealed. The courts have a particular responsibility not to take any liberties in substituting a legal term with a more familiar or graphic designation. Ignorance of the law cannot be a defence for those who are empowered to apply it. Yet, at the appeal, the original sentence of 13 years was upheld and one of the judges argued:, "...the sentence is to be varied because the judge characterized the offence as 'rape'. It was a rape. That Parliament has chosen to categorize rape and other sexual offences as sexual assault does not change the accuracy of that description applied to this particular assault" (1985, 548).

This is the consequence of what might be called "judicial sclerosis", which hinders the ability of a judge to see things according to a new set of conditions. The inability to be flexible combined with discretionary latitude create structural impediments which may sometimes limit the effectiveness of the new legislation.

Recommendations

1. Upon receiving a related case for consideration, the Supreme Court of Canada should set out the appropriate parameters in terms of the actions and elements which constitute a sexual assault. This will result in less confusion regarding the required elements constituting a sexual assault and will enable more equitable application of the legislation.

2. The Supreme Court should consider and provide clarification in the following areas:

(a) The inclusion of reasonable and appropriate secondary sexual characteristics is to be used in the definition of a sexual assault. The presence of sexual connotation or degradation for the purposes of sexual gratification should be based on a reasonable and objective evaluation not by way of including only primary sexual organs or excluding all secondary sexual characteristics in defining sexual assault.

(b) A sexual assault should not be equated with the former offences of indecent assault or rape in order to be considered valid. The intent of the new legislation was to move away from the previous rigidly defined sexual elements (i.e. penetration of the vagina by a penis) and to focus on the aspect of force.

(c) Parameters must also prevent the inclusion of spontaneous and unintentional incidents in the definition of sexual assault. The charging of persons for acts such as unsolicited hand-kisses or hugs would be appropriately dealt with under the assault section as opposed to sexual assault. Including any and all offences with a remote sexual connotation will only serve to hinder the integrity and effective prosecution of cases under the new legislation.

Corroboration and Recent Complaint

The former requirement for corroborative evidence, such as cuts, bruises, torn clothing, or witnesses to an offence which gave credence to a victim's complaint, has been taken out (Sec. 246.4). Legally, a conviction can now be obtained without additional proof that a complainant's testimony is truthful. Nevertheless, the uncertainty of prosecuting on the basis of one person's word against that of another has implications which are unique to sexual assault cases. Women's (and girls') credibility is still undermined by the traditional view that complaints may be-motivated by personal factors such as vengeance or guilt. False accusations are no more likely in cases of sexual assault than in any other cases. Attitudes among the members of the judiciary must change in the wake of the legal reform.

In a similar manner, rules relating to the matter of recent complaint have been repealed (Sec. 246.5). Formerly, it was believed that the victim of a "genuine" sexual assault would complain to someone at the first opportunity. This assumption failed to consider the effect a sexual assault may have on some victims. Embarrassment, ambivalent feelings about reporting a family member or significant other, fear of reprisal, or sheer confusion may cause a delay in responding.

Pertinent to both procedural issues is the following judicial interpretation from the Ontario Supreme Court:

"I permitted the complainant to testify that she caused the police to be called almost immediately after exiting the accused's care. I did not, however, permit her to testify as to what she told the police. I did, however, permit her and the police to testify that she made a statement. I did additionally, permit the other witnesses to describe her emotional condition and her state of dress. As well, a doctor testified to her physical condition a few hours after the alleged assault" (*R. v. Page*, 1984).

It is obvious that the matters of corroboration and recent complaint can be construed in a manner which overrides the original intention of the revised legislation. If evidence such as cited in the above case is emphasized to the extent that it detracts from the importance of the complainant's testimony, it may also be used in its absence to cast serious doubt on her credibility.

Recommendation

1. Corroborative evidence such as visible injuries to the victim and early reporting of the offence should not be used in determining the veracity of the charge, and the absence of these elements should not be interpreted as supporting the innocence of the accused.

Sexual Background of the Victim

The questioning of the victim as to sexual activity with anyone other than the accused has always existed in some form under sexual offences legislation. The first substantive amendments occurred in 1976, at which time the victim could be cross-examined regarding prior sexual conduct but was not compelled to answer. In addition, the accused was not permitted to lead evidence which refuted her testimony. However, once these questions had been asked the damage was done. In the eyes of the jury, a refusal to respond could very well be interpreted as having something to conceal, without regard to the obvious infringement of the victim's right to have the sexual offence in question the focus of attention.

In an effort to reduce harassment and entrapment of the victim by defence counsel, the 1976 amendments to the Criminal Code placed the following restrictions on such questioning.

> (1)reasonable notice must be given to the prosecution with the particulars of the evidence sought to be adduced and,
>
> (2)the judge, after an in-camera hearing would decide whether the exclusion of that evidence would prevent the just determination of an issue of fact in the proceedings, including the credibility of the complainant (Sec. 142.C.C.1976).

While at face value the above provisions appeared to have effectively curtailed the innuendo and surprise "attacks" on victims by way of questioning from defence counsel, the judge was then placed in control of decisions made regarding the admissibility of evidence of prior sexual activity. In effect, while restrictions were placed on the questioning by defence counsel, no such restrictions were placed on the judge in deciding whether the information sought was necessary for a "just determination of the case". It is also noteworthy that while inappropriate defence questions were to be abruptly stopped and stricken from the court record, the statement would have already been made, and the innuendo would have been planted in the minds of the jury members.

A further development concerning the 1976 amendments occurred when the Supreme Court interpreted the 1976 amendments in *Forsythe* v. R. (1980) as referred to by Boyle (1984). The court indicated that the victim was required to testify as a witness at an in-camera hearing and that her evidence could be refuted in evidence led by the accused. This decision not only nullified the new provisions but provided less protection to the victim than did the pre–1976 provisions. At this point it became apparent that victims were not protected from personal questioning of a sexual nature – questioning which had no valid relationship to the offence being tried save conjecture or victim-character assassination for the benefit of the defence's case.

With the advent of the new sexual assault legislation in 1983, the provisions for questioning on the sexual background of the victim were clarified. Parameters were set by which judges could ascertain the validity of such questioning, instead of using their own discretion. The new stipulations read as follows:

> 246.6 (1) In proceedings in respect of an offence under section 246.1, 246.2 or 246.3, no evidence shall be adduced by or on behalf of the accused concerning the sexual activity of the complainant with any person other than the accused unless:
>
> (a)it is evidence that rebuts evidence of the complainant's sexual activity or absence thereof that was previously adduced by the prosecution;
>
> (b)it is evidence of specific instances of the complainant's sexual activity tending to establish the identity of the person who had sexual contact with the complainant on the occasion set out in the charge; or
>
> (c)it is evidence of sexual activity that took place on the same occasion as the sexual activity that forms the subject-matter of the charge, where that evidence relates to the consent that the accused alleges he believed was given by the complainant.
>
> (2)No evidence is admissible under paragraph (1)(c) unless:
>
> (a)reasonable notice in writing has been given to the prosecutor by or on behalf of the accused of his intention to adduce the evidence

together with particulars of the evidence sought to be adduced; (C.C. 1983)

Provision (a) concerns admissibility of evidence of sexual activity of the victim by defence counsel where it has been introduced by the crown. The evidence initially given by the crown may include reference either to the victim's sex life or to the absence of one. Provision (b) basically refers to those instances where the accused asserts that he is not the person who committed the offence. Provision (c) is ambiguous, implicitly reinforcing the myth that if a female says yes to one person then consent to others may be inferred when these acts occur on the same occasion.

The first provision of the restriction (Sec. 246.4(1)(a)) has been subject to several appeal challenges by the accused which have ruled in favour of the crown in compliance with the new provision. The first case, *R. v. Wiseman et al.* from the Ontario District Court (1986), concerned evidence given by the victim at the preliminary hearing that she told the accused to let her up and that she did not think it was right that they should use someone else's home. The accused contended that such evidence amounted to sexual activity which should allow the accused to call evidence in reply. The request by the accused was denied on two grounds: (1) the evidence brought out by the crown at the preliminary hearing does not apply to the provision which relates to trial, while (2) the statements made by the victim did not relate to any statements regarding sexual activity.

Another case, *R. v. Gran* (1984), involved an appeal by the accused on the grounds that the trial judge had erred in disallowing cross-examination of the victim with respect to her allegation that she had been sexually assaulted several months earlier. The trial judge disallowed the appeal because the evidence had not been given during the complainant's examination-in-chief, even though such evidence could be described as being of a sexual nature.

An examination of the cases tried under the new legislation indicates that the sexual background of the victim, while further clarified, continues to be a consideration in sexual assault proceedings. The case of *R. v. J.A.* (1984) concerned the sexual assault of a 16-year-old female by her 22-year-old brother who was acting in the capacity of a parent and sole provider for his mother, three brothers and the sister he assaulted. The female complied out of fear upon orders from her brother. The judge stated his contempt for the breach of trust involved between an adult and child, especially when the offender is in a position of authority over the child. However, the severity of the offence was reduced in the eyes of the judge by the following circumstances:

> Although, as I have said, this type of behavior is both socially and morally wrong, such occurrences may not warrant the same harsh sentences imposed by Canadian courts confronted with an incestuous relationship between a father and his daughter or between someone acting in *loco parentis* and a young girl. This also holds true if the sister involved in that incestuous relationship with a brother is not of previously chaste character. I hasten to add that previous sexual experiences encountered by a sister do not allow a brother to take advantage of that, but one must realize that the damage, the physical damage, the psychological trauma may not be the same.

Consequently, the offender was given a suspended sentence and placed on two years' probation.

A case which was appealed to the New Brunswick

Court of Appeal by the crown concerned the sentence given to two defendants accused of sexual assault (*R. v. Cormier*, 1985). They were given six months and three months imprisonment, respectively. The crown argued that the trial judge had erred in stating that the victim's reputation and lifestyle reduced the seriousness of the offence without any evidence to indicate that the victim would consent to the advances of the accused. The sentences were revised by the Appeal Court to four years' and two years' imprisonment.

Recommendations

1. Discussion of the sexual background (past sexual activity) of the victim should be prohibited altogether from sexual assault trials. This information bears no relevance to the charges at hand and only serves to detract from the seriousness of the offence being tried. Questioning of the sexual background of the victim initiated by the defence counsel, although stricken from the court record upon crown/judicial objections, should result in charges of contempt of court for defence counsel. These statements preclude a fair hearing of the charges and plant suspicions of the victim's credibility in juries.

2. The onus is on the crown to ensure that the past sexual background of the victim is kept out of the proceedings by way of quickly voicing objection to any such statements made by defence counsel. The judge cannot be relied on to monitor any and all statements or innuendo of past sexual activity. Similarly, the crown is cautioned against introducing the presence or absence of past sexual activity for the victim. This will open the door to a rebuttal from the accused and detract from the real issue, the sexual assault charge.

Sexual Assault of a Spouse

Husbands (and wives) can now be prosecuted under the new sexual assault legislation, regardless of whether they are living together or apart at the time of the offence. Although this new law shows no discrimination on the basis of sex, it primarily deals with the sexual assault of wives by their husbands. Prior to 1983, a husband did not need his wife's consent to have sexual intercourse with her, and he was protected by law in enforcing his wife's "duty" to succumb to his sexual demands.

Canada's first decision under section 246.8 was heard in March 1983 in Grand Prairie, Alberta. Following a guilty plea from the estranged husband of the victim, the judge stated: "I am of the view, and I believe it is common ground, that the degree of trauma associated with a sexual attack is affected by the relationship, if any, between the parties. And I think it cannot be said that the trauma suffered by the victim is as great where there has been a past history of lawful sexual relations with the accused as it would if she were attacked by a stranger" (*R. v. McDonald*, 1983). The assailant received a one-year prison term and one year's probation.

Our data and several other studies have shown that the majority of sexual assaults occur in the home between persons who are known to each other. The trauma associated with a breach of trust between two persons in this type of offence is considerable and must not be minimized by such misleading statements as the one above.

There have been a few decisions favourable to the victims, but sentences have been relatively short compared to cases of similar circumstances which did not involve spouses. Common to all these cases is the extensive injury to the complainants. This corroborative evidence appears to be necessary in practice even though the legal requirement for corroboration has been removed. None of the cases uncovered in our investigation of the new legislation have disclosed a single spousal sexual assault case heard in a Canadian courtroom in which a complainant did not have corroborative evidence. The following excerpt from a case described in Weekly Criminal Bulletin exemplifies this point: "Moreover, it could not be said that the accused could have had an honest belief in the consent of his wife to sexual intercourse, particularly given the degree of violence prior to the act of sexual intercourse" (*R.* v. A., 1985). The assailant was convicted and sentenced to one year's imprisonment and two years' probation.

The accused in the following case attacked his estranged wife as she entered her car. A guilty plea resulted in one year in prison plus three on probation: "He drove to another location where his own car was parked and tied her wrists with twine to the steering wheel. He forced her to change into a transparent white dress and garter belt. He then drove to another location, masturbated and tried unsuccessfully to have sexual intercourse with her. He ordered her to pose nude in various positions and invited another man to witness it. The entire episode lasted throughout the night for about eight hours" (*R. v. Ryan*, 1985).

Sentencing of husbands does not seem to reflect the gravity of their offences. An even more blatant example is illustrated in the following case. The first Manitoba decision concerning the sexual assault of a spouse resulted in a conviction and sentence of six months' imprisonment with one year's probation (*R. v. Guiboche*, 1983). According to the *Winnipeg Free Press*, the husband: "...pursued and caught her and began punching her in the face. He threw her to the ground and began choking her...then dragged his wife along the ground a short distance, pulled her pants to her knees and had intercourse with her against her will...Medical evidence presented at the trial noted (she)...required eight stitches to close cuts to her nose and mouth" (Sept. 8, 1983).

The second conviction in Manitoba (*R. v. Martens*, 1987) for the sexual assault of a spouse occurred in March 1987. The offender was given a three-month sentence for "sexual assault causing bodily harm", which was mitigated by the offender's wife who sent a letter to the judge asking for leniency. Women's groups and the Manitoba Bar Association criticized the sentence, stating that the consideration of the letter by the judge in court was inappropriate.

It must be emphasized that the first step has been taken by removing spousal immunity from the Criminal Code. Nevertheless judicial attitudes must shift along with the legal revision to portray offences against wives to be as serious as assaults against others. Beliefs about women's masochistic tendencies and men's rights to have obedient wives linger on. Meanwhile women's continued dependence on men and their lengthy socialization to be victims keep them silent.

Sexual and physical abuse of wives is a contradiction of the "ideal" institution of marriage, which has us believing that the home is a sanctuary. There is an abundance of research documenting the extensive physical abuse suffered by wives (for example, Martin 1977; Klein 1981). Sexual abuse often accompanies battering as another form of intimidation and expression of power. Sexual assault of wives has not been considered a crime long enough for society and the victims themselves to perceive it as an offence. Thus, sexual assault will have an even lower incidence of reporting than battering. We are not likely to see any significant change until more cases proceed to trial. The stigma associated with sexual assault is even more demeaning to wives than that of battering because it is less clear that an offence has been committed when battering does not accompany the sexual assault. As more cases are made public with fair objective judgments in favour of women who are sexually assaulted in marital relationships, perhaps we will begin to see how extensive the problem of marital assault is.

Recommendations

1. Low sentences given for cases of spousal sexual assault should be appealed by the crown. The fact that the victim and the offender are or were involved in a marital relationship should not negate the objective realities of the violence of a sexual assault which may or may not involve injury.

2. The reporting of spousal sexual assault will only increase when more cases reach the courtroom and the offence can be viewed as a valid one meriting penalties that are equivalent to those imposed for other assaults.

Prior Relationship

Although the credibility of a complainant can no longer be based on past sexual conduct, in the event of a prior relationship with the accused, prejudices inherent in this scenario are reflected in sentencing. For example, a lenient sentence of 90 days to be served intermittently along with two years' probation was handed down to an offender who had tied up his victim and had intercourse with her against her will. "However, the accused had had a sexual relationship with the woman in the past and there was no injury to the woman" (*R. v. Naqitarvik*, 1985).

Another 90-day sentence with three years' probation was imposed on an accused who forced a woman to commit various sexual acts after she had accepted a motorcycle ride from him. Although the victim tried to fight off her attacker, he threatened and overpowered her. It was stated that the accused and the victim were known to each other (*R. v. Ashbee*, 1985).

Alternately, a sentence of two years (increased to five years on appeal) was imposed on an offender who attacked a woman who was walking down the street. He dragged her into bushes, choked her and had forced sexual intercourse with her. This is as close to the classic stereotype of assault as one could conceive. The difference in attitude between the latter and the former two cases is reflected in the appeal judge's comment: "An assault of this nature involving the grabbing of someone minding their own business, going down a public street, is a most serious offence. It is not to be compared to the social engagement that has gone wrong. It is something which this court takes a very serious view of. The trial judge's sentence was manifestly inadequate" (*R. v. Mitchell*, 1984).

The disparities perceived then, to a great extent, depend on the attitudes of those who are making the assessments (i.e. police, prosecutors, judges, juries) and it is obvious that sexual assaults, although they may be similar in effect, are not treated similarly.

The issue of prior relationship is somewhat related to the spousal immunity clause which was removed from the old legislation. Although prior relationship is not itself directly addressed in the new law, the failure of wives to report their husbands is akin to nonreporting by victims who have previously had relationships with offenders. Since closeness of relationship between victims and offenders correlates with a low incidence of reporting, it is not surprising that the response of the courts continues to reflect the old attitudes which have not been seriously challenged with a significant increase of reporting cases. If husbands are successfully prosecuted for sexually assaulting their wives, this will certainly have an effect on cases in which there was a prior relationship.

Recommendation

1. Criteria used for determining seriousness of sexual assaults need to be standardized in practice, according to the three-tiered structure set out under new legislation. The existence of a prior relationship should not be considered. Nonconsent at the time of the offence is the salient point.

Young Victims of Sexual Assault

Unique obstacles ensue when convictions are sought for sexual assaulters of young children.[1] The corroboration requirement which has been removed from sexual assault may still bear relevance for victims of "tender years", particularly where sworn evidence cannot be obtained from

1 In January 1988 Bill C-15 came into effect. The amendments deal specifically with child sexual abuse under the Criminal Code and the Canada Evidence Act. The major provisions include much greater latitude in obtaining evidence from children and the use of videotaped testimony of young victims in court. These changes bring great potential in allowing for the testimony of young sexual abuse victims in criminal proceedings. To date, there have been too few cases to provide any feedback on the impact of Bill C-15.

a young victim. The new corroboration provision, section 246.4, states that the conviction of the accused charged with any of the new sexual assault offences (sections 246.1, 246.2, 246.3) and incest (section 150) will not require corroboration to obtain a conviction and that the judge shall not issue any cautionary warning to the jury in the absence of such evidence. However, as Boyle (1984) points out, the provision is unclear as to whether such an exception is applicable to instances of unsworn testimony. The confusion around the acceptability of young victim's testimony is the result of a contradictory provision in the Criminal Code relating to the testimony of young witnesses. The provision, Section 586, reads:

> No person shall be convicted of an offence upon the unsworn evidence of a child unless the evidence of the child is corroborated in a material particular by evidence that implicates the accused.

The crown is then left in a precarious position regarding the admissibility of the young victim's testimony.

The use of a sworn oath as a requirement for testifying in court is in itself subject to criticism. First, the oath does not guarantee honest testimony. Rather, it is the duty of the legal counsel in court to question witnesses to arrive at the accuracy of the testimony given. In this sense, the oath is more a symbolic gesture than a functional procedure. Second, the oath presumes a respect for the truth and an understanding of the consequences of telling lies.

While the accused has the benefit of safeguards against being falsely convicted for sexual assault via provisions restricting children's testimony, there are no corresponding safeguards for the protection of the young sexual assault victim in the court proceedings. What of the preoccupation surrounding the ability of children to tell the truth and to separate fact from fiction? In fact, children may be more likely to relate events reliably. The relative sophistication of adults in comparison to children may facilitate deceit, whereas the more limited life experiences of the child will diminish this likelihood. Carpenter, who has done research on child victims, relates the following on the possibility of children lying about sexual offences: "There is no evidence in the literature or among the service providers that children are unable to distinguish fact from fantasy in these situations. Of course the younger the child the more unlikely it is that the child would or even could imagine such things, given the detail and accuracy with which children repeat these incidents" (Cited in Rush 1980, 155).

Cases considered under the sexual assault legislation (prior to the introduction of Bill C-15 in January 1988) are illustrative of the problematic aspects for young victims. A sexual assault case from British Columbia, *R. v. Andrew F.* (1985) resulted in an acquittal of a male babysitter for the sexual assault of a five-year-old female child. While medical evidence supported the fact that the child had had sexual intercourse, she could not be sworn as a witness. The veracity of the charge against the accused was questioned, as it was unclear whether the child had actually experienced what she was relating or whether she was remembering prior discussion with her parents, police and others. A determination was made that the young child's testimony was unreliable whereupon the accused was acquitted.

A further example concerned the sexual assault of a child where there was no question that the assault had occurred, although the evidence given by the victim against the accused was considered to be uncorroborated and lacking confirmatory evidence. The court considered- the frailties of young children's evidence. The victim was described as being reluctant to testify even though she said she was not embarrassed or intimidated. As a consequence, there was reasonable doubt as to the guilt of the accused and he was acquitted (*R. v. Breckinridge*, 1984).

In *R. v. Bird* from the Ontario County Court in 1984, the accused was acquitted of sexual assault of a ten-year-old female. The only direct evidence against the accused came from the young victim, and there were discrepancies noted in her testimony from the preliminary hearing to the trial. Even though corroboration was no longer necessary under the sexual assault legislation, the court had reasonable doubt as to the accuracy of the accusations made by the victim. It was also noted that the alleged acts of the accused were totally out of character for him.

Conversely, the following two cases are illustrative of convictions secured for sexual assaults on young victims with the help of independent corroborative evidence. The first case, *R. v. R.S.* from the Ontario County Court (1985), involved the sexual assault of a twelve-year-old victim by her stepfather. The court noted that it must be extremely cautious in convicting an accused with only the testimony of a young victim even though the evidence was obtained under oath. However, while corroboration was not necessary, there was independent and substantial corroboration of her evidence.

Similarly, in *R. v. Sarabando* (1985), from the same court, an accused was convicted of sexual assault of a fourteen-year-old involving the fondling and kissing of the victim against her wishes. While it was mentioned that the victim did not relate most of the details in her discussion with the police, it was noted that her emotional state and independent evidence substantiated her claims. As these cases illustrate, while courts refer to the abolition of the necessity of corroboration, its use is still regarded as essential for obtaining a conviction in some circumstances.

Concern for the protection of children from sexual assault, with particular abhorrence reserved for sexual assaults on children by persons in positions of trust or authority, is commonly stated throughout Canadian courtrooms. However, the sentences given for convictions do not generally reflect the professed condemnation of such actions by adults against children. From our review of child sexual assault cases we found that low sentencing was a consistent trend.

For example, in *R. v. Smaaslet* (1984; 1985) an accused appealed his sentence of 90 days imprisonment for the fondling of an eleven-year-old he was babysitting. While the Court of Appeal expressed concern over breaches of trust and the protection of children, it proceeded to determine that the 90-day sentence should be served intermittently as opposed to consecutively.

Another case involved the trial of a male charged with sexual intercourse with a female under fourteen. The victim was the ten-year-old child of his common-law wife (*R. v. Gallant*, Ont. Dist. Ct. 1985). Once again, the court emphasized the seriousness of the violation of the parental trust and cited it as an aggravating factor. Yet, the court proceeded to note that there was no physical harm to the child, the offender was no longer living with the victim's mother and the offender, while having a criminal record, had employment. The offender was sentenced to seven months' imprisonment followed by two years' probation.

Another case involved the crown's appeal of a sentence of fifteen months' imprisonment given to a father convicted of sexual assault with a weapon on his fourteen-year-old daughter. (*R. v. Thom*, 1985) The offences included sexual assault and the striking of his daughter with firewood. The Court of Appeal judges saw the sentence as fitting and disallowed the appeal.

A final case concerned charges of sexual assault by a grandfather on his thirteen-year-old granddaughter. Two charges were involved and on one occasion sexual intercourse had occurred. At trial the offender was described as being intoxicated during the offences, having no criminal record and a good employment record. It was also noted that the victim had not suffered any emotional trauma from the offences. The grandfather was given a suspended sentence with probation for two years. A crown appeal on sentence resulted in the determination that nine months' imprisonment with two years' probation was adequate (*R. v. Billie*). Surprisingly, this sentence was deemed appropriate in terms of repugnance for the offences and for general deterrence.

A common theme in many of the above cases is the emotional and physical impact on young victims. The issue of harm to the child is minimized by members of the judiciary by drawing attention to the apparent absence of emotional trauma or physical injury. This contention callously neglects the extensive literature on the lasting and devastating effects of sexual abuse on children (Finkelhor, 1979). During this critical stage of development, children's self-concept is easily transformed so that they learn to see themselves as sexual objects. There is an erosion of trust that takes place, trust that should be inherent between a child and an adult caretaker. Again, the issue of an imbalance of power arises. During our interviews with victims, stories of incestuous experiences, sometimes blocked out of memory for years, always reemerged, manifested through self-destructiveness, suicide attempts and depression. Children are left with scars, whether or not they are obvious at the time of the abuse.

A final issue affecting young victims of sexual assault is the emotional impact of relating the details of the offence to an array of adults including teachers, social workers, police and lawyers. All these discussions and interviews occur before the trial. If the case reaches the court, the child will also be required to testify in front of a number of adults and be subjected to a cross-examination by defence counsel. The trauma for young children, who may find questioning about sexual offences difficult to understand and even more difficult to discuss, may be intensified when the offender is a parent, relative or family friend.

The terror experienced by young victims during the pre-court phase and the eventual prospect of testifying in court are effective in preventing many of the charges from being tried in a court of law. O'Hara reported that police in Vancouver investigated 85 reports of child sexual assault from October to December 1985 with only 33 cases resulting in charges being laid. A reluctance to proceed by victims or parents saw more than one-half of those charges being discontinued (*Maclean's*, Jan. 1986, 47).

Recommendations

1. The child victim of sexual assault must be listened

to, must be supported, and above all else must be protected during the legal proceedings as much as is possible without violating the rights of the accused. The inherent distrust of children's evidence must end. The onus is on all those in the criminal justice system, from the police through to the judges in the courtroom, to give children a fair hearing.

2. Evidence given by children promising to tell the truth should be afforded the same weight as sworn evidence. Visual or verbal aids should be acceptable alternatives for children to articulate their ability to distinguish between the truth and lies. The formal sworn testimony process (as it applied prior to Bill C-15) is irrelevant to children who are not equipped to deal with the abstract concepts of truth and lies in isolation from more simplistic, though no less accurate, alternative methods of obtaining sworn testimony.

3. The necessity of corroboration for young victims should be abolished. Although this has been addressed in Bill C-15 by removing the cautionary section in the Criminal Code which warns against unsworn evidence given by young witnesses, there is still uncertainty about the relative weight of unsworn evidence. The corroboration prohibition should apply unequivocally to young victims who promise to tell the truth so that all sexual assault victims would be accorded the same protection under the Criminal Code.

4. The use of videotaped evidence should be allowed for child victims of sexual abuse. Properly conducted videotaped interviews can permit child victims to describe in their own way what occurred. The appropriate use of such interviews should reduce the number of times the young victim must recount the attack to police, crown at-

torneys, medical professionals, social workers and others. The introduction of tapes as courtroom evidence can ease the burden and trauma of providing direct testimony.

5. Sexual assault of children by a parent or relative should be considered as serious a crime as assault by a stranger. Belief in the sanctity and continuity of the family has over-ridden our abhorrance of the crime. A family where the sexual abuse of children is occurring does not deserve special protection; the main focus should be on the well-being of the child in that environment.

6. The offence of incest should be abolished from the Criminal Code. The sexual assault of children by blood relatives should not be accorded special status and should be tried under the new sexual assault provisions. Incest is akin to the former charge of "rape" in that it also requires sexual intercourse as a necessary element. The new legislation considers the the use of force or coersion rather than the sexual nature of the offence. Incest, as it is defined, ignores the blended families found in today's society by differentiating between blood relatives and other persons in positions of trust or authority.

Publication Ban on the Victim's Identity
Section 442(3) of the Criminal Code enforces a mandatory publication ban on the name of a victim. This provision has been held for victims of sexual assault under the new sexual assault legislation. Under the old legislation, the onus was on the crown to initiate the publication ban proceedings. In an Ontario sexual assault case, a newspaper challenged the constitutionality of the ban on the basis of the freedom of the press which is guaranteed by the Charter of Rights and Freedoms (*Canadian Newspapers v. Attorney General for Canada, Ontario*

Lawyers Weekly, February 22, 1985). In February of 1985, the Ontario Court of Appeal held that the ban under section 442(3) was of no force and effect. The publication ban should be left to judicial discretion according to the decision. The judge in the Court of Appeal stated: "However, in an exceptional case where it [publication ban] is not merited, the presiding judge should have an opportunity to refuse to make it." The decision is slated for appeal to the Supreme Court of Canada. The judgment from the Ontario Court of Appeal is viewed as an important one with respect to the new sexual assault legislation which was enacted with the intent of facilitating the reporting of sexual assault. The decision allowing for judicial discretion on the publication of a victim's name may act to discourage victims from reporting an assault.

Recommendation

1. The Supreme Court of Canada should consider the mandatory publication ban on the victim's name in sexual assault cases as a necessary safeguard to encourage increased reporting of sexual assaults in line with the intent of the new sexual assault legislation.

The 1983 Sexual Assault legislation has the potential to constitute a marked improvement over the old rape laws. However, as we have seen, legal reform will not automatically change the system of inequality. Along with government initiatives, new definitions and meanings must be introduced and supported within the legal system. Patriarchal ideology still dominates the thoughts and behaviour of society's inhabitants. The legal system is set up to protect the status quo. Thus, nothing less than a concerted effort from without (through the power structure) and within (through changes in attitudes and practices) will adequately deal with gender inequality.

CHAPTER VIII

Conclusion

ALTHOUGH there are variations in status among women (just as there are with men), all females share some measure of powerlessness in relation to males. Defined in terms of femininity, the prevailing conceptions of what are "appropriate" feminine traits and the relegation of women to the (undervalued) roles of wife and mother are paramount to their status as second class citizens of society. Token recognition of a few women scattered throughout the authority system disguises the glaring resistance most women encounter when they deviate from the norms of mainstream society. Our analysis of sexual assault places violence against females within this context. Most victims of sexual assault experience opposition, both socially and structurally. This opposition appears in the form of "blaming the victim", which is manifested through harsh judgment from others, the victim's self-depreciation and an oftentimes insensitive response from the criminal justice system.

Our research indicates that even when the victim initiates legal proceedings, the majority of perpetrators slip through the cogs in the "wheel of justice". We found that nearly three-quarters of the charges studied were diverted from the legal system and that most of this filtering occurred at the police level. This corresponds to the concern many of the victims initially expressed when they were asked why they did not report an assault – that is, fear of the police not believing them. When we took this expressed concern a step further to consider why they were apprehensive, we found stereotyped beliefs about sexual assault were shared by the victim and members of the criminal justice system. The most frequent reason for the filtering out of charges was an "unfounded" designation by the police. In this regard, it was apparent that the police, in exercising their discretionary power, had to speculate on whether the charges would be accepted at the subsequent crown and court levels. Stereotypical definitions of "genuine" offences are formed in relation to judicial and societal responses which have repeatedly shown considerable indifference toward sexual assaults that do not conform to specific unwritten "guidelines". The degree to which the victim is held responsible depends upon how closely she observed socially prescribed behaviour. The victim who hitchhikes, frequents bars or knows her assailant thus becomes suspect. Our research also demonstrates that victims themselves ascribe to these beliefs under such circumstances.

The extent of self-blame experienced by victims is encountered in the second most frequent reason for the filtering out of charges: the victim withdraws charges. First-hand accounts of specific reasons for the victim's withdrawal were not available from the police files, apart from general fear of police, refusing to enter the legal process, and wanting to forget the assault. However, accounts from the interviews with victims indicate that the factors considered most important by the victim in deciding whether or not to contact the police are more fundamental. Her relationship to the offender, attitudes of others, self-blame and the extent of injury she suffered were the significant variables.

Cases studied at the criminal justice level indicated that roughly 30 percent of charges resulted in convictions. Most of these convictions were based on reduced charges which also carried lesser penalties. Only 10 percent of the convictions pertained to original charges laid by police.

There is considerable evidence stemming from both studies which indicates similarities in the data. The victims in each of the studies were predominantly young (19 years and under), unmarried and most were students at the time of the offence. In addition, the information received from victims, that they are more likely to report offences when the offenders are strangers (followed by "general knowledge", "acquaintance" and least often when the offenders are "family friend", "boyfriend" and "relative") was confirmed by the data from the police files. Victims are less able and/or willing to identify someone they are familiar with as having committed a crime against them. For those reports that were made to the police, half were initiated by the victim in both studies. This is consistent with the reported assaults as being more readily defined by the victim as meriting legal action.

As is evident from our research, there is little encouragement for victims to report sexual assaults in the expectation of achieving some sense of justice. However, the current state of underreporting not only exacerbates the problem of dealing effectively with the offence in the legal system, it leaves victims without redress and the perpetrators of the crime unaccountable. The legal system clearly must accept some of the responsibility for improving the circumstances. This can be achieved by handling sexual assault charges based on their own merit as opposed to stereotyping "genuine" offences and classifying "appropriate" charges which only result in the filtering out of the majority of charges.

Eradicating myths about sexual assault is an arduous task in a male-dominated society and the new legislation in and of itself cannot remedy the situation. The law is only as innovative as the individuals who use, interpret, and apply it. If victims do not report, the pervasiveness of the offence remains cloaked in secrecy. As long as the legal system and, indeed, society as a whole retain the traditional beliefs which place the onus of the deed on the victim, she will be discouraged from reporting the offence and entering into the legal process.

The new legislation carries with it many of the same problems which existed under the old rape laws. Our analysis of the cases tried under the new legislation reveal that there is still a preoccupation with victim accountability, which is reflected in the number of acquittals and low sentences. The strength of socialization is once again demonstrated as we discover that the implementation of revised laws does not necessarily coincide with the formulation of new beliefs about the offence. For example, although the corroboration provision was removed, we found, over and over again, the need for proof that the assault took place as the victim indicated. The apprehension of accepting the word of women (and children) for such an accusation is still omnipresent. Although it is known that this phenomenon is exclusive to sexual assault cases, the intellectualized knowledge reflected in the revised laws has not yet been internalized.

The notion of breaking down the old structures and re-establishing new institutions devoid of discrimination is an overwhelming concept. Yet, it would appear that, given the imbalance of male/female power, this idea is the only answer. Affirmative action is one practical method of dealing with institutional discrimination. This translates into increasing the representation of qualified women at the higher levels of the social structure, reflecting their actual proportion of the population. This does not refer to tokenism but is rather an acknowledgement of competence among women. In addition, confronting issues such as reproductive freedom for women, child care support systems and wages and pensions for homemakers are important steps toward equality for women.

Education is one of the most effective means of offering new insight to oppressed groups, as well as their oppressors. Recognition of myths and stereotypes helps to dispel them. This is a challenge to educators in every sphere of society. Efforts of the women's movement toward raising the collective consciousness of society have produced sexual assault centres, sexual harassment policies in the workplace, implementation of programs responding to wife battering and child abuse, human rights legislation, as well as the revised sexual assault legislation. While these innovations have resulted in a degree of awareness and advancement, they must be accompanied by continued strong advocacy to bring about significant changes. Assignment of new meanings must stem from the position that the dependent status of females legitimates the assumption of male authority. The progression from authority to violence is only a matter of degree.

REFERENCES

Abbreviations used in the text

CACSW Canadian Advisory Committee on the Status of Women
MACSW Manitoba Action Committee on the Status of Women
NCW National Council on Welfare

Secondary Sources

Amir, Menachim. 1971. *Patterns in Forcible Rape*. Chicago: University of Chicago Press.

Bart, Pauline. 1975. Rape doesn't end with a kiss. *Viva* 11(9): 39-41, 100-101.

Blishen, Bernard R. 1967. Socio-economic index for occupations in Canada. *Canadian Review of Sociology and Anthropology* 4(1): 41-53.

Boyd, Monica. 1984. *Canadian Attitudes Toward Women: Thirty Years of Change*. Ottawa: Labour Canada.

Boyle, Christine L. 1984. *Sexual Assault*. Toronto: Carswell Co. Ltd.

Brickman, Julie, John Briere, Margaret Ward, Marnie Kalef, Adeena Lungen. 1980. Preliminary report of the Winnipeg Rape Incidence Project; Paper presented at the annual meeting of the Canadian Psychological Association, Quebec City, June.

Brodyaga, Lisa. 1975. *Rape and Its Victims: Report for Citizens, Health Facilities and Criminal Justice Agencies*. Washington, DC: Law Enforcement Assistance Administration, U.S. Government Printing Office.

Brownmiller, Susan. 1975. *Against Our Will: Men, Women and Rape*. New York: Bantam Books.

Buckle, S., and L. Buckle. 1977. *Bargaining For Justice, Case Disposition and Reform in the Criminal Courts*. New York: Praeger Publishers.

Canadian Advisory Council on the Status of Women. 1985a. *Women and Part-Time Work*. Ottawa.
– 1985b. *Women and Work*. Ottawa.

Carrow, Debra. 1980. *Rape: Guidelines for a Community Response, An Executive Summary.* U.S. Department of Justice. Washington, D.C.: Government Printing Office.

Chambliss, William J., and R. Seidman. 1971. *Law, Order and Power.* Reading, MA: Addison-Wesley Publishing Company, Inc.

Chappell, Duncan. 1975. *Forcible Rape: A National Survey of the Response By Prosecutors.* Washington, D.C.: Batelle Law and Justice Study Center.

Clark, Lorenne, and Debra Lewis. 1977. *Rape: The Price of Coercive Sexuality.* Toronto: The Women's Press.

Cole, George F. 1976. The decision to prosecute. *Readings in Criminal Justice,* R.H. Moore, ed. Indianapolis: The Bobbs-Merril Company Inc.

Conklin, John E. 1972. *Robbery and the Criminal Justice System.* Philadelphia: J.B. Lippincott.

Connidis, Ingrid. 1979. Problems in the use of official statistics for criminal justice system research. *Canadian Journal of Criminology* 21(4): 397-415.

Criminal Code. R.S.C. 1970, c.C-34, s.143, as amended 1980-81-82, c.125 s.19.

Curtis, Lynn A. 1974. *Criminal Violence: National Patterns and Behaviour.* Lexington, Mass.: Lexington Books.

Davis, K. 1969. *Discretionary Justice: A Preliminary Inquiry.* Baton Rouge: Louisiana State University Press.

Dean, C. W., and M. deBruyn-Kops. 1982. *The Crime and Consequences of Rape.* Springfield, Ill.: Charles C. Thomas Company.

Donnerstein, E., and Daniel Linz. 1984. Sexual violence in the media: a warning. *Psychology Today* 18 (January): 14-15.

Egan, Patricia, ed. 1985. The Canadian Law List, 1985. Aurora, Ontario: The Canada Law Book Inc.

Elizabeth Fry Society of Manitoba and Y.W.C.A. 1985. Making street connections. Winnipeg: unpublished study.

Ennis, Philip H. 1967. *Criminal Victimization in the United States: A Report of a National Survey*. Chicago: National Opinion Research Center.

Finkelhor, David. 1979. What's wrong with sex between adults and children? ethics and the problem of sexual abuse. *American Journal of Orthopsychiatry* 49(4): 692-97.

Freidland, Martin L. 1965. *Detention Before Trial: A Study of Criminal Cases Tried in Magistrates' Courts*. Toronto: University of Toronto Press.

Gager, Nancy, and C. Schurr. 1976. *Sexual Assault: Confronting Rape in America*. New York: Grossett and Dunlap.

Galvin, Jim, and K. Polk. 1983. Attrition in case processing: is rape unique?*Journal of Research in Crime and Delinquency* 20: 126-54.

Griffiths, C. T., J. Klein and S. Verdun-Jones. 1980. *Criminal Justice in Canada, An Introductory Text*. Vancouver: Butterworth and Company.

Grosman, Brian. 1969. *An Inquiry Into the Exercise of Discretion*. Toronto: The University of Toronto Press.

Grosman, Brian. 1970. The role of the prosecutor in Canada. *The American Journal of Comparative Law* 18: 498-507.

Groth, A. Nicholas. 1979. *Men Who Rape: The Psychology of the Offender*. New York: Plenum Press.

Hann, R.G. 1973. *Decision-Making, The Canadian Criminal Court System: A Systems Analysis*. Vol. II. Toronto: University of Toronto Press.

Heumann, Milton. 1978. *Plea Bargaining: The Experiences of Prosecutors, Judges and Defence Attorneys*. Chicago: University of Chicago Press.

Hirsch, Miriam F. 1981. *Women and Violence*. New York: Van Nostrand Reinhold.

Hogarth, J. 1974. *Studies on Sentencing*. Ottawa: Information Canada.

Kilpatrick, Dean G., Lois J. Veronen and Patrick A. Resick. 1979. The aftermath of rape: recent empirical findings. *American Journal of Orthopsychiatry*. 49(4): 658-69.

Kinnon, Dianne. 1981. *Report on Sexual Assault in Canada*. Ottawa: Canadian Advisory Council on the Status of Women.

Klein, Dorie. 1981. Violence against women: some considerations regarding its causes and its elimination. *Crime and Delinquency* 27(1):64-80.

Klein, John. 1976. *Lets Make a Deal*. New York: D. C. Heath and Company.

LaFave, Wayne R. 1970. The prosecutor's discretion in the United States. *American Journal of Comparative Law* 18: 532-48.

LaFree, Gary D. 1982. Variables affecting guilty pleas and convictions in rape cases: toward a social theory of rape processing.Social Forces 58(3): 833-50.

Lagino, Helen. 1980. Pornography, freedom and oppression: a closer look. *Take Back The Night: Women on Pornography*, L. Lederer, ed. New York: Thomas Morrow.

Lautt, Melanie. A report on prostitution in the prairies.Fraser Commission Report on Pornography and Prostitution. Report No. 9.

Lederer, Laura, ed.. 1980. *Take Back the Night: Women on Pornography*. New York: Thomas Morrow.

Lott, Bernice, Mary Ellen Reilly, and Dale R. Howard. 1982. Sexual assault and harassment: a campus community case study.Signs: Journal of Women in Culture and Society 8(2).

Lovelace, Linda, and M. McGrady. 1980. *Ordeal.* Seacaucus, NJ: Citadel Press.

Lowman, John. 1984. Prostitution in Vancouver: the genesis of a social problem. Fraser Commission Report on Pornography and Prostitution. Report No. 8, Vol. II.

Manitoba Action Committee on the Status of Women. 1984. Presentation to the Fraser Commission on Pornography and Prostitution. Winnipeg, April, 1984.

Manitoba Advisory Council on the Status of Women. 1979. *The Royal Commission Report Ten Years Later.* Winnipeg.
Manitoba Bar Association. 1986. *Headnotes and Footnotes.*

Martin, Del. 1977. *Battered Wives.* New York: Pocketbooks.

McCahill, Thomas, L. Meyer and A. Fischman. 1979. The Aftermath of Rape. Lexington, Mass.: D.C. Heath and Company.

Meyer, Linda Carol. 1979. Rape cases in Philadelphia: court outcome and victim response. Ph.D. Dissertation, University of Pennsylvania, 1979.

National Council on Welfare. 1985. *Poverty Profile.* Ottawa.

Notman, N.T., and C. C. Nadelson. 1980. Psychodynamic and life-stage considerations in the response to rape. *The Rape Crisis Intervention Handbook*, Sharon L. McCombie, ed. New York: Plenum Press.

Ohara, Jane. 1986. The search for solutions to sexual abuse.MacLean's (January 27): 46-47.

Reiss, Albert J., Jr. 1974. Discretionary jusice. *Handbook of Criminology*, D. Glaser, ed. Chicago: Rand McNally College Publishing Co.

Robin, Gerald D. 1977. Forcible rape: institutionalized sexism in the criminal justice system.Crime and Delinquency (April): 136-58.

Rush, Florence. 1980. *The Best Kept Secret: Sexual Abuse of Children.* Englewood Cliffs, NJ: Prentice-Hall, Inc.

Russell, Diana E.H. 1984. *Sexual Exploitation: Rape, Child Sexual Abuse and Workplace Harassment.* Sage Library of Social Research, Vol 155. Beverly Hills, Cal.: Sage Publications Inc.

Ryan, William. 1974. The art of savage discovery: how to blame the victim. *Victimology,* Israel Drapkin and Emilio Viano, eds. Lexington, Mass: D.C. Heath and Co.

Schram, Donna. 1978. Forcible rape. *Final Project Report.* National Institute of Law Enforcement and Criminal Justice. Washington, DC: United States Department of Justice.

Senate Committee on Health, Welfare and Science. 1980. *Child at Risk.* Ottawa: Canadian Government Publishing Centre.

Skelton, Carol, and Barry Burkhart. 1980. Sexual assault: determinants of victim disclosure.Criminal Justice and Behavior7(9):229-36.

Solicitor General of Canada. 1984. *Canadian Urban Victimization Survey.* Ottawa

Stanley, Marily G. 1985. The experience of the rape victim with the criminal justice system prior to Bill C-127. Ottawa: Department of Justice, Policy Planning and Development Branch.

Statistics Canada. 1983. *The Canada Census of 1981.* Ottawa: Supply and Services Canada.

- 1984. *Women in the Work World.*

- 1987. *Issue of Earnings of Men and Women, 1986.* Ottawa.

Supply and Services Canada. 1982. *Images of Women: Task Force on Sex-Role Stereotyping in Broadcast Media.* Ottawa.

Veers, J.E., and D.F. Cousineau. 1980. The heathen Canadians: demographic correlates of nonbelief. Pacific Sociological Review (23): 199-216.

Weis, Kurt, and Sandra S. Borges. 1973. Victimology and rape: the case of the legitimate victim. *Issues in Criminology* 8(2): 71-116.

Williams, Joyce E. and Karen Holmes. 1981. *The Second Assault: Rape and Public Attitudes.* Westport, Conn.: Greenwood Press.

Williams, Kristen M. 1978. *The Prosecution of Sexual Assaults.* Institute for Law and Social Research. Washington, DC: National Institute of Law Enforcement and Criminal Justice.

Wilson, Paul R. 1978. *The Other Side of Rape.* Queensland, Australia: University of Queensland Press.

Wilson, Paul R., and David Nias. 1976. *Love's Mysteries: The Psychology of Sexual Attractiveness.* London: Open Books.

Women and Part-Time Work. Canadian Advisory Council on the Status of Women. June, 1985.

Women and Work. Canadian Advisory Council on the Status of Women. February, 1985.

Women in the Work World. Statistics Canada. September, 1984.

Zwarun, Suzanne. 1985. Chatelaine grades the province on women's issues. *Chatelaine* April: 70-74.

Cases

R. v. A., (1985), 14 W.C.B., (Y.T. Terr. Ct.)
R. v. Andrew F., (1985), 14 W.C.B., (B.C.)
R. v. Ashbee, (1985), 14 W.C.B., (Ont. C.A.)
R. v. Billie, 14 W.C.B., (B.C.C.A.)
R. v. Bird, 13 W.C.B., (Ont. C.C.)
R. v. Breckinridge, 13 W.C.B., (Ont. Dist. Ct.)

R. v. Burden, (1982), (B.C.C.A.)
R. v. Chase, (1984), 40 C.R. (3d), (N.B.C.A.)
R. v. Cook, (1985), 46 C.R. (3d), (B.C.C.A.)
R. v. Cormier, (1985), C.C.L., (N.B.C.A.)
R. v. Daychief, (1985) 6 W.W.R., (Alta. C.A.)
R. v. Forsythe, (See Boyle, 1984)
R. v. Gallant, (1985), 14 W.C.B., (Ont. Dist. Ct.)
R. v. Gardynik, (1984), 42 C.R. (3d), (Ont. C.A.)
R. v. Gran, (1984), 13 W.C.B., (B.C.C.A.)
R. v. Guiboche, (Sept. 9, 1983), Winnipeg Free Press
R. v. J.A., (1984), N.W.T.R., (N.W.T. Terr. Ct.)
R. v. Martens (Feb. 27, 1987), Winnipeg Free Press
R. v. McDonald, (1983) (Alta.)
R. v. Mitchell, (1984), (Alta. C.A.)
R. v. Naqitarvik, (1985), 14 W.C.B., (N.W.T. Terr. Ct.)
R. v. Page, (1984), 40 C.R., (Ont. S.C.)
R. v. R.S., (1985), 13 W.C.B., (Ont. C.C.)
R. v. Ryan, (1985), C.C.L., (B.C.C.A.)
R. v. Sarabando, (1985), 13 W.C.B., (Ont. C.C.)
R. v. Smaaslet, (1985), C.C.L., (B.C.C.A.)
R. v. Taylor, (1985), 40 C.R. (3d) 269, (Alta, C.A.)
R. v. Thom, (1985), 14 W.C.B., (B.C.C.A.)
R. v. Thorne, (1985), 13 W.C.B., (Ont. C.A.)
R. v. Wiseman et al., (1986), 22 C.C.C. (3d)

Index